Understanding SQL

MARTIN GRUBER

San Francisco ■ Paris ■ Düsseldorf ■ London

Acquisitions Editor: Dianne King
Editors: Michael L. Wolk, Eric Stone, Lyn Cordell
Technical Editor: Jon Forrest
Word Processors: Scott Campbell, Deborah Maizels
Book Designer: Julie Bilski
Chapter Art and Layout: Charlotte Carter
Screen Graphics: Delia Brown
Typesetter: The Typesetting Shop, Inc.
Proofreader: Ed Lin
Cover Designer: Thomas Ingalls + Associates
Cover Photographer: Michael Lamotte
Screen reproductions produced by XenoFont

Library of Congress Card Number: 89-51772
ISBN 0-89588-644-8
Manufactured in the United States of America
10 9 8 7 6 5 4 3 2 1

This book is dedicated to Lee and Janet Fesperman for getting me involved in this whole thing in the first place, and to my mother for her encouragement and support.

ACKNOWLEDGMENTS

I would like to thank FFE Software for allowing me to use FirstSQL in the production of this book.

CONTENTS AT A GLANCE

TABLE OF CONTENTS

INTRODUCTION

SQL (USUALLY PRONOUNCED "SEQUEL") STANDS for Structured Query Language. It is a language that enables you to create and operate on *relational databases*, which are sets of related information stored in tables.

The database world is becoming increasingly integrated, and this has led to a clamor for a standard language that can be used to operate in many different kinds of computer environments. A standard language allows users to learn one set of commands and use it to create, retrieve, alter, and transfer information regardless of whether they are working on a personal computer, a workstation, or a mainframe. In our increasingly interconnected computer world, a user equipped with such a language has tremendous power to utilize and integrate information from a variety of sources in a great number of ways.

Because of its elegance and independence from machine specifics, as well as its support by the industry leaders in relational-database technology, SQL has become, and will for the foreseeable future remain, that standard language. For this reason, anyone who expects to work with databases in the nineties needs to know SQL.

The SQL standard is defined by ANSI (American National Standards Institute) and is currently accepted as well by ISO (International Standards Organization). However, most commercial database programs extend SQL beyond the ANSI definition, adding other features that they think will be useful. Sometimes they violate the standard in minor ways, although good ideas tend to be copied and become "defacto" or "marketplace" standards. In this book, we will basically be following the ANSI standard, but with an eye towards the most common variations. You should consult the documentation on the software package(s) you will be using to see where they vary from the standard.

WHO CAN USE THIS BOOK?

This book requires no more than a minimal knowledge of computers and databases. SQL is actually considerably easier to use than many languages that are less compact because you don't have to define the procedures used to achieve the desired results. This book will lead you through the language step by step, providing examples along the way and exercises for each chapter to sharpen your comprehension and skills. You will be able to perform useful tasks almost immediately; then you will build more complex skills layer by layer.

Because SQL is part of so many programs that run on so many different computers, no assumptions can be made about the specific context in which you are using it. This book is designed to be as general purpose as possible. You will be able to apply what you learn here directly to any context in which SQL is used.

Although this book is designed to be accessible to database beginners, it presents SQL in considerable depth. Examples are designed to reflect a variety of situations, many of which commonly occur in business environments. Certain examples are fairly complex in the interest of showing all the implications of a particular feature. The discussion of SQL is not restricted to what is technically correct, but also explores the implications of various features and approaches. We believe you will not find another book on SQL which has the accessibility and the depth of this one.

HOW IS THIS BOOK ORGANIZED?

The chapters of this book are arranged so that each one will introduce a new group of related concepts and features. Every chapter builds on what came before and concludes with practice questions to sharpen and solidify your understanding. (Answers to the practice questions are in Appendix A.)

The first seven chapters introduce the basic concepts of relational databases and of SQL, and then proceed to lay out the basics of queries. Queries are commands used to retrieve information from a database; they are the most common and, at times, probably the most complex aspect of SQL. Chapters 8 through 14 introduce more advanced query techniques, specifically how to query more than one table at a time, and how to combine queries in various ways. Other aspects of SQL—how to create tables, how to enter values into them, and how to grant and deny access to tables that you create—are covered in Chapters 15 through 23. Chapter 24 shows you how to access information about the structure of your database. In Chapter 25, you will learn how to put SQL into programs written in other languages.

Depending on how you will be using SQL, some of the later information may be unnecessary for you to study. Not all users create tables or even enter values into them. As a tutorial, this book is written so that one chapter will flow into the next, but you can feel free to skim sections that you may not need to use. This is one reason we put all the query instruction together at the beginning. Queries are basic; you will need to understand them in order to use most of the other functions of SQL. But the reverse is not necessarily true.

We will use a single set of tables to derive the bulk of the book's examples. You will become quite familiar with these tables, and thus be able to understand clearly the points being made with them.

Here is a chapter-by-chapter summary of the contents of this book:

- Chapter 1 shows you what a relational database is, including the important concept of the primary key, and gives examples similar to real-life situations. It also contains the three tables from which we will derive the bulk of our examples in this book and explains their contents.

- Chapter 2 orients you to the world of SQL. It covers such general issues as: the structure of the language, the different types of data recognized by SQL, and some common SQL conventions and terminology.

- Chapter 3 shows you how to create queries and introduces several techniques to refine them. After reading this chapter, you will be able to do useful work with SQL.

- Chapter 4 illustrates how two types of standard mathematical operators, relationals (=, <, > =, and so on) and Booleans (AND, OR, NOT), are used in SQL.
- Chapter 5 introduces some operators that are used in a manner similar to the relational operators but are specific to the SQL language. Also in this chapter, the issue of missing data is brought up and NULL values are defined.
- Chapter 6 teaches you about a set of operators that derive data from tables, rather than simply extracting it. This enables you to have summary data about the values in your tables that is up to the second.
- Chapter 7 shows some things you can do to the output of a query, such as performing mathematical operations on it, inserting text in it, and ordering it in various ways.
- Chapter 8 shows how a single query can draw information from more than one table at a time. This process defines a relationship between the tables, extending the ways in which you can interrelate the data in your database.
- Chapter 9 demonstrates that the same technique that enables you to query multiple tables at once can enable you to define special interrelationships between the items of data in a single table.
- In Chapter 10, you will learn how to execute one query and have its output control what happens to another query.
- Chapter 11 extends the technique introduced in Chapter 10. Here you will learn how to have one query control another by being executed repeatedly.
- Chapter 12 introduces a new kind of SQL special operator. EXISTS is an operator that acts on an entire query rather than on a simple value.
- Chapter 13 introduces the operators ANY, ALL, and SOME. These operators, like EXISTS, operate on entire queries.

- Chapter 14 introduces the command that enables you to combine the output of multiple queries directly, rather than having one control another.
- Chapter 15 introduces the commands that determine what the values are in a database—that is, the commands to insert, delete, and update values.
- Chapter 16 extends the power of the commands introduced in the previous chapter by showing how they can be controlled by queries.
- Chapter 17 shows you how to create a table.
- Chapter 18 elaborates on the creation of tables by showing you how you can make them reject certain kinds of changes automatically.
- Chapter 19 explores the relationships built into your database when, for a logical reason, a value located somewhere in a table has to be the same as a value located elsewhere.
- Chapter 20 talks about the view, a "window" that shows the partial contents of some other table. Even if you do not expect to create tables as such, you may want to look over views, because they are quite useful, and are commonly created by many users who don't create tables.
- Chapter 21 concentrates on the complex issue of changing the values in a view. When you change the values in a view, you actually change them in the underlying table. This brings up some special problems that are also treated in this chapter.
- Chapter 22 talks about privileges—who has the ability to query tables, who has the ability to change their contents, how these abilities can be given to and taken from users, and so on.
- Chapter 23 is something of a catchall for general features that don't fit in anywhere else. Specifically, we will discuss when changes to the database become permanent, and how SQL deals with simultaneous actions.

- Chapter 24 describes how SQL databases keep your database structured, and shows you how to access and use this information.
- Chapter 25 focuses on the special problems and procedures associated with putting SQL commands inside other languages. It includes SQL features relevant only to the embedded form, such as cursors and the FETCH command.

The appendices of this book contain the answers to the sample problems (Appendix A), an extra copy of the sample tables (Appendix E), some detailed information on different types of data (Appendix B) and on common nonstandard features (Appendix C), as well as a reference guide to SQL commands (Appendix D).

CONVENTIONS OF THIS BOOK

SQL consists of instructions you give a database program, telling it to perform some action. Although these are commonly called "statements" in database jargon, we shall, for the most part, use the term "commands" to emphasize that these are directions that have effects.

Words in italics are terminology. In the text, terms are italicized when they are first explained; in the syntax of commands, they are italicized to indicate that they stand for something besides themselves.

In our examples, we will show you the text you should enter into your database program, and then show you the output as it appears in one database product (FirstSQL, a database program for the IBM PC). Output from other products may look different, but the content will be the same.

1

Introducing Relational Databases

BEFORE YOU CAN USE SQL, YOU MUST UNDERSTAND what relational databases are. In this chapter, we will explain this, and show you how relational databases are useful. We won't be discussing SQL specifically here, so if you already understand these concepts fairly well, you may wish to merely skim this chapter. In any case, you should look at the three tables that are introduced and explained at the chapter's end; these will be the basis of most of our examples in this book. A second copy of them is available in Appendix E, and we recommend copying them for your reference.

WHAT IS A RELATIONAL DATABASE?

A *relational database* is a body of related information stored in two-dimensional tables. Think of an address book. There are many entries in the book, each of which corresponds to a given individual. For each individual, there may be several independent pieces of data, such as name, telephone number, and address. Suppose you were to format this address book as a table with rows and columns. Each row (also called a *record*) would correspond to a certain individual; each column would contain a value for each type of data—name, telephone number, and address represented in each row. The address book might look like this:

NAME	*TELEPHONE*	*ADDRESS*
Gerry Farish	(415)365-8775	127 Primrose Ave., SF
Celia Brock	(707)874-3553	246 #4 3rd St., Sonoma
Yves Grillet	(762)976-3665	778 Modernas, Barcelona

What you have here is the foundation of a relational database as defined at the beginning of this discussion—a two-dimensional (row and column) table of information. Relational databases seldom consist of a single table, however. Such a table is little more than a filing system. By creating several tables of interrelated information, you can perform more complex and powerful operations on your data. The power of the database lies in the relationships that you can construct between the pieces of information, rather than in the pieces of information themselves.

RELATING TABLES TO EACH OTHER

Let us use the example of our address book to discuss a database that would actually be used in a business situation. Suppose the individuals in our first table (the address book) are patients in a hospital. In another table, we could store additional information about these patients. The columns of the second table might be labelled Patient, Doctor, Insurer, and Balance.

PATIENT	*DOCTOR*	*INSURER*	*BALANCE*
Farish	Drume	B.C./B.S.	$272.99
Grillet	Halben	None	$44.76
Brock	Halben	Health, Inc.	$9077.47

Many powerful functions could be performed by extracting information from these tables according to specific criteria, especially when the criteria involve relating pieces of information from different tables to one another. For example, suppose Dr. Halben wanted the phone numbers of all of his patients. To extract this information, he could relate the table with the phone numbers of patients (the address book) to the table that shows which patients are his. Although, in this simple example, he could also do this in his head and produce the phone numbers of patients Grillet and Brock, these tables could easily be larger and more complex. Relational-database programs were developed to process large and complex collections of data of this kind, which obviously are quite common in the business world. Even if the hospital database contained hundreds or thousands of names—as is probably the case in practice—a single SQL command could give Dr. Halben the information he needed almost instantly.

THE ORDER OF THE ROWS IS ARBITRARY

To maintain maximum flexibility, the rows of a table are, by definition, in no particular order. This is an aspect of database that differs from our address book. The entries in an address book are usually ordered alphabetically. In relational-database systems, one powerful capability that users have is the ability to order the information however they want to as they retrieve it.

Consider the second table. Sometimes you might want to see this information ordered alphabetically by name, sometimes by the balance in ascending or descending order, and sometimes grouped by doctor. Imposing a set order on the rows would interfere with the user's ability to be flexible, so the rows are always considered to be unordered. For this reason, you cannot simply say, "I want to look at the fifth row of a table." Regardless of the order in which the data is entered or of any other criteria, there is, by definition, no such fifth row. The rows of the table are considered to be in no particular sequence.

IDENTIFYING ROWS (THE PRIMARY KEY)

For this and other reasons, you need to have a column in your table that uniquely identifies each row. Typically, this column contains a number—a patient number assigned to each patient, for example. Of course, you could also use the patient's name, but it is possible to have several Mary Smiths; in that case, you would have no simple way to distinguish these patients from one another. This is why numbers are more commonly used. This unique column (or unique group of columns), used to identify each row and keep all rows distinct, is referred to as the *primary key* of the table.

The primary key of a table is vital to the structure of the database. It is the heart of your filing system; when you want to find a specific row in a table, you refer to it by the primary key. In addition, primary keys guarantee that your data has a certain integrity. If the primary key is properly used and maintained, you will know that no row of a table is empty and that every row is different from every other row. We will discuss keys further when we talk about referential integrity in Chapter 19.

COLUMNS ARE NAMED AND NUMBERED

Unlike the rows, the columns (also called *fields*) of a table are ordered and named. Thus, in our address-book table, it is possible to refer to the "address column" or to "column 3". Naturally, this means that each column of a given table must have a different name to avoid ambiguity. It is best if these names indicate the content of the field. In the sample tables in this book, we will use some abbreviations as column names, such as *cname* for customer name, and *odate* for order date. We have also given each table a single numeric column as a primary key. The next section will explain these tables and their keys in detail.

A SAMPLE DATABASE

Tables 1.1, 1.2, and 1.3 constitute a relational database that is small enough to follow easily, but complex enough to illustrate the major concepts and practices involved in using SQL. These tables are printed in this chapter and also in Appendix E. Since they will be used to illustrate the various features of SQL throughout this book, we recommend you copy them for easy reference.

You will notice that the first column of each table contains numbers whose values are different for every row. As you may have guessed, these are the primary keys of the tables. Some of these numbers also appear in columns of other tables. There is nothing wrong with this. It indicates a relationship between the rows that use a value taken from a primary key, and the row where that value is used in the primary key itself.

Table 1.1: Salespeople

SNUM	SNAME	CITY	COMM
1001	Peel	London	.12
1002	Serres	San Jose	.13
1004	Motika	London	.11
1007	Rifkin	Barcelona	.15
1003	Axelrod	New York	.10

Table 1.2: Customers

CNUM	CNAME	CITY	RATING	SNUM
2001	Hoffman	London	100	1001
2002	Giovanni	Rome	200	1003
2003	Liu	San Jose	200	1002
2004	Grass	Berlin	300	1002
2006	Clemens	London	100	1001
2008	Cisneros	San Jose	300	1007
2007	Pereira	Rome	100	1004

Table 1.3: Orders

ONUM	AMT	ODATE	CNUM	SNUM
3001	18.69	10/03/1990	2008	1007
3003	767.19	10/03/1990	2001	1001
3002	1900.10	10/03/1990	2007	1004
3005	5160.45	10/03/1990	2003	1002
3006	1098.16	10/03/1990	2008	1007
3009	1713.23	10/04/1990	2002	1003
3007	75.75	10/04/1990	2004	1002
3008	4723.00	10/05/1990	2006	1001
3010	1309.95	10/06/1990	2004	1002
3011	9891.88	10/06/1990	2006	1001

For example, the snum field of the Customers table indicates to which salesperson a customer is assigned. The snum number relates to the Salespeople table, which gives information about these salespeople. Obviously, the salespeople to whom the customers are assigned should exist—that is to say, the snum values in the Customers table should also be present in the Salespeople table. If this is the case, we say that the system is in a state of *referential integrity*. This issue will be more thoroughly and formally explained in Chapter 19.

The tables themselves are intended to resemble a real-life business situation, where you would use SQL to keep track of the salespeople, their customers, and the customers' orders. Let's take a moment to look at these three tables and the meaning of their various fields.

Here's an explanation of the columns in Table 1.1:

FIELD	***CONTENT***
snum	A unique number assigned to each salesperson (an "employee number").
sname	The name of the salesperson.
city	The location of the salesperson.
comm	The salesperson's commission on orders in decimal form.

Table 1.2 contains the following columns:

FIELD	***CONTENT***
cnum	A unique number assigned to each customer.
cname	The name of the customer.
city	The location of the customer.
rating	A numeric code indicating level of preference given this customer. Higher numbers indicate greater preference.
snum	The number of the salesperson assigned to this customer (from the Salespeople table).

And here are the columns in Table 1.3:

FIELD	***CONTENT***
onum	A unique number given to each purchase.
amt	The amount of the purchase.

odate	The date of the purchase.
cnum	The number of the customer making the purchase (from the Customers table).
snum	The number of the salesperson credited with the sale (from the Salespeople table).

SUMMARY

Now you know what is meant by a relational database, a concept that sounds more complicated than it really is. You also have learned some fundamental principles about how tables are structured—how rows and columns work, how primary keys distinguish rows from one another, and how columns can refer to values in other columns. You are aware that record is a synonym for row, and that field is a synonym for column. Both terminologies are encountered in discussions of SQL, and we will use them interchangeably in this book.

You are now familiar with the sample tables. Brief and simple as they are, they are adequate to demonstrate most of the features of the language, as you shall see. On occasion, we will introduce another table or postulate some different data in one of these tables to show you some other possibilities.

Now you are ready to dive into SQL itself. The next chapter gives you a bird's-eye view of the language, orienting you to the terrain and putting a lot of the material you may need to refer back to in one familiar place.

Putting SQL to Work

1. Which field of the Customers table is the primary key?
2. What is column 4 of the Customers table?
3. What is another word for row? For column?
4. Why can you not ask to see the first five rows of a table?

(See Appendix A for answers.)

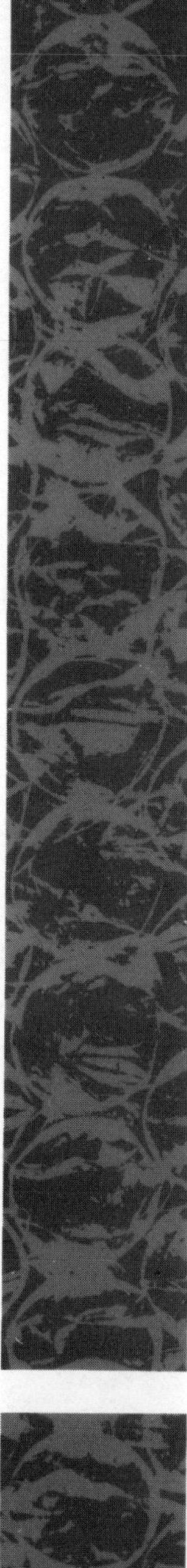

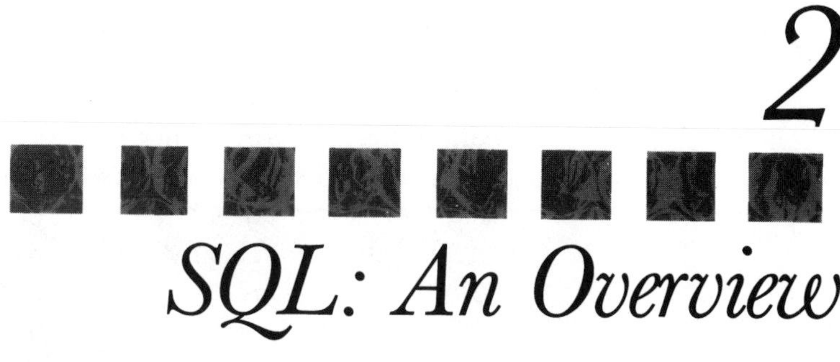

2

SQL: An Overview

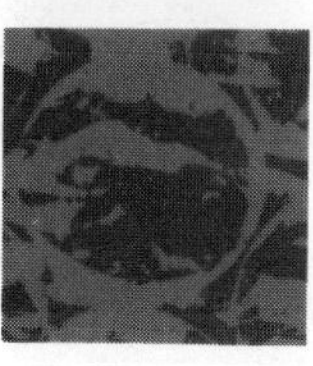

THIS CHAPTER WILL ACQUAINT YOU WITH THE structure of the SQL language as well as with certain general issues, such as the types of data that fields can contain and some of the areas of ambiguity that exist in SQL. It is intended to provide a context for the more specific information in subsequent chapters. You do not need to remember every detail mentioned in this chapter. The overview presented here consolidates, in one easily located area, many of the details that you may have to refer back to as you proceed to master the language. We have put all this at the beginning of the book to orient you to the world of SQL without oversimplifying it and to give you a familiar place to refer back to when you have questions. This material will become much clearer when we move into the specifics of SQL commands, starting in Chapter 3.

HOW DOES SQL WORK?

SQL is a language oriented specifically around relational databases. It eliminates a lot of the work you would have to do if you were using a general-purpose programming language, such as C. To build a relational database in C, you would have to start from scratch. You would have to define an object called a table that could grow to have any number of rows, and then create step-by-step procedures for putting values in it and retrieving them. If you wanted to find some particular rows, you would have to enumerate each step of the process like this:

1. Look at a row of the table.
2. Perform a test to see if it is one of the rows you want.
3. If so, store it somewhere until the whole table is examined.
4. See if there are any more rows in the table.
5. If there are more rows, go back to step 1.
6. If there are no more rows, output all values stored in step 3.

(Of course, this is not an actual set of C instructions, just an English-language rendition of the logical steps that would be involved.)

SQL, however, spares you all this. Commands in SQL can operate on entire groups of tables as single objects and can treat any quantity of information extracted or derived from them as a single unit as well.

HOW DOES ANSI FIT IN?

As we mentioned in the Introduction, the SQL standard is defined by *ANSI* (the American National Standards Institute). SQL was not invented by ANSI. It is essentially a product of IBM research. But other companies picked up on SQL right away; in fact, at least one company (Oracle) beat IBM to the punch with a marketable SQL product.

After there were a number of competing SQL products on the market, ANSI defined the standard to which they would all conform (defining such standards is ANSI's function). Doing this after the fact, however, presents some problems. The resulting ANSI standard is somewhat limited; also what ANSI specifies is not always what is found most useful in practice, so products attempt to conform to the ANSI standard without letting it limit them too much. This, in turn, leads to occasional inconsistencies that we will explain as we encounter them. Database products usually give ANSI SQL additional features and frequently relax many of its more limiting restrictions. Therefore, common variations from ANSI will be explored as well. Although we obviously cannot cover every exception or variation, successful ideas tend to be copied and used similarly in different products even when they are not specified by ANSI. ANSI is sort of minimum standard—you can do a lot more than it does, but you should produce the results it specifies when performing a task it defines.

INTERACTIVE VS EMBEDDED SQL

In a sense, there are two SQL's: interactive and embedded. For the most part, the two forms operate the same way, but they are used differently.

Interactive SQL is used to operate directly on a database to produce output for human consumption. In this form of SQL, you enter a command now, it is executed now, and you can see the output (if any) immediately.

Embedded SQL consists of SQL commands put inside of programs that are mostly written in some other language (such as COBOL or Pascal). This can make these programs more powerful and efficient. However, enabling these languages to deal with SQL's structure and its style of data management does require some extensions to interactive SQL. The output of SQL commands in embedded SQL is "passed off" to variables or parameters usable by the program in which it is embedded.

In this book, we will present SQL in its interactive form. This will enable us to discuss commands and their effects without worrying about how they interface with other languages. Interactive SQL is also the form most useful to nonprogrammers. What you learn about interactive SQL basically applies as well to the embedded form. The changes needed to use the embedded form will be dealt with in the last chapter of this book.

THE SUBDIVISIONS OF SQL

In both the interactive and the embedded forms of SQL, there are multiple sections, or subdivisions. Since you are likely to encounter this terminology when reading about SQL, we will provide some explanation. Unfortunately, these terms are not used consistently in all implementations. They are emphasized by ANSI and are useful on a conceptual level, but many SQL products do not treat them separately in practice, so they essentially become functional categories of SQL commands.

Data Definition Language (or DDL, also called Schema Definition Language in ANSI) consists of those commands that create the objects (tables, indexes, views, and so on) in the database. Data Manipulation Language (DML) is a set of commands that determine which values are present in the tables at any given time. Data Control Language (DCL) consists of features that determine whether a user is permitted to perform a particular action. This is considered part of DDL in ANSI. Don't let these names put you off. These are not different languages per se, but divisions of SQL commands into groups according to their functions.

THE VARIOUS TYPES OF DATA

Not all the types of values that can occupy the fields of a table are logically the same. The most obvious distinction is between numbers and text. You can't put numbers in alphabetical order or subtract one name from another. Since relational-database systems are based on the relationships between pieces of information, the various types of data must be clearly distinguished from one another, so that the appropriate processes and comparisons can be applied.

In SQL, this is done by assigning each field a *data type* that indicates the kind of value the field will contain. All of the values in a given field must be of the same type. In the Customers table, for example, cname and city are strings of text, whereas rating, snum, and cnum are numbers. For this reason, you could not enter Highest or None into the rating field, which has a numeric data type. This limitation is fortunate because it imposes some structure on your data. You frequently will be comparing some or all of the values in a given field, so that you can perform an action on some rows and not on others. You could not do this if the field's values had mixed data types.

Unfortunately, the definition of these data types is a major area in which many commercial database programs and the official SQL standard are not always in synch. The ANSI SQL standard recognizes only text and number types, whereas many commercial programs use other special types as well. Notably, DATE and TIME are almost defacto standard types (although the exact format varies). Some packages also support types such as MONEY, BINARY. (Binary is a special number system used by computers. All of the information in a computer is represented by binary numbers and then converted to other systems so we can more easily use and understand it.)

ANSI defines several different types of number values, the distinctions between which are frequently subtle and sometimes confusing. The exact ANSI data types are enumerated in Appendix B. The complexity of the ANSI numeric types can, at least in part, be explained by the effort to make embedded SQL compatible with a variety of other languages.

Two ANSI number types, INTEGER and DECIMAL (which can be abbreviated as INT and DEC, respectively), will be adequate for our purposes, as well as the purposes of many practical business applications. Of course, an INTEGER can be thought of as a DECIMAL that allows no digits to the right of the (implied) decimal point.

The type for text is CHAR (or CHARACTER), which refers to a string of text. A field of type CHAR has a definite length, which is the maximum number of characters that can be entered into that field. Most implementations also have a nonstandard type called VARCHAR, which is a text string that can be of any length up to an implementation-defined maximum (typically 254 characters). CHARACTER and VARCHAR values are enclosed in single quotes such as 'text'. The difference between CHAR and VARCHAR is that CHAR has to reserve enough memory for the maximum length of the string. VARCHAR allocates memory as needed.

The character types consist of all the printable characters, including the numbers. However, the number 1 is not the same as the character '1'. The character '1' is just another printable piece of text, not recognized by the system as having the numeric value 1. 1 + 1 = 2, but '1' + '1' does not equal '2'. CHARACTER values are stored in the computer as binary values, but appear to the user as printable text. The conversion follows a format defined by the system you are using. This conversion format will be one of the two standard types (possibly with extensions) used in computer systems: ASCII (used in all personal and most small computers) and EBCDIC (used in some larger computers). Certain operations, such as alphabetical ordering of field values, will vary with the format. Implications of these two formats will be discussed in Chapter 4.

We shall follow the market, not ANSI, in using the type called DATE. (In an implementation that did not recognize the DATE type, you could declare a date as a character or numeric field, but this makes many operations more difficult.) You should refer to the documentation on the software package you will be using to find out exactly what data types it supports.

SQL INCONSISTENCIES

As you may have gathered from the preceding discussion, there are inconsistencies within the world of SQL itself. SQL emerged from the commercial database world as a tool, and was later turned into an ANSI standard. Unfortunately, what ANSI specifies is not always what is found most useful in practice, so products attempt to conform to the ANSI standard without letting it limit them too much. ANSI is a sort of minimum standard—you can do a lot more than it does, but you should be able to produce the same results as it does when performing the same task.

WHAT IS A USER?

SQL is mostly found in computer systems that have more than one user, and need to differentiate between them (your family PC may have any number of users, but it usually has no way of distinguishing one from another). Typically, in such a system, each user has some sort of authorization code that identifies him or her (the terminology varies). When beginning a session with the computer, the user *logs on*, which tells the computer which user, identified by an authorization ID, is speaking. Any number of people using the same authorization ID are a single user as far as the computer is concerned; likewise, a person can be many users (generally at different times) by using different authorization ID's.

SQL follows this pattern. Actions in most SQL environments are credited to a specific authorization ID, which usually corresponds to a user. A table or other object is owned by a user, who has authority over what happens to it. A user may or may not have the privilege to perform an action on an object he or she does not own. For our purposes, we will assume any user has the privileges needed to perform any action, until we get around to discussing privileges specifically in Chapter 22.

The special value USER can be used as an argument to a command. It indicates the authorization ID of the user issuing the command.

CONVENTIONS AND TERMINOLOGY

Keywords are words that have a special meaning in SQL. They are understood to be instructions, not text or names of objects. We will indicate keywords by printing them in all CAPS. You should take care not to confuse keywords with terminology. SQL has certain special terms that are used to describe it. Among these are such words as query, clause, and predicate, which are important in describing and understanding the language but do not mean anything to SQL itself.

Commands, or *statements*, are instructions given by you to a SQL database. Commands consist of one or more logically distinct parts called *clauses*. Clauses begin with a keyword for which they are generally named, and consist of keywords and arguments. Examples of clauses you will encounter are "FROM Salespeople" and "WHERE city = 'London'." *Arguments* complete or modify the meaning of a clause. In the examples above, "Salespeople" is the argument, and FROM is the keyword of the FROM clause. Likewise, "city = 'London' " is the argument of the WHERE clause. *Objects* are structures in the database that are given names and stored in memory. They include base tables, views (the two kinds of tables), and indexes.

When we show you how commands are formed, we will generally do so by example. There is, however, a more formal method of describing commands using standardized conventions. We will make some use of this in later chapters, it is good for you to understand these conventions in case you encounter them in other SQL documents. Square brackets ([ ]) will indicate portions that can optionally be omitted, and ellipses (. . .) will indicate that the preceding may be repeated any number of times. Words indicated in angle brackets (<>) are special terms that will be explained as they are introduced. We have simplified the standard SQL terminology considerably, but without changing the effect.

SUMMARY

Whew! You have quickly covered a lot of ground in this chapter. But our intention has simply been to fly high over the SQL territory, so you could have an idea of its overall shape. When we return to the ground in the next chapter, things will become much more concrete. Now you know a fair amount about SQL —how it is structured, how it is used, how it conceives of data, how and by whom it is defined (and some inconsistencies emerging from that), and some of the conventions and terminology used to describe it. This is a lot of information for a single chapter; we don't expect you to remember all of the details, but you can refer to details as you need to. The important thing is the big picture.

In Chapter 3, we will go hands-on, showing exactly how commands are formed and what they do. We will introduce the SQL command used to extract information from tables, which is easily the most widely used command in SQL. By the end of that chapter, you will be able to extract highly specific information from your database.

Putting SQL to Work

1. What is the most basic distinction between data types in SQL?
2. Does ANSI recognize the data type DATE?
3. Which subdivision of SQL is used to put values in tables?
4. What is a keyword?

(See Appendix A for answers.)

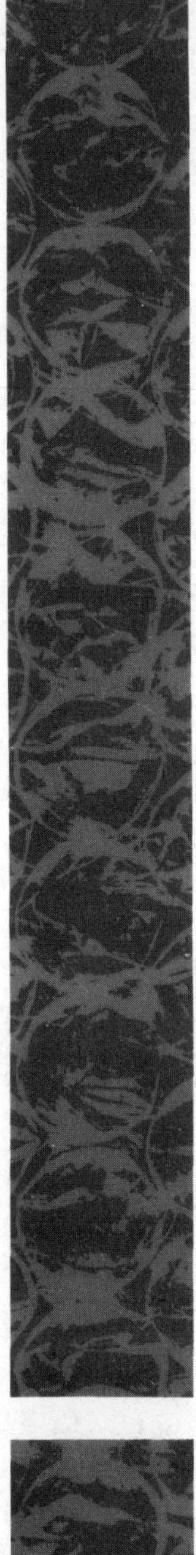

3

Using SQL to Retrieve Information from Tables

IN THIS CHAPTER WE WILL SHOW YOU HOW TO retrieve information from tables. You will learn how to omit or to reorder columns and how to eliminate redundant data from your output automatically. Finally, you will learn how to define a condition—a test, if you will—that you can use to determine which rows of a table are used to derive output. This last feature, to be further described in later chapters, is one of the most elegant and powerful in SQL.

MAKING A QUERY

As we pointed out before, SQL stands for Structured Query Language. Queries are probably the most frequently used aspect of SQL. In fact, there is a category of SQL users who are unlikely to ever use the language for anything else. For this reason, we will begin our discussion of SQL with a discussion of the query and how it is implemented in this language.

What is a query? A query is a command you give your database program that tells it to produce certain specified information from the tables in its memory. This information is usually sent directly to the screen of the computer or terminal you are using, although, in many cases, it can also be sent to a printer, stored in a file (as an object in the computer's memory), or given as input to another command or process.

WHERE DO QUERIES FIT IN?

Queries are usually considered as part of DML. However, because a query does not change the information in the tables at all, but merely shows it to the user, we shall consider queries a category unto themselves and define DML commands as those that affect, rather than simply reveal, the contents of a database.

Queries in SQL are all constructed from a single command. The structure of this command is deceptively simple, because you can extend it enough to allow some highly sophisticated evaluating and processing of data. This command is called SELECT.

THE SELECT COMMAND

In its simplest form, the SELECT command simply instructs the database to retrieve information from a table. For example, you could produce the Salespeople table by typing the following:

```
SELECT snum, sname, city, comm
   FROM Salespeople;
```

The output for this query is shown in Figure 3.1.

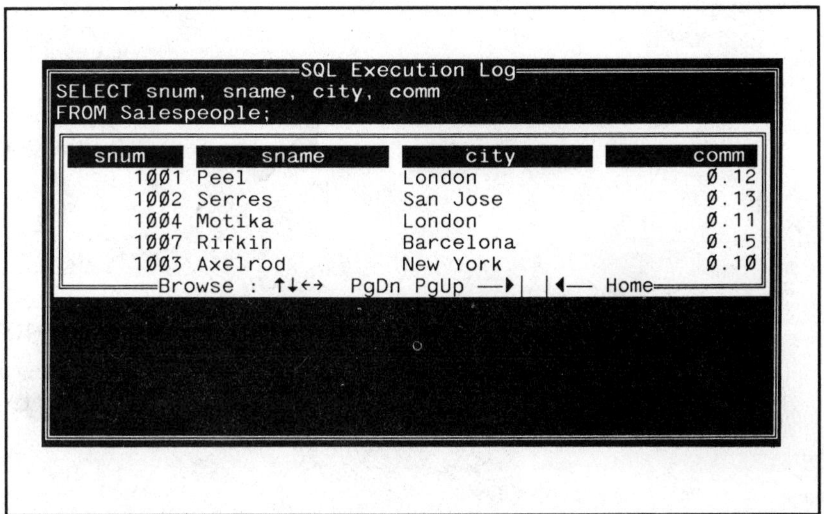

Figure 3.1: The SELECT command

In other words, this command simply outputs all of the data in the table. Most programs will also provide column headings as above, and some allow elaborate formatting of the output, but that is beyond the specifications of the standard. Here is an explanation of each part of the command:

SELECT — A keyword that tells the database this command is a query. All queries begin with this word followed by a space.

snum, sname . . .	This is a list of the columns from the table that are being selected by the query. Any columns not listed here would not be included in the output of the command. This, of course, would not delete them or their information from the tables because a query does not affect the information in the tables; it only exhibits the data.
FROM Salespeople	FROM is a keyword, like SELECT, which must be present in every query. It is followed by a space and then the name of the table being used as the source of the information. In this case that table is Salespeople.
;	The semicolon is used in all interactive SQL commands to tell the database that the command is complete and ready to be executed. A substitute on some systems is a backslash (\) on a line by itself after the end of the command.

It is worth noting here that a query of this nature will not necessarily order its output in any particular way. The same command executed on the same data at different times may not even produce the same ordering. Usually, the rows come out in the order in which they are found in the table but, as we stated in the previous chapter, that order is arbitrary. It will not necessarily be the order in which the data is entered or stored. You *can* order output from SQL commands directly through the use of a special clause. Later, we will explain how to do this. For now, simply recognize that, in the absence of explicit ordering, there is no definite order to your output.

Our use of the return (the Enter key) is arbitrary. We could just as easily have typed the query on one line as follows:

```
SELECT snum, sname, city, comm FROM Salespeople;
```

Since SQL uses the semicolon to indicate the end of a command, most SQL programs treat the return (made by pressing the Return or Enter key) as a space. It is a good idea to use returns and indentation as we did previously to make your commands easier to read and correct.

SELECTING EVERYTHING THE EASY WAY

If you want to see every column of a table, there is an optional abbreviation you can use. The asterisk (*) can be substituted for a complete list of the columns as follows:

```
SELECT *
     FROM Salespeople;
```

This will produce the same result as our previous command.

SELECT IN BRIEF

In summation, the SELECT command begins with the keyword SELECT, followed by a blank. After this comes a list of the names of the columns you wish to see, separated by commas. If you wish to see all of the columns of a table, you can replace this list with an asterisk (*). The keyword FROM is next, followed by a space and the name of the table that is being queried. Finally, a semicolon (;) must be used to end the query and indicate that the command is ready to be executed.

LOOKING ONLY AT CERTAIN COLUMNS OF A TABLE

The power of the SELECT command lies in its ability to extract highly specific information from a table. First, we will introduce the ability to look only at specified columns of a table. This is done easily by simply omitting the columns you do not wish to see from the SELECT portion of the command. For example, this query

```
SELECT sname, comm
    FROM Salespeople;
```

will produce the output shown in Figure 3.2.

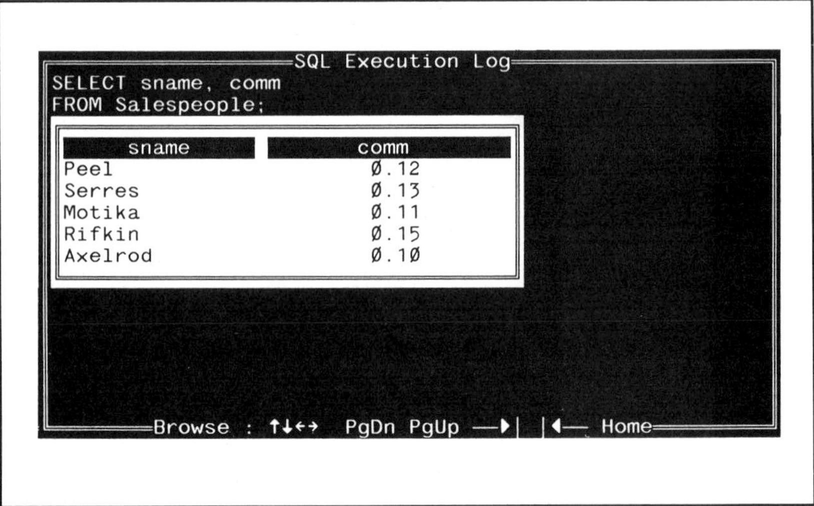

Figure 3.2: Selecting certain columns

There may be tables that have a large number of columns containing data, not all of which is relevant to the purpose at hand. Therefore, you will find the ability to pick and choose your columns quite useful.

COLUMN REORDERING

Even though the columns of a table are, by definition, ordered, this does not mean that you have to retrieve them in that order. An asterisk (*) will produce all the columns in their proper order, but if you indicate the columns separately, you can put them in any order you want. Let's look at the Orders table, placing the order date first, followed by the salesperson number, the order number, and the amount:

```
SELECT odate, snum, onum, amt
     FROM Orders;
```

This query's output is shown in Figure 3.3.

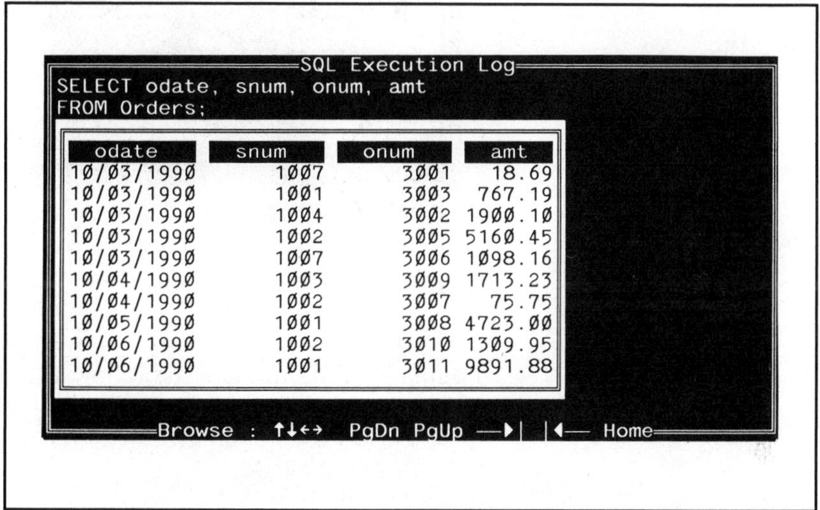
SQL Execution Log
SELECT odate, snum, onum, amt
FROM Orders;

odate	snum	onum	amt
10/03/1990	1007	3001	18.69
10/03/1990	1001	3003	767.19
10/03/1990	1004	3002	1900.10
10/03/1990	1002	3005	5160.45
10/03/1990	1007	3006	1098.16
10/04/1990	1003	3009	1713.23
10/04/1990	1002	3007	75.75
10/05/1990	1001	3008	4723.00
10/06/1990	1002	3010	1309.95
10/06/1990	1001	3011	9891.88

Browse : ↑↓←→ PgDn PgUp —▸| |◂— Home

Figure 3.3: Rearranging columns

As you can see, the structure of the information in the tables is merely a foundation for its active restructuring with SQL.

ELIMINATING REDUNDANT DATA

DISTINCT is an argument that provides a way for you to eliminate duplicate values from your SELECT clause. Suppose you want to know which salespeople currently have orders in the Orders table. You don't need to know how many orders each one has; you need only a list of salesperson numbers (snum's). You could enter

```
SELECT snum
     FROM Orders;
```

to get the output shown in Figure 3.4.

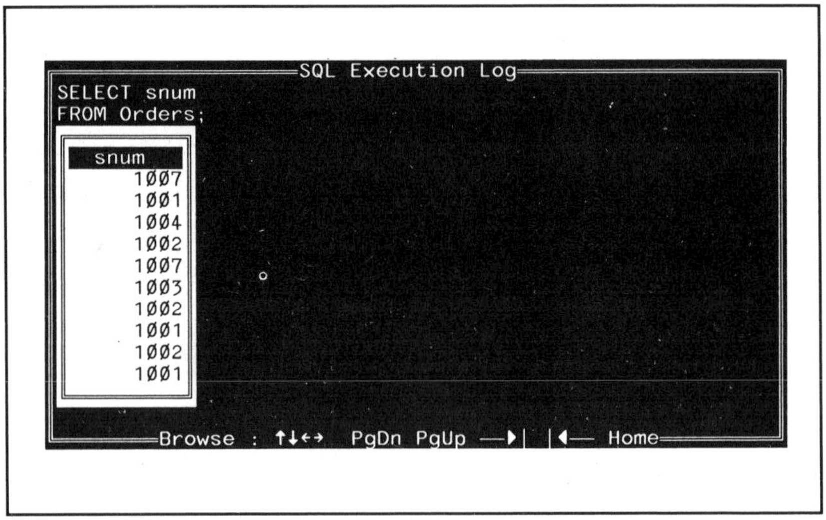

```
SQL Execution Log
SELECT snum
FROM Orders;

 snum
 1007
 1001
 1004
 1002
 1007
 1003
 1002
 1001
 1002
 1001

Browse : ↑↓←→  PgDn PgUp —▶| |◀— Home
```

Figure 3.4: SELECT with duplicates

To produce a list without duplications, which would be easier to read, you could enter the following:

```
SELECT DISTINCT snum
   FROM Orders;
```

The output for this query is shown in Figure 3.5.

In other words, DISTINCT keeps track of which values have come up before, so they will not be duplicated on the list. This is a useful way to avoid redundant data, but it is important that you be aware of what you are doing. If you should not have redundant data, you should not use DISTINCT, because it can hide a problem. For example, you might assume that all your customers' names are different. If someone put a second Clemens in the Customers table, however, and you use SELECT DISTINCT cname, you would not even see evidence of the duplication. You might get the wrong Clemens. Since you don't expect redundancy in this case, you shouldn't use DISTINCT.

THE PARAMETERS OF DISTINCT DISTINCT can be specified only once in a given SELECT clause. If the clause

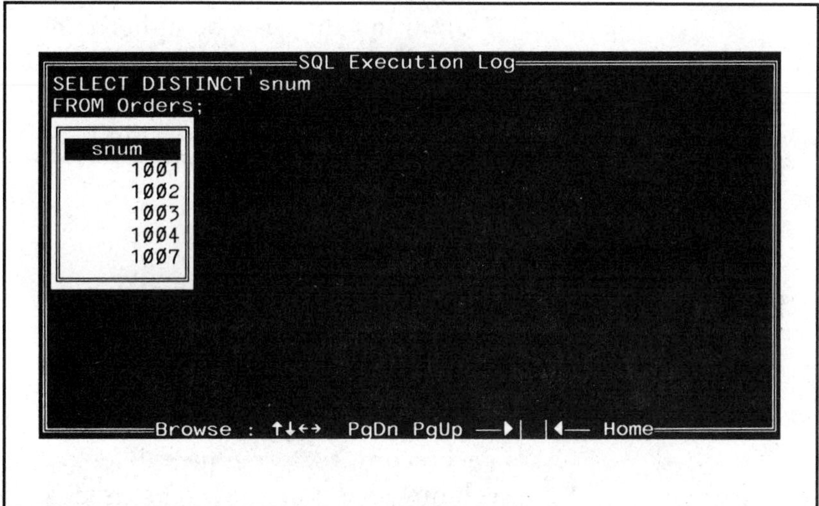

Figure 3.5: SELECT without duplicates

selects multiple fields, DISTINCT eliminates rows where all of the selected fields are identical. Rows in which some values are the same and some different will be retained. DISTINCT, in effect, applies to the entire output row, not a specific field (except when used within aggregate functions, as explained in Chapter 6), so it makes no sense to repeat it.

DISTINCT VS ALL As an alternative to DISTINCT, you may specify ALL. This has the opposite effect: duplicate output rows are retained. Since this is also what happens if you specify neither DISTINCT nor ALL, ALL is essentially a clarifier, rather than a functional argument.

QUALIFIED SELECTION—THE WHERE CLAUSE

Tables tend to get very large as time goes on, and more and more rows are added. As it is usually only certain rows that interest you at a given time, SQL enables you to define criteria to determine which rows are selected for output. The WHERE clause of the SELECT command allows you to define a *predicate*, a condition that can be either true or false for any row of the table. The command extracts only those rows from the table for which the predicate is true. For example, suppose you want to see the names and commissions of all salespeople in London. You could enter this command:

```
SELECT sname, city
   FROM Salespeople
   WHERE city = 'London';
```

When a WHERE clause is present, the database program goes through the entire table one row at a time and examines each row to determine if the predicate is true. Therefore, for the Peel record, the program will look at the current value of the city column, determine that it is equal to 'London', and include this row in the output. The Serres record will not be included, and so on. The output for the above query is shown in Figure 3.6.

Notice that the city column is not included in the output, even though its value is used to determine which rows are selected. This is perfectly alright. It is not necessary for the columns used

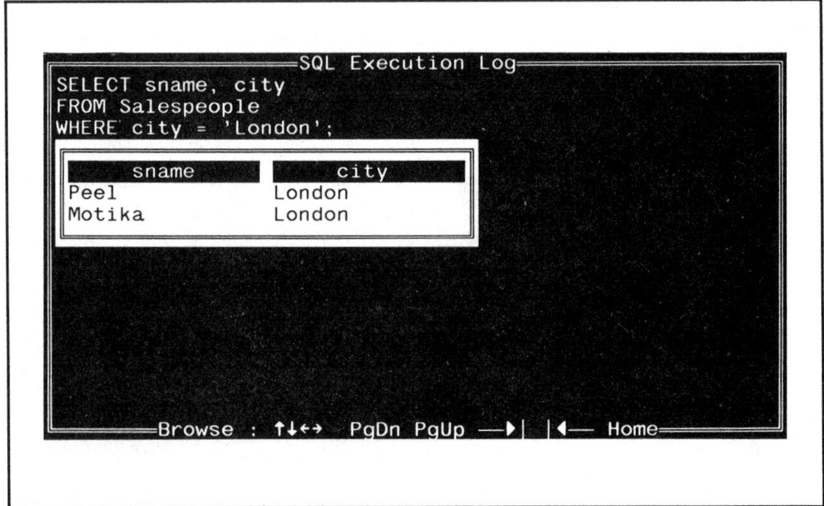

Figure 3.6: SELECT with a WHERE clause

in the WHERE clause to be present among those selected for output.

Let's try an example with a numeric field in the WHERE clause. The rating field of the Customers table is intended to separate the customers into groups based on some criteria that can be summarized by such a number. Perhaps it is a form of credit rating or a rating based on the volume of previous purchases. Such numeric codes can be useful in relational databases as a way of summarizing complex information. We can select all customers with a rating of 100, as follows:

```
SELECT *
    FROM Customers
    WHERE rating = 100;
```

The single quotes are not used here because rating is a numeric field. The results of the query are shown in Figure 3.7.

The WHERE clause is compatible with the previous material in this chapter. In other words, you can still use column numbers, eliminate duplicates, or reorder columns in SELECT commands that use WHERE. However, you substitute column

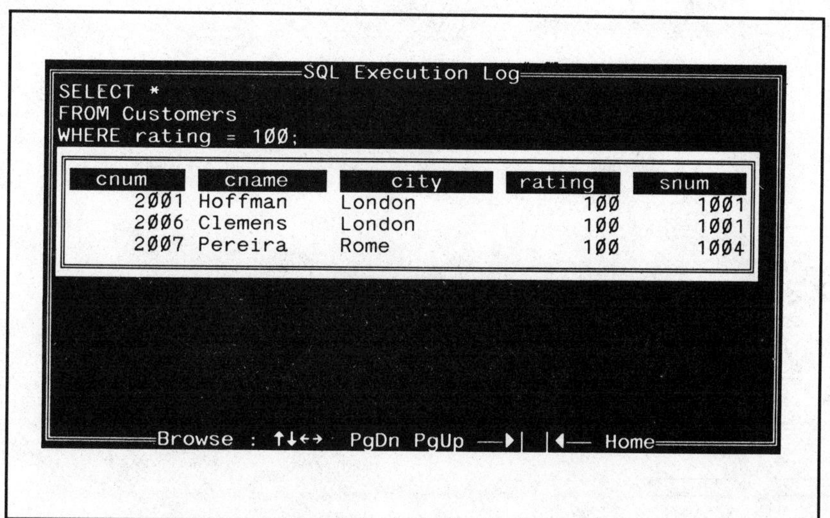

SQL Execution Log

```
SELECT *
FROM Customers
WHERE rating = 100;
```

cnum	cname	city	rating	snum
2001	Hoffman	London	100	1001
2006	Clemens	London	100	1001
2007	Pereira	Rome	100	1004

Browse : ↑↓←→ PgDn PgUp —▶| |◀— Home

Figure 3.7: SELECT with a numeric field in the predicate

numbers for names only in the SELECT clause, not in the WHERE clause itself.

SUMMARY

Now you know several ways to make a table give you the information that you want, rather than simply spilling out its contents. You can reorder the columns of the table or eliminate any of them. You can decide whether or not you want to see duplicate values.

Most importantly, you can define a condition called a predicate that determines whether or not a particular row of a table, possibly from among thousands, will be selected for output. Predicates can become very sophisticated, giving you great precision in controlling which rows are selected by a query. It is this ability to decide exactly what you want to see that makes SQL queries so powerful. The next several chapters will consist, for the most part, of features that expand the power of predicates. In Chapter 4, you will be exposed to operators other than equals that are used in predicate conditions and to ways of combining multiple conditions into a single predicate.

Putting SQL to Work

1. Write a SELECT command that produces the order number, amount, and date for all rows in the order table.
2. Write a query that produces all rows from the customer table for which the salesperson's number is 1001.
3. Write a query that produces the salesperson table with the columns in the following order: city, sname, snum, comm.
4. Write a SELECT command that produces the rating followed by the name of each customer in San Jose.
5. Write a query that will produce the snum values of all salespeople with orders currently in the Orders table without any repeats.

(See Appendix A for answers.)

4

Using Relational and Boolean Operators to Create More Sophisticated Predicates

IN CHAPTER 3, YOU LEARNED THAT PREDICATES CAN evaluate an equals statement as true or false. They can also evaluate other kinds of relationships besides equalities. This chapter will explore the other relational operators used in SQL. You will also learn how to use Boolean operators to change and combine predicate values. With Booleans, a single predicate can contain any number of conditions. This allows you to produce quite sophisticated predicates. The use of parentheses to structure these complex predicates will also be explained.

RELATIONAL OPERATORS

A *relational operator* is a mathematical symbol that indicates a certain type of comparison between two values. You have already seen how equalities, such as 2 + 3 = 5 or city = 'London', are used. But there are other relational operators as well. Suppose you want to see all Salespeople with commissions above a certain amount. You would use a greater-than type of comparison. These are the relational operators that SQL recognizes:

=	Equal to
>	Greater than
<	Less than
>=	Greater than or equal to
<=	Less than or equal to
<>	Not equal to

These operators have the standard meanings for numeric values. For character values, their definition depends on the conversion format, ASCII or EBCDIC, that you are using. SQL compares character values in terms of the underlying numbers as defined in the conversion format. Even character values, such as '1', which represent numbers, do not necessarily equal the number they represent.

You can use relational operators to represent alphabetical order—for example, 'a' < 'n' means a precedes n in alphabetical order—but this is limited by the parameters of the conversion format. In both ASCII and EBCDIC, characters are less than all other characters that they precede in alphabetical order, provided all are of a single case (upper or lower). In ASCII, all uppercase characters are less than all lowercase characters, so that 'Z' < 'a', and all numbers are less than all characters, so that '1' < 'Z'. Both of these are reversed in EBCDIC. To keep the discussion simple, we will assume from here on that you are using the ASCII format. Consult your system documentation if you are unsure of which format you are using or how it works.

The values being compared here are called scalar values. *Scalar values* can be produced by scalar expressions; 1 + 2 is a scalar expression that produces the scalar value 3. Scalar values can be characters or numbers, although obviously only numbers are used with arithmetic operators, such as + or *. Predicates typically compare scalar values using either relational operators or special SQL operators to see if the comparison is true. Some SQL operators are explained in Chapter 5.

Suppose you wanted to see all customers with a rating above 200. Since 200 is a scalar value, as are the values in the rating column, you would use a relational operator to compare them:

```
SELECT *
    FROM Customers
    WHERE rating > 200;
```

The output for this query is shown in Figure 4.1.

Of course, if we also wanted to see the customers with a rating equal to 200, we would use the predicate

```
rating > = 200
```

BOOLEAN OPERATORS

Basic Boolean operators are also recognized in SQL. Boolean expressions are those that are either true or false, like predicates. Boolean operators relate one or more true/false values and produce a single true/false value. The standard Boolean operators recognized in SQL are AND, OR, and NOT. Other, more complex, Boolean operators exist (such as "exclusive or"), but these

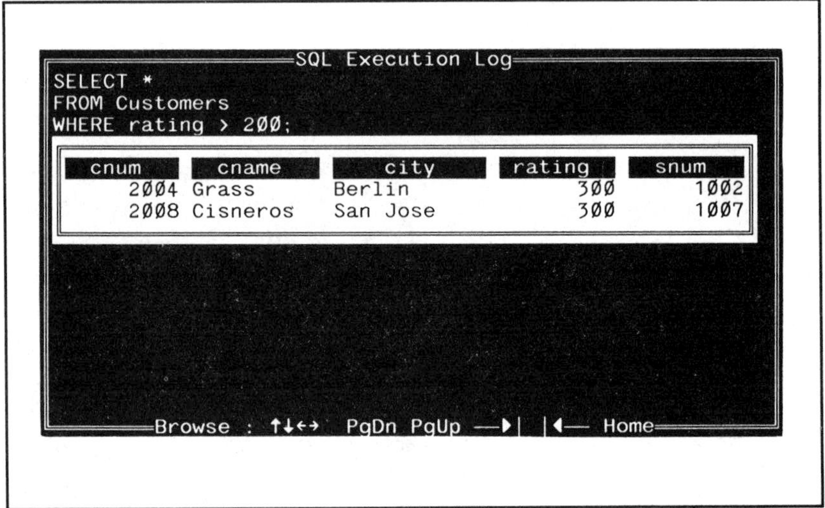

Figure 4.1: Using greater than (>)

can be built from our three simple pieces. As you may be aware, Boolean true/false logic is the entire basis of digital computer operation; so, actually, everything SQL (or any other language) does can be reduced to Boolean logic. These are the Boolean operators and how they work:

- AND takes two Booleans (in the form A AND B) as arguments and evaluates to true if they are both true.
- OR takes two Booleans (in the form A OR B) as arguments and evaluates to true if either is true.
- NOT takes a single Boolean (in the form NOT A) as an argument and changes its value from false to true or from true to false.

By relating predicates with Boolean operators, you can greatly increase their sophistication. Suppose you want to see all customers in San Jose who have a rating above 200:

```
SELECT *
   FROM Customers
   WHERE city = 'San Jose'
      AND rating > 200;
```

(Of course, as we stated before, the returns are for readability only.) The output for this query is shown in Figure 4.2. There is only one customer who fills the bill.

If you used OR, you would get all customers who were either located in San Jose *or* had a rating above 200

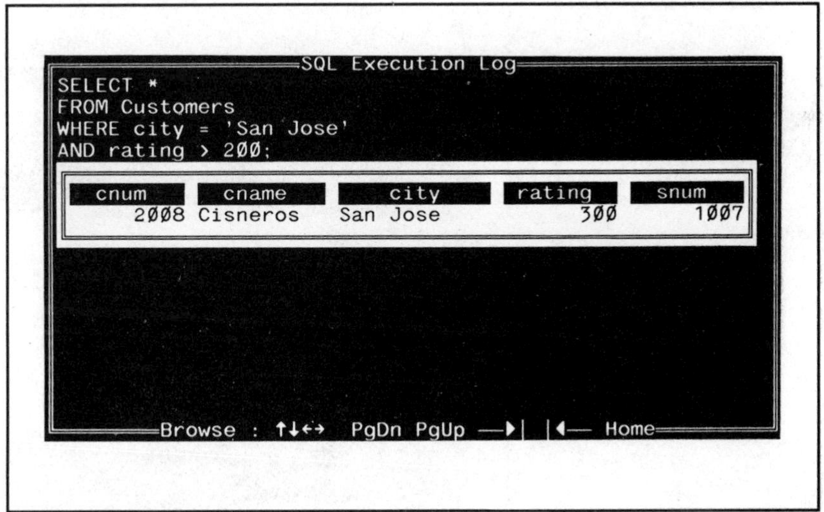

Figure 4.2: SELECT using AND

```
SELECT *
    FROM Customers
    WHERE city = 'San Jose'
        OR rating > 200;
```

The output for this query is shown in Figure 4.3.

NOT can be used to reverse the value of a Boolean. Here is an example of a NOT query:

```
SELECT *
    FROM Customers
    WHERE city = 'San Jose'
        OR NOT rating > 200;
```

This query's output is shown in Figure 4.4.

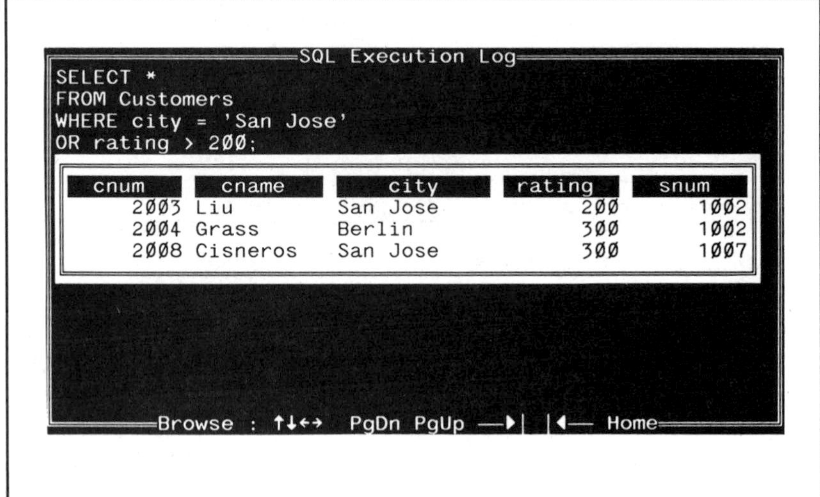

SQL Execution Log

```
SELECT *
FROM Customers
WHERE city = 'San Jose'
OR rating > 200;
```

cnum	cname	city	rating	snum
2003	Liu	San Jose	200	1002
2004	Grass	Berlin	300	1002
2008	Cisneros	San Jose	300	1007

Browse : ↑↓←→ PgDn PgUp —▶| |◀— Home

Figure 4.3: SELECT using OR

SQL Execution Log

```
SELECT *
FROM Customers
WHERE city = 'San Jose'
OR NOT rating > 200;
```

cnum	cname	city	rating	snum
2001	Hoffman	London	100	1001
2002	Giovanni	Rome	200	1003
2003	Liu	San Jose	200	1002
2006	Clemens	London	100	1001
2008	Cisneros	San Jose	300	1007
2007	Pereira	Rome	100	1004

Browse : ↑↓←→ PgDn PgUp —▶| |◀— Home

Figure 4.4: SELECT using NOT

All of the records except Grass were selected. Grass was not in San Jose, and his rating was greater than 200, so he failed both tests. Each of the other rows met one *or* the other (or both) of these criteria. Notice that the NOT operator must precede a Boolean whose value it is to change, not be located before the relational operator as you might do in English. It is *incorrect* to enter

```
rating NOT > 200
```

as a predicate, even though that is how we would say it in English. This brings up another point. How would SQL evaluate the following?

```
SELECT *
    FROM Customers
    WHERE NOT city = 'San Jose'
        OR rating > 200;
```

Does the NOT apply only to the city = 'San Jose' expression, or to both that and the rating > 200 expression? As written, the correct answer would be the former. SQL will apply NOT only to the Boolean expression immediately following it. You could obtain another result with this command:

```
SELECT *
    FROM Customers
    WHERE NOT (city = 'San Jose'
        OR rating > 200);
```

SQL understands parentheses to mean that everything inside them will be evaluated first and treated as a single expression by everything outside them (which is the standard interpretation in mathematics). In other words, SQL takes each row and determines if the city = 'San Jose' or the rating > 200. If either condition is true, the Boolean expression inside the parentheses is true. However, if the Boolean expression inside the parentheses is true, the predicate as a whole is false, because NOT turns the trues into falses and vice versa. The output for this query is shown in Figure 4.5.

Here is a deliberately complex example. See if you can follow its logic (the output is shown in Figure 4.6):

```
SELECT *
    FROM Orders
```

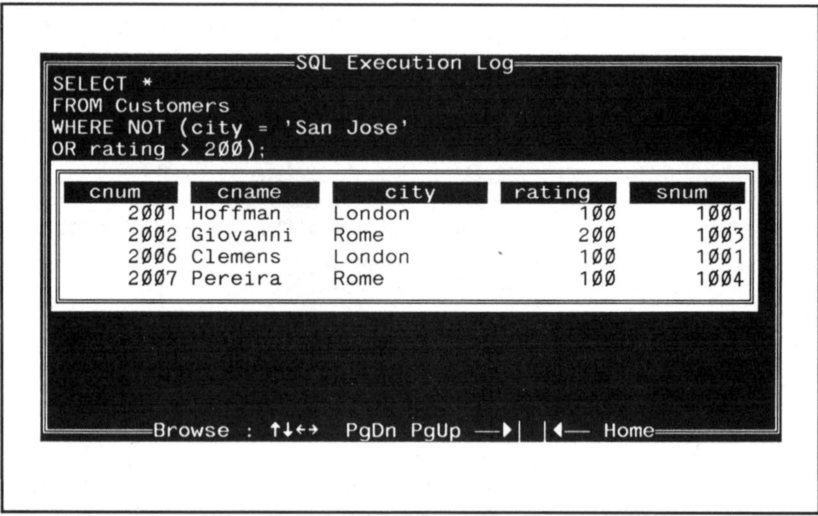

Figure 4.5: SELECT with NOT and parentheses

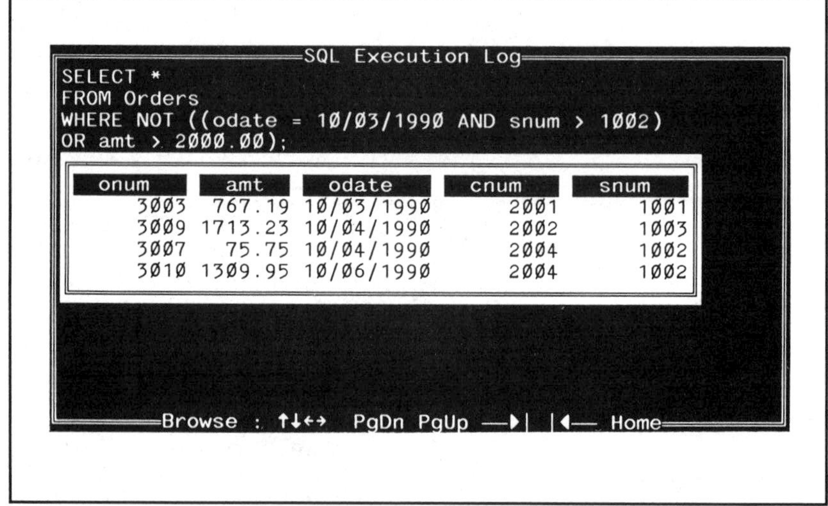

Figure 4.6: A complex query

```
WHERE NOT ((odate = 10/03/1990 AND snum > 1002)
      OR amt > 2000.00);
```

Although Boolean operators are simple individually, they are not so simple when combined into complex expressions. The way to evaluate a complex Boolean is to evaluate the Boolean expression(s) most deeply nested in parentheses, combine these into a single Boolean value, and then combine this with the higher nested values.

Here is a detailed explanation of how the example above was evaluated. The most deeply nested Boolean expressions in the predicate—odate = 10/03/1990 and snum > 1002—are joined by an AND, forming one Boolean expression that will evaluate to true for all rows that meet both of these conditions. This compound Boolean expression (which we will call Boolean number 1, or B1 for short) is joined with the amt > 2000.00 expression (B2) by an OR, forming a third expression (B3), which is true for a given row if either B1 or B2 is true for that row. B3 is wholly contained in parentheses preceded by a NOT, forming the final Boolean expression (B4), which is the condition of the predicate. Thus B4, the predicate of the query, is true whenever B3 is false and vice versa. B3 is false whenever B1 and B2 are both false. B1 is false for a row if the order date of the row is not 10/03/1990 or if its snum value is not greater than 1002. B2 is false for all rows with an amount that is not above 2000.00. Any row with an amount above 2000.00 would make B2 true; as a result, B3 would be true, and B4 false. Therefore, all such rows are eliminated from the output. Of the remaining rows, those on October 3 with snum greater than 1002 (such as the row for onum 3001 on October 3 with snum of 1007), make B1 true, thereby making B3 true, and the predicate of the query false. These are also eliminated. The output shows the rows that are left.

SUMMARY

In this chapter, you have greatly extended your fluency with predicates. Now you can find values that relate to a given value in any one of a number of ways—all definable with the various relational operators. You can also use the Boolean operators AND and OR to combine multiple conditions, each of which could stand alone in predicates, into a single predicate. The Boolean operator NOT, as you have seen, can reverse the meaning of a condition or group of conditions. All of the Boolean and relational operators can have their effect controlled by the use of parentheses, which determine the order in which the operations are performed. These operations can be taken to any level of complexity; you have had some taste of how conditions that are quite involved can be built up out of these simple parts.

Now that we have shown how standard mathematical operators are used, we can move on to operators that are exclusive to SQL. This we will do in Chapter 5.

Putting SQL to Work

1. Write a query that will give you all orders for more than $1,000.
2. Write a query that will give you the names and cities of all salespeople in London with a commission above .10.
3. Write a query on the Customers table whose output will exclude all customers with a rating < = 100, unless they are located in Rome.
4. What will be the output from the following query?

```
SELECT *
     FROM Orders
     WHERE (amt < 1000 OR
          NOT (odate = 10/03/1990
               AND cnum > 2003));
```

5. What will be the output of the following query?

```
SELECT *
     FROM Orders
     WHERE NOT ((odate = 10/03/1990 OR snum
      > 1006)
          AND amt > = 1500);
```

6. What is a simpler way to write this query?

```
SELECT snum, sname, city, comm
     FROM Salespeople
     WHERE (comm > + .12 OR
     comm < .14);
```

(See Appendix A for answers.)

5

Using Special Operators in Conditions

IN ADDITION TO THE RELATIONAL AND BOOLEAN operators we discussed in Chapter 4, SQL uses the special operators IN, BETWEEN, LIKE, and IS NULL. In this chapter, you will learn how to use them, as you would the relational operators, to produce more sophisticated and powerful predicates. The discussion of IS NULL will involve the implications of missing data and of the NULL value that indicates data is missing. You will also learn a variation in the usage of NOT that is applicable to these operators.

THE IN OPERATOR

IN explicitly defines a set in which a given value may or may not be included. Based on what you have learned up to now, if you wanted to find all salespeople that were located in either Barcelona or London, you would have to use the following query (its output is shown in Figure 5.1):

```
SELECT *
    FROM Salespeople
    WHERE city = 'Barcelona'
        OR city = 'London';
```

Here is an easier way to get the same information:

```
SELECT *
    FROM Salespeople
    WHERE city IN ('Barcelona', 'London');
```

The output for this query is shown in Figure 5.2.

As you can see, IN defines a set by explicitly naming the members of the set in parentheses, separated by commas. It then checks the various values of the named field to try to find a match. If it does, the predicate is true. When the set contains numeric rather than character values, of course, the single quotes are omitted. Let's find all customers matched with salespeople 1001, 1007, and 1004. The output for the following query

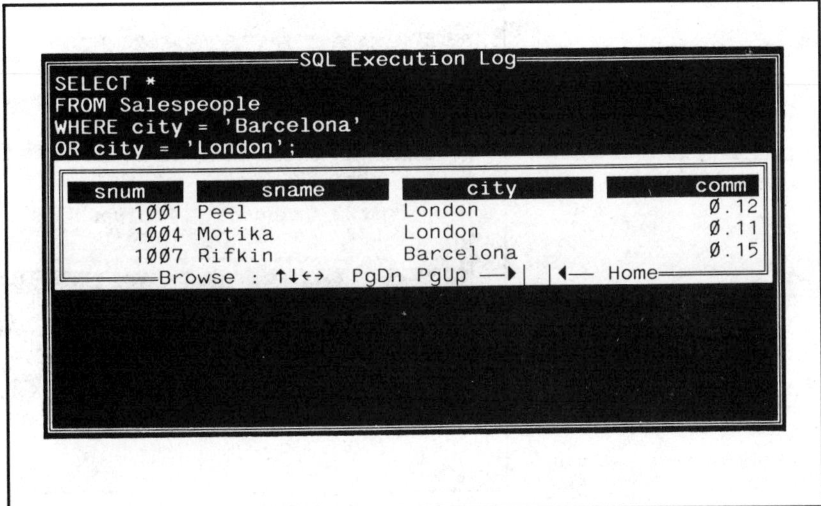

SQL Execution Log
SELECT *
FROM Salespeople
WHERE city = 'Barcelona'
OR city = 'London';
snum sname city comm
1001 Peel London 0.12
1004 Motika London 0.11
1007 Rifkin Barcelona 0.15
Browse : ↑↓←→ PgDn PgUp —▶| |◀— Home

Figure 5.1: Finding salespeople in Barcelona or London

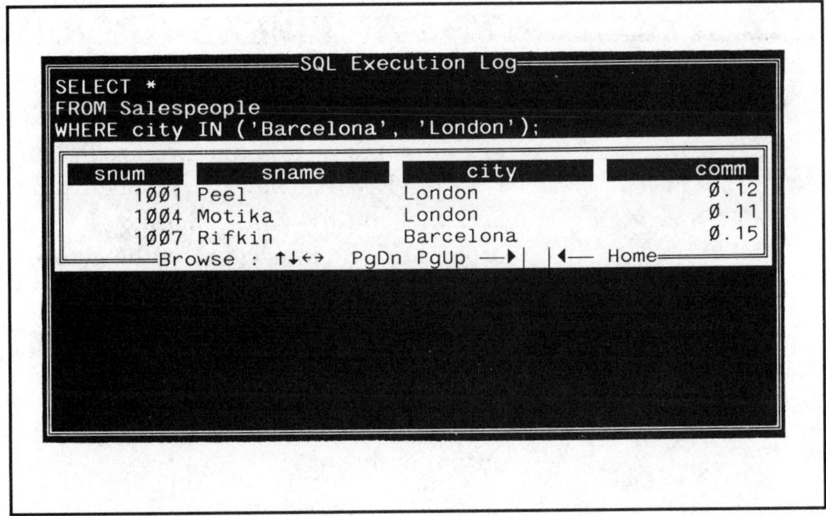

Figure 5.2: SELECT using IN

is shown in Figure 5.3:

```
SELECT *
    FROM Customers
    WHERE snum IN (1001, 1007, 1004);
```

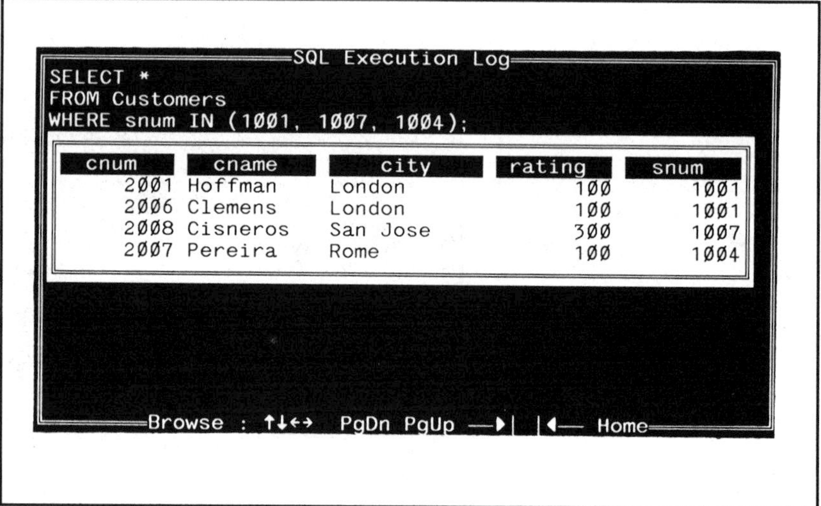

```
SQL Execution Log
SELECT *
FROM Customers
WHERE snum IN (1001, 1007, 1004);

 cnum   cname      city       rating  snum
 2001   Hoffman    London       100   1001
 2006   Clemens    London       100   1001
 2008   Cisneros   San Jose     300   1007
 2007   Pereira    Rome         100   1004

Browse : ↑↓←→  PgDn PgUp —▶| |◀— Home
```

Figure 5.3: SELECT using IN with numbers

THE BETWEEN OPERATOR

The BETWEEN operator is similar to IN. Rather than enumerating a set as IN does, BETWEEN defines a range that values must fall in to make the predicate true. You use the keyword BETWEEN followed by the beginning value, the keyword AND and the ending value. Unlike IN, BETWEEN is sensitive to order, and the first value in the clause must be first in alphabetic or numeric order. (Notice that, unlike English, SQL does not say (*value*) "is BETWEEN" (*value*) and (*value*), but simply (*value*) "BETWEEN" (*value*) and (*value*). This applies as well to the LIKE operator.) The following will extract from the Salespeople table all salespeople with commissions between .10 and .12 (the output is shown in Figure 5.4):

```
SELECT *
   FROM Salespeople
   WHERE comm BETWEEN .10 AND .12;
```

Notice that the BETWEEN operator is inclusive; that is, values matching either of the two boundary values (in this case, .10 and .12) cause the predicate to be true. SQL does not directly

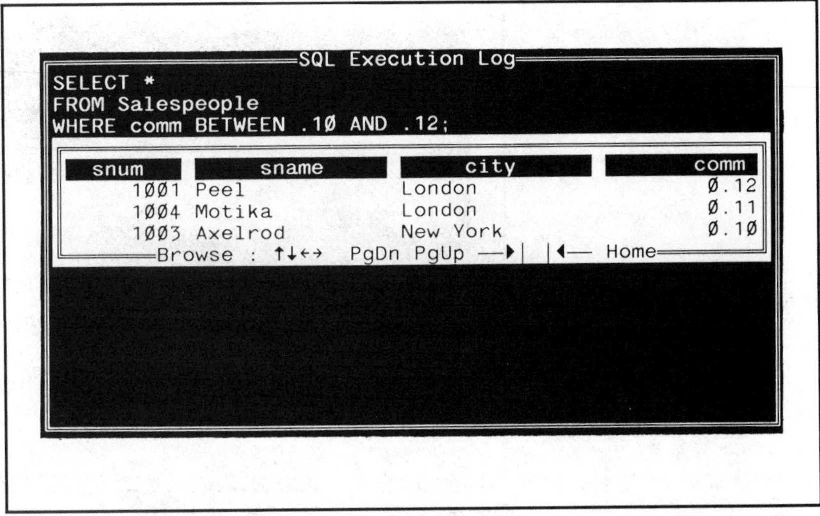

Figure 5.4: SELECT using BETWEEN

support a noninclusive BETWEEN. You must either define your boundary values so that an inclusive interpretation is acceptable, or do something like this:

```
SELECT *
   FROM Salespeople
   WHERE (comm BETWEEN .10, AND .12)
      AND NOT comm IN (.10, .12);
```

The output for this query is shown in Figure 5.5.

Admittedly, this is a bit clumsy, but it does show how these new operators can be combined with Boolean operators to produce more complex predicates. Basically, you use IN and BETWEEN just as you do relational operators to compare values, one of which happens to be a set (for IN) or a range (for BETWEEN).

Also like relational operators, BETWEEN operates on character fields in terms of the ASCII equivalents. This means you can use it to select ranges from alphabetical ordering. It is important when you do this to be consistent in your use of capitalization.

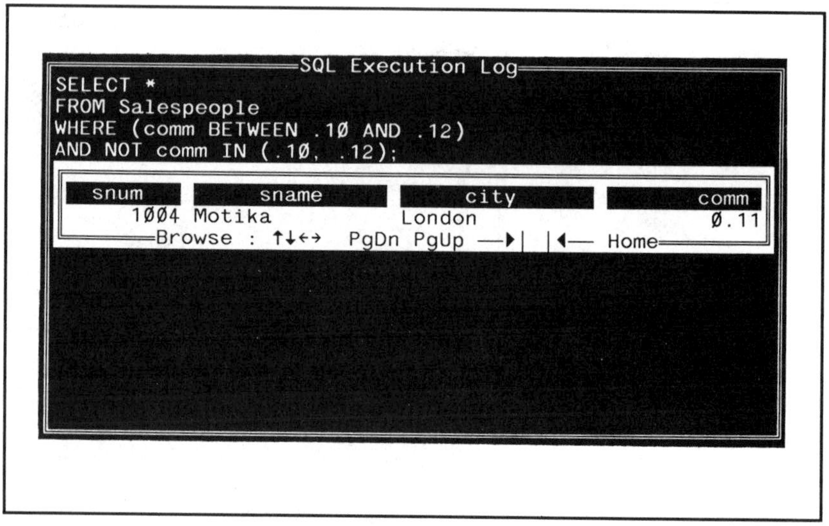

```
SQL Execution Log
SELECT *
FROM Salespeople
WHERE (comm BETWEEN .10 AND .12)
AND NOT comm IN (.10, .12);

snum   sname     city      comm
1004   Motika    London    0.11
Browse : ↑↓←→  PgDn PgUp —▶|  |◀— Home
```

Figure 5.5: Making BETWEEN noninclusive

This query selects all customers whose names fall in a certain alphabetical range:

```
SELECT *
   FROM Customers
   WHERE cname BETWEEN 'A' AND 'G';
```

The output for this query is shown in Figure 5.6.

Notice that Grass and Giovanni are omitted, even though BETWEEN is inclusive. This is because of the way BETWEEN compares strings of unequal length. The string 'G' is shorter than the string 'Giovanni', so BETWEEN pads the 'G' with blanks. The blanks precede the letters in alphabetical order (in most implementations), so Giovanni is not selected. The same applies to Grass. It is important to remember this if you are using BETWEEN to extract alphabetical ranges. You will usually go one letter beyond the last letter you want to include, or add a z (several if necessary) after your second boundary value.

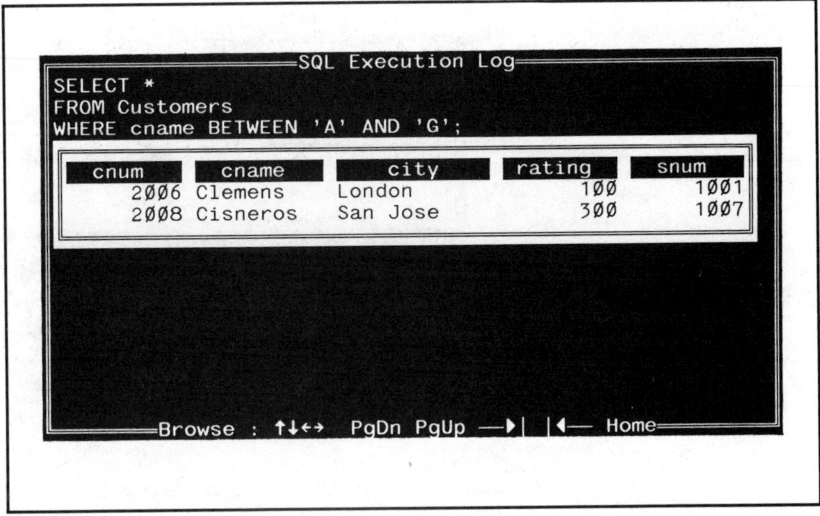

Figure 5.6: Using BETWEEN alphabetically

THE LIKE OPERATOR

LIKE can be applied only to fields of types CHAR or VARCHAR, against which it is used to find substrings. In other words, it searches a character field to see if part of it matches a string. To do this, it uses *wildcards*, special characters that will match anything. There are two types of wildcards used with LIKE:

- The underscore character (_) stands for any single character. For example, 'b_t' will match 'bat' or 'bit' but it will not match 'brat'.
- The percent sign (%) stands for a sequence of any number of characters (including zero characters). '%p%t' will match 'put', 'posit', or 'opt', but not 'spite'.

Let's find all the customers whose names begin with G (the output is shown in Figure 5.7):

```
SELECT *
    FROM Customers
    WHERE cname LIKE 'G%';
```

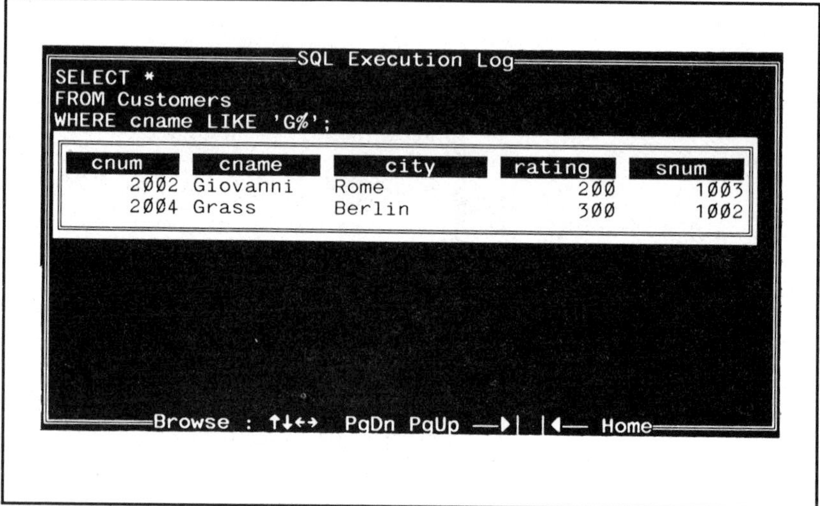

Figure 5.7: SELECT using LIKE with %

LIKE can be handy if you are searching for a name or other value, and you cannot remember all of it. Suppose you were unsure whether to spell the name of one of your salespeople Peal or Peel. You can simply use the part you know and the wildcards will find all possible matches (the output of this query is shown in Figure 5.8):

```
SELECT *
    FROM Salespeople
    WHERE sname LIKE 'P_ _l%';
```

The underscore wildcards each represent a single character, so a name like Prettel would not show up. The % wildcard at the end of the string is necessary in many implementations if the length of the sname field is greater than the number of characters in the name Peel (which it obviously is here, because some of the other sname values are longer than four characters). In such a case, the sname field value is actually stored as the name Peel, followed by a series of spaces. Therefore, the character 'l' is not considered the end of the string. The % wildcard simply matches all the spaces. This would not be necessary if the sname field were of type VARCHAR.

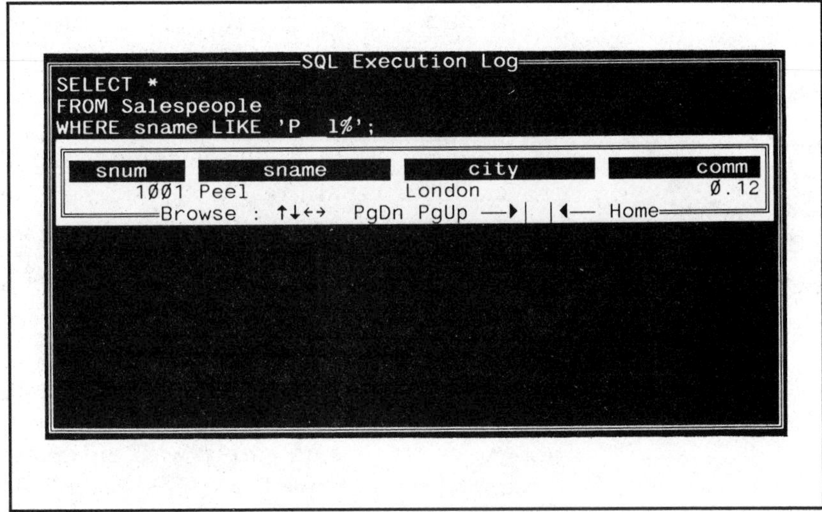

Figure 5.8: SELECT using LIKE with _ (underscore)

So what do you do if you need to search for a percent sign or an underscore in a string? In a LIKE predicate, you can define any single character as an escape character. An *escape character* is used immediately before a percent sign or underscore in the predicate, and means that the percent sign or underscore will be interpreted as a character rather than a wildcard. For example, we could search our sname column for the presence of underscores, as follows:

```
SELECT *
    FROM Salespeople
    WHERE sname LIKE '%/_%'ESCAPE '/';
```

With the current data there is no output, because we have not included any underscores in our salespeople's names. The ESCAPE clause defines '/' as an escape character. The escape character is used in the LIKE string, followed by a percent sign, an underscore, or itself (to be explained shortly), which will be searched for in the column, rather than treated as a wildcard. The escape character must be a single character and applies only to the single character immediately following it. In the example above, both the beginning and ending percent signs are still treated as wildcards; only the underscore represents itself.

As mentioned above, the escape character can also be used on itself. In other words, if you want to search the column for your escape character, you will simply enter it twice. The first one acts as an escape character meaning "take the following character literally as a character," and the second one is that character—the escape character itself. Here is the preceding example revised to search for occurrences of the string '_/' in the sname column:

```
SELECT *
    FROM Salespeople
    WHERE sname LIKE '%/_//%'ESCAPE '/';
```

Again there is no output with the current data. The string being matched consists of any sequence of characters (%), followed by the underscore character (/_), the escape character (//), and any sequence of trailing characters (%).

WORKING WITH NULL VALUES

Frequently, there will be records in a table that do not have values for every field, either because the information is not complete, or because the field simply does not apply to every case. SQL provides for these instances by allowing you to enter a NULL into the field in place of a value. A NULL is not *in* the field at all, strictly speaking. When a field value is NULL, it means that the database program has specially marked that field as not having any value for that row (record). This is different from simply assigning a field a value of zero or a blank, which the database will treat the same as any other value. Also, since NULL is technically not a value, it does not have a data type. It can be placed in any type of field. Nonetheless, a NULL in SQL is frequently referred to as a NULL value.

Suppose you have a new customer who has not yet been assigned a salesperson. Rather than wait for the salesperson to be assigned, you want to enter the customer into the database now, so that he or she does not get lost in the shuffle. You can enter a row for the customer with a NULL for snum and fill in that field with a value later, when a salesperson is assigned.

THE IS NULL OPERATOR

Since NULL indicates missing values, you cannot know what the result of any comparison involving a NULL would be. When a NULL is compared to any value, even another NULL, the result is neither true nor false, but *unknown*. An unknown Boolean generally behaves the same as a false—a row that produces an unknown value in the predicate will not be selected by the query—with the notable exception that, while NOT (false) equals true, NOT (unknown) still equals unknown. Therefore, an expression such as "city = NULL" or "city IN (NULL)" will be unknown, regardless of the city value.

Often you will need to distinguish between false and unknown —between rows containing column values that fail a predicate condition and those containing NULL in those columns. For this reason, SQL provides the special operator IS, which is used with the keyword NULL to locate NULL values.

To find all records in our Customers table with NULL values in the city column, we could enter:

```
SELECT *
    FROM Customers
    WHERE city IS NULL;
```

This currently produces no output because we have no NULL values in our sample tables. NULL values are very important, and we will be returning to them later.

USING NOT WITH SPECIAL OPERATORS

The special operators we have covered in this chapter can be immediately preceded by the Boolean NOT. This is in contrast to relational operators, which must have the NOT before the entire expression. For example, if we want to eliminate NULLs from our output, rather than finding them, we would use NOT to reverse the meaning of the predicate:

```
SELECT *
    FROM Customers
    WHERE city IS NOT NULL;
```

In the absence of NULLs (which is currently the case), this would produce the entire Customers table. It is the equivalent of entering

```
SELECT *
    FROM Customers
    WHERE NOT city IS NULL;
```

which is also acceptable.

We can also use NOT with IN:

```
SELECT *
    FROM Salespeople
    WHERE city NOT IN ('London', 'San Jose');
```

This is another way of saying

```
SELECT *
    FROM Salespeople
    WHERE NOT city IN ('London', 'San Jose');
```

The output for this query is shown in Figure 5.9.

You can use NOT BETWEEN and NOT LIKE the same way.

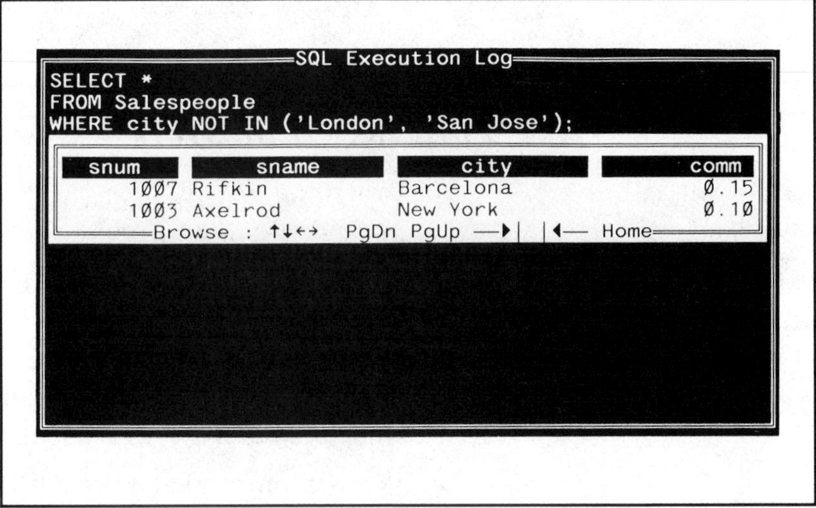

Figure 5.9: Using NOT with IN

SUMMARY

Now you can construct predicates in terms of relationships specially defined by SQL. You can search for values in a certain range (BETWEEN) or in an enumerated set (IN), or you can search for character values that match text within parameters that you define (LIKE).

You have also learned some things about how SQL deals with missing data—a reality of the database world—by using NULLs in place of values. You can extract or exclude NULLs from your output by using the IS NULL (or IS NOT NULL) operator. Now that you have an entire set of both standard mathematical and special operators at your disposal, you are ready to move on to special SQL functions that operate on entire groups of values, rather than on single values. This is the subject of Chapter 6.

Putting SQL to Work

1. Write two queries that will produce all orders taken on October 3rd or 4th, 1990.
2. Write a query that selects all of the customers serviced by Peel or Motika. (Hint: the snum field relates the two tables to one another.)
3. Write a query that will produce all of the customers whose names begin with a letter from A to G.
4. Write a query that selects all customers whose names begin with C.
5. Write a query that selects all orders save those with zeroes or NULLs in the amt (amount) field.

(See Appendix A for answers.)

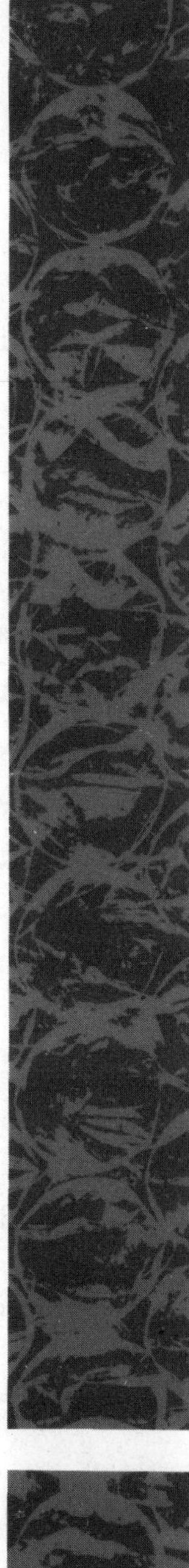

6

Summarizing Data with Aggregate Functions

IN THIS CHAPTER, YOU WILL MOVE BEYOND SIMPLY using queries to extract values from the database and discover how you can use them to derive information from those values. This is done with aggregate or summary functions that take groups of values from a field and reduce them to a single value. You will learn how to use these functions, how to define the groups of values to which they will be applied, and how to determine which groups are selected for output. You will also see under what conditions you can combine field values with this derived information in a single query.

WHAT ARE THE AGGREGATE FUNCTIONS?

Queries can produce generalizations about groups of values as well as field values. It does this through the use of aggregate functions. Aggregate functions produce a single value for an entire group of table entries. Here is a list of these functions:

- COUNT produces the number of rows or nonNULL field values that the query selected.
- SUM produces the arithmetic sum of all selected values of a given field.
- AVG produces the average (mean) of all selected values of a given field.
- MAX produces the largest of all selected values of a given field.
- MIN produces the smallest of all selected values of a given field.

HOW DO YOU USE AGGREGATE FUNCTIONS?

Aggregate functions are used like field names in the SELECT clause of queries and, with one exception, take field names as arguments. Only numeric fields can be used for SUM and AVG. For COUNT, MAX, and MIN, numeric or character fields can be used. When used with character fields, MAX and MIN will translate to ASCII equivalents, which is to say that, generally speaking, MIN will mean first, and MAX last, in alphabetical order (the issue of alphabetical ordering is discussed in more detail in Chapter 4).

To find the SUM of all of our purchases from the Orders table, we could enter the following query, whose output is shown in Figure 6.1:

```
SELECT SUM(amt)
   FROM Orders;
```

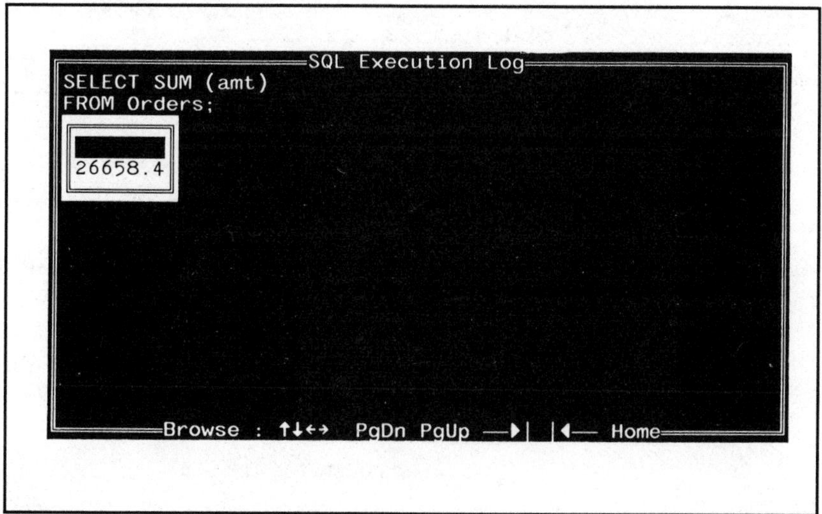

Figure 6.1: Selecting a sum

This, of course, differs substantially from selecting a field in that it returns a single value, regardless of how many rows are in the table. Because of this, aggregate functions and fields cannot be selected at the same time, unless the GROUP BY clause (described shortly) is used.

Finding the average amount would be a similar operation (the output of the following query is shown in Figure 6.2):

```
SELECT AVG(amt)
   FROM Orders;
```

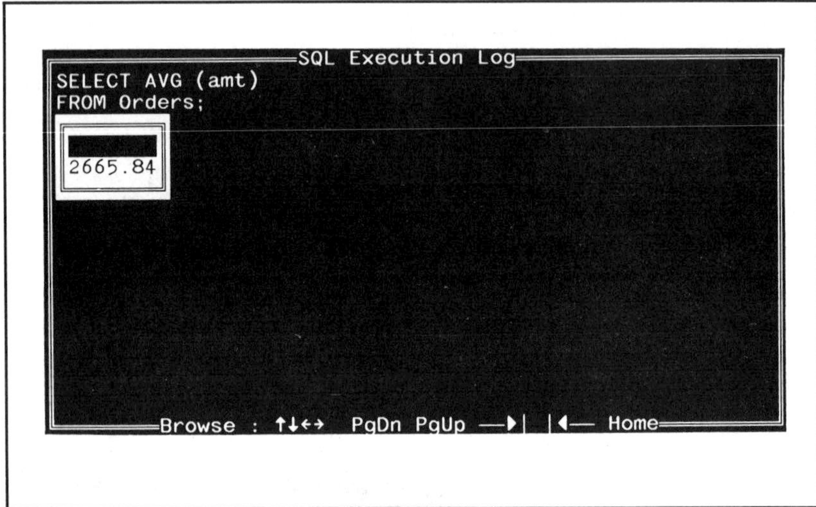

Figure 6.2: Selecting an average

SPECIAL ATTRIBUTES OF COUNT

The COUNT function is slightly different. It counts the number of values in a given column, or the number of rows in a table. When it is counting column values, it is used with DISTINCT to produce a count of the number of different values in a given field. We could use it, for example, to count the number of salespeople currently listing orders in the Orders table (the output is shown in Figure 6.3):

```
SELECT COUNT (DISTINCT snum)
    FROM Orders;
```

THE USE OF DISTINCT Notice in the above example that DISTINCT, followed by the name of the field it is being applied to, is placed in parentheses, not immediately after SELECT as we have seen before. This use of DISTINCT with COUNT when applied to individual columns is required by the ANSI standard, but many programs do not enforce this requirement.

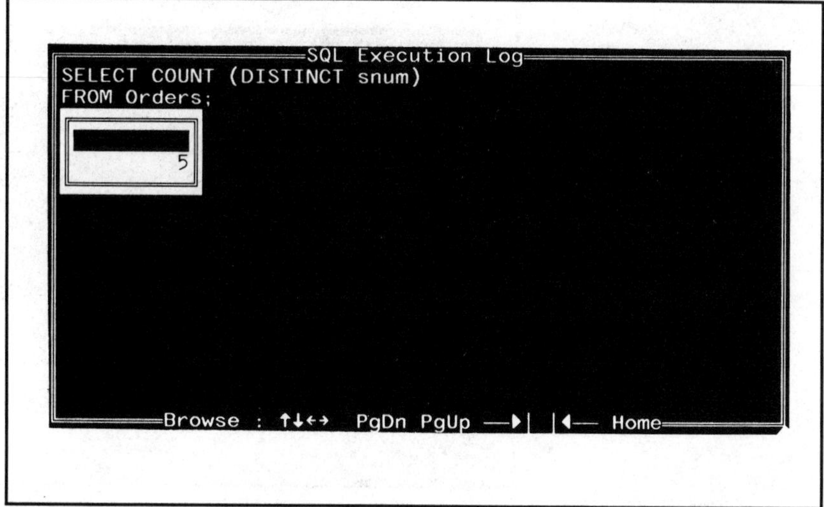

Figure 6.3: Counting field values

You can select multiple COUNTs of DISTINCT fields in a single query, which, as we have seen in Chapter 3, is not the case when you select DISTINCT rows.

DISTINCT can be used in this way with any aggregate function, but it is most often used with COUNT. With MAX and MIN, it simply has no effect, and with SUM and AVG, you usually want to include repeated values, because these legitimately affect the total and the average of all column values.

USING COUNT WITH ROWS RATHER THAN VALUES To count the total number of rows in a table, use the COUNT function with an asterisk in place of a field name, as in the following example, the output of which is shown in Figure 6.4:

```
SELECT COUNT(*)
    FROM Customers;
```

COUNT with the asterisk includes both NULLs and duplicates, so DISTINCT cannot be used. For this reason, it can produce a higher number than the COUNT of a particular field,

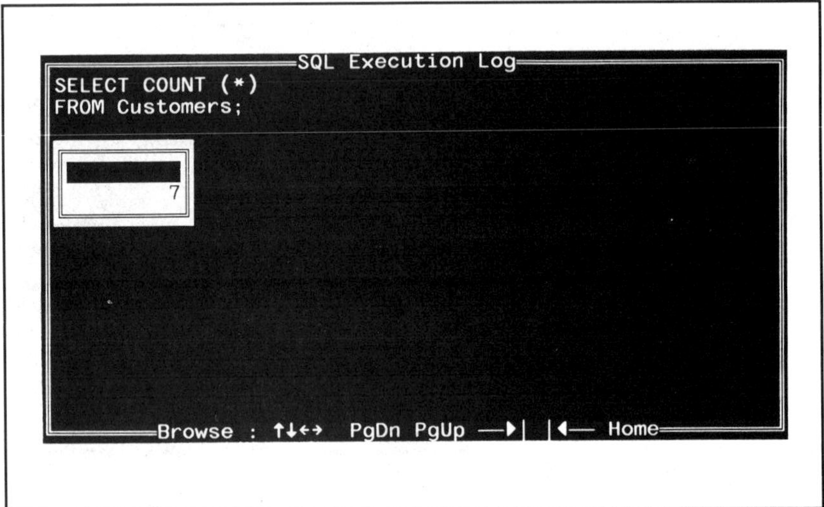

Figure 6.4: Counting rows instead of values

which eliminates all rows that have redundant or NULL data in that field.

DISTINCT has been eliminated for COUNT (*), because it should have no effect in a well-designed and maintained database. In such a database, there should be neither rows that are entirely NULL nor duplicates (the former contain no data, and the latter are completely redundant). If, on the other hand, fully NULL or redundant rows are present, you probably don't want COUNT to suppress this information.

INCLUDING DUPLICATES IN AGGREGATE FUNCTIONS

Aggregate functions can also (in many implementations) take the argument ALL, which is placed before the field name, like DISTINCT, but means the opposite: to include duplicates. ANSI technically doesn't allow this for COUNT, but many implementations relax this restriction. The differences between ALL and * when used with COUNT are

- ALL still takes a fieldname as an argument.
- ALL will not count NULL values.

Since * is the only argument that includes NULLs and it is used only with COUNT, functions other than COUNT disregard NULLs in any case. The following command will COUNT the number of nonNULL rating fields in the Customers table (including repeats):

```
SELECT COUNT (ALL rating)
    FROM Customers;
```

AGGREGATES BUILT ON SCALAR EXPRESSIONS

Up until now, you have used aggregate functions with single fields as arguments. You can also use aggregate functions with arguments that consist of scalar expressions involving one or more fields. (If you do this, DISTINCT is not allowed.) Suppose the Orders table had another column that held the prior outstanding balance (blnc) for each customer. You would find the current balance by adding the order amount to the prior balance. You could find the largest outstanding balance as follows:

```
SELECT MAX (blnc + amt)
    FROM Orders;
```

For each row of the table, this query will add the blnc and the amt for that customer and select the largest value it finds. Of course, since customers may have multiple orders, their outstanding balance is evaluated separately for each order. Presumably, the order with the most recent date would have the greatest outstanding balance. Otherwise, an old balance could be selected by the above query.

In fact, there are many situations in SQL where you can use scalar expressions with or in place of fields, as you will see in Chapter 7.

THE GROUP BY CLAUSE

The GROUP BY clause allows you to define a subset of the values in a particular field in terms of another field, and apply an aggregate function to the subset. This enables you to combine fields and aggregate functions in a single SELECT statement. For example, suppose you wanted to find the largest order taken by each salesperson. You could do a separate query for each, selecting the MAX amt from the Orders table for each snum value. GROUP BY, however, let's you put it all in one command:

```
SELECT snum, MAX(amt)
    FROM Orders
    GROUP BY snum;
```

The output for this query is shown in Figure 6.5.

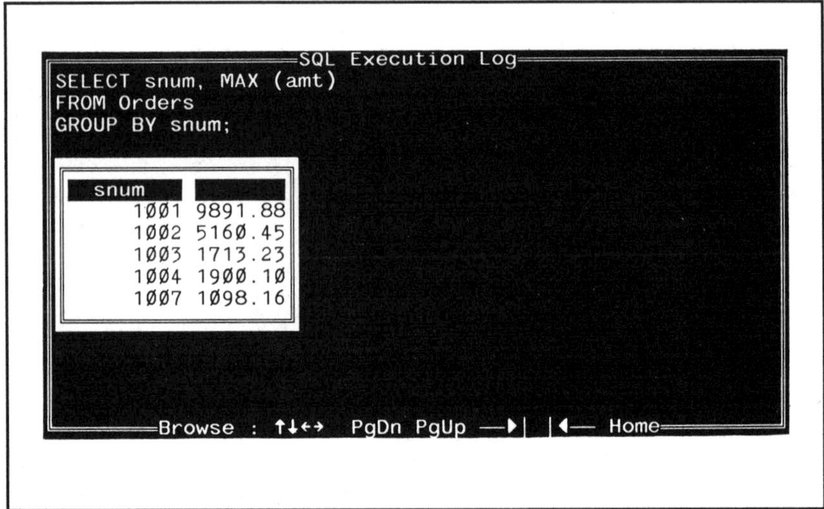

Figure 6.5: Finding maximum amounts for each salesperson

GROUP BY applies the aggregate functions independently to a series of groups that are defined by having a field value in common. In this case, each group consists of all the rows with the same snum value, and the MAX function is applied separately to each such group. This means the field to which GROUP BY applies has, by definition, only one value per output group, as do the aggregate functions. The result is a compatibility that allows aggregates and fields to be combined in this way.

You can also use GROUP BY with multiple fields. To refine the above example further, suppose you wanted to see the largest order taken by each salesperson on each date. To do this, you would group the Orders by date within salesperson, and apply the MAX function to each group, like this:

```
SELECT snum, odate, MAX(amt)
    FROM Orders
    GROUP BY snum, odate;
```

The output for this query is shown in Figure 6.6.

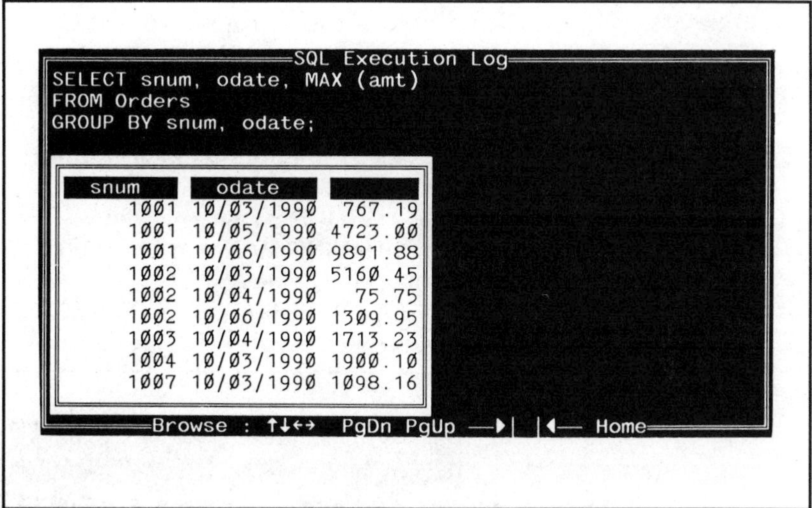

Figure 6.6: Finding each salesperson's largest orders for each day

Of course, empty groups—that is, dates when the current salesperson had no orders—are not shown.

THE HAVING CLAUSE

Suppose, in the previous example, you had wanted to see just the maximum purchases over $3000.00. You cannot use aggregate functions in a WHERE clause (unless you use a subquery, explained later), because predicates are evaluated in terms of a single row, whereas aggregate functions are evaluated in terms of groups of rows. This means you could *not* do something like the following:

```
SELECT  snum, odate, MAX(amt)
     FROM Orders
     WHERE MAX(amt) > 3000.00
     GROUP BY snum, odate;
```

This would be rejected in a strict ANSI interpretation. To see the maximum purchases over $3000.00, you would use the HAVING clause. The HAVING clause defines criteria used to eliminate certain groups from the output, just as the WHERE clause does for individual rows. The correct command would be the following:

```
SELECT  snum, odate, MAX(amt)
     FROM Orders
     GROUP BY snum, odate
     HAVING MAX (amt) > 3000.00;
```

The output for this query is shown in Figure 6.7.

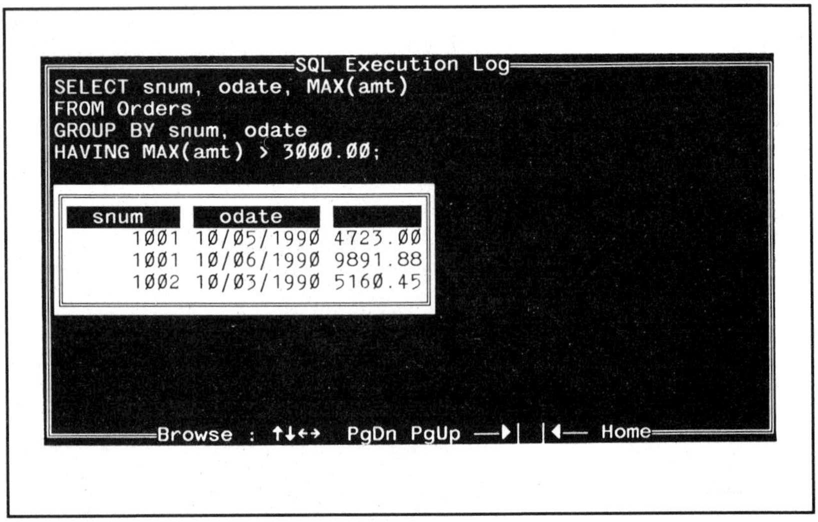

```
=============== SQL Execution Log ===============
SELECT snum, odate, MAX(amt)
FROM Orders
GROUP BY snum, odate
HAVING MAX(amt) > 3000.00;

   snum       odate
   1001  10/05/1990  4723.00
   1001  10/06/1990  9891.88
   1002  10/03/1990  5160.45

=Browse : ↑↓←→  PgDn PgUp  —▸|  |◂—  Home=
```

Figure 6.7: Eliminating groups of aggregate values

Arguments to the HAVING clause follow the same rules as those to the SELECT clause of a command using GROUP BY. They must have a single value per output group. The following command would be illegal:

```
SELECT snum, MAX(amt)
    FROM Orders
    GROUP BY snum
    HAVING odate = 10/03/1988;
```

The odate field cannot be referenced by the HAVING clause because it can have (and indeed does have) more than one value per output group. To avoid this situation, the HAVING clause must reference only aggregates and fields chosen by GROUP BY. Here is the correct way to state the above query (the output is shown in Figure 6.8):

```
SELECT snum, MAX(amt)
    FROM Orders
    WHERE odate = 10/03/1990
    GROUP BY snum;
```

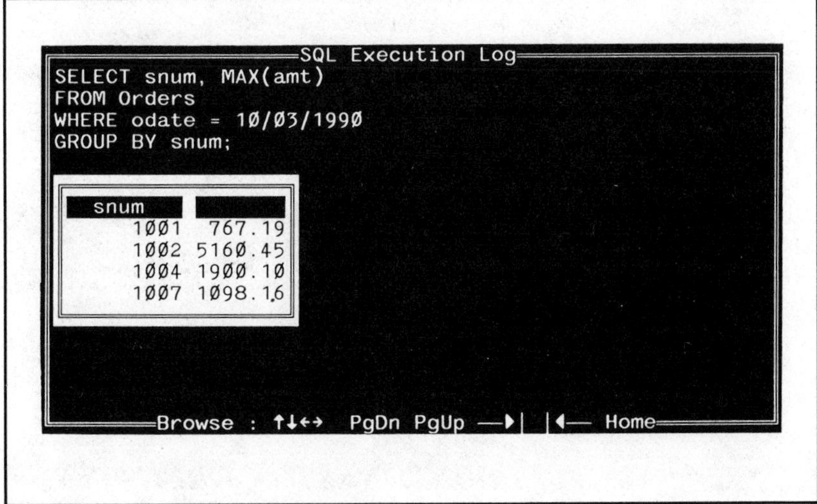

Figure 6.8: Each salesperson's maximum for October 3

Of course, since odate is not and cannot be a selected field, the significance of this data is less self evident than in some other examples. The output should probably include something that says, "these are the largest orders for October 3." In Chapter 7, we will show you how to insert text in your output.

As mentioned, HAVING can take only arguments that have a single value per output group. In practice, references to aggregate functions are the most common, but fields chosen by GROUP BY are also permissible. For instance, we could look at the largest orders for Serres and Rifkin:

```
SELECT snum, MAX(amt)
    FROM Orders
    GROUP BY snum
    HAVING snum IN (1002, 1007);
```

The output for this query is shown in Figure 6.9.

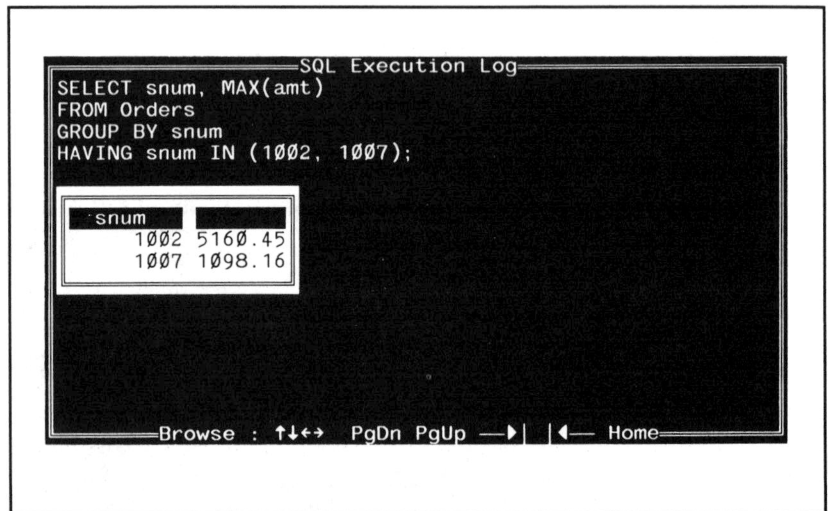

Figure 6.9: Using HAVING with GROUP BY fields

DON'T NEST AGGREGATES

In a strict interpretation of ANSI SQL, you cannot take an aggregate of an aggregate. Suppose you wanted to find out which day had the higher total amount ordered. If you tried to do this:

```
SELECT odate, MAX ( SUM (amt) )
    FROM Orders
    GROUP BY odate;
```

Your command would probably be rejected. (Some implementations don't enforce this restriction, which is advantageous because nested aggregates can be useful, even if they are somewhat problematic.) In the above command, for example, SUM is to be applied to each odate group, and MAX to all of the groups, producing a single value for all the groups. Yet the GROUP BY clause implies that there should be one row of output for each odate group.

SUMMARY

Now you are using queries a little differently. The ability to derive, rather than simply locate, values is very powerful. It means that you may not necessarily have to keep track of certain information if you can formulate a query to derive it. A query will give you up-to-the-minute results, whereas a table of totals or averages will be only as good as the last time it was updated. This is not to suggest that aggregate functions can completely supplant the need to track information such as this independently.

You can apply these aggregates to groups of values defined by a GROUP BY clause. These groups have a field value in common, and they can reside within other groups that have a field value in common. Meanwhile, predicates are still used to determine which rows the aggregate function is applied to. Combined, these features make it possible to produce aggregates based on tightly defined subsets of the values in the field. Then you can define another condition to exclude certain of the resulting groups with the HAVING clause.

Now that you have become adept with many facets of how a query produces values, we will show you, in Chapter 7, some things that you can do with the values it produces.

Putting SQL to Work

1. Write a query that counts all orders for October 3.
2. Write a query that counts the number of different non-NULL city values in the Customers table.
3. Write a query that selects each customer's smallest order.
4. Write a query that selects the first customer, in alphabetical order, whose name begins with G.
5. Write a query that selects the highest rating in each city.
6. Write a query that counts the number of salespeople registering orders for each day. (If a salesperson has more than one order on a given day, he or she should be counted only once.)

(See Appendix A for answers.)

7

Formatting Query Output

THIS CHAPTER WILL EXTEND YOUR ABILITY TO work with the output produced by queries. You will learn how to insert text and constants among the selected fields, how to use the selected fields in mathematical expressions, whose results will then become the output, and how to make the values you output emerge in a specified order. This last feature includes the ability to order your output by any column, any values derived from a column, or both of these.

STRINGS AND EXPRESSIONS

Many SQL-based databases provide special features that allow you to refine the output from your queries. Naturally, these vary greatly from product to product, and discussion of them is beyond our scope here. However, there are a few features built into the SQL standard that allow you to do more than simply output field values and aggregate data.

SCALAR EXPRESSIONS WITH SELECTED FIELDS Let's suppose you want to perform simple numeric computations on the data to put it in a form more appropriate to your needs. SQL allows you to place scalar expressions and constants among the selected fields. These expressions can supplement or replace fields in the SELECT clauses, and they can involve one or more selected fields themselves. For example, you might consider it desirable to present your salespeople's commissions as percentages rather than decimal numbers. Simple enough:

```
SELECT snum, sname, city, comm * 100
    FROM Salespeople;
```

The output from this query is shown in Figure 7.1.

OUTPUT COLUMNS The last column of the preceding example is unlabeled because it is an output column. *Output columns* are columns of data created by a query, rather than being directly extracted from a table. You create them whenever you use

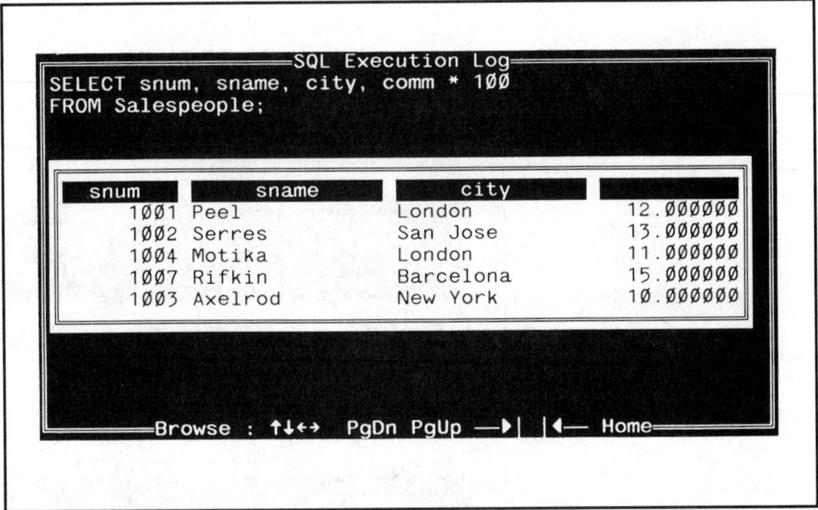

SQL Execution Log

```
SELECT snum, sname, city, comm * 100
FROM Salespeople;
```

snum	sname	city	
1001	Peel	London	12.000000
1002	Serres	San Jose	13.000000
1004	Motika	London	11.000000
1007	Rifkin	Barcelona	15.000000
1003	Axelrod	New York	10.000000

Browse : ↑↓←→ PgDn PgUp —▶| |◀— Home

Figure 7.1: Putting an expression in your query

aggregate functions, constants, or expressions in a query's SELECT clause. Because the names of columns are one of the attributes of a table, columns that do not come from tables have no names. Other than the fact that they are unlabeled, output columns can be treated the same as columns extracted from tables in almost all situations.

PUTTING TEXT IN YOUR QUERY OUTPUT The letter 'A', when signifying nothing but itself, is a *constant*, just as the number 1 is. You have the ability to insert constants in the SELECT clause of a query, including text. However, character constants, unlike numeric constants, cannot be used in expressions. You can have the expression 1 + 2 in your SELECT clause, but you cannot use an expression such as 'A' + 'B'; this is reasonable if we keep in mind that 'A' and 'B' here are simply letters, not variables or symbols for anything besides themselves. Nonetheless, the ability to insert text in the output from your queries is quite handy.

You could refine the previous example by marking the commissions as percentages with the percent sign (%). This enables you to put such items as symbols and comments in the output, as in the following example (the output is shown in Figure 7.2):

```
SELECT snum, sname, city, ' %', comm * 100
    FROM Salespeople;
```

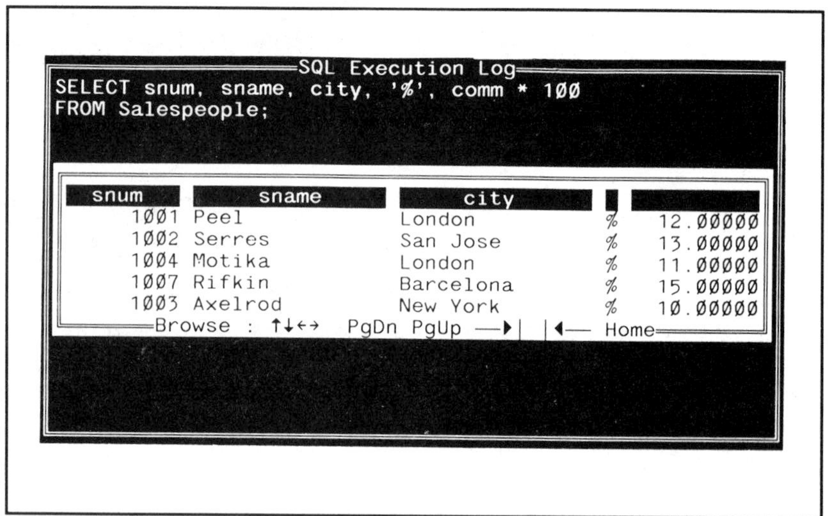

Figure 7.2: Inserting characters in your output

Notice that the space before the percent is inserted as part of the string. This same feature can be used to label output with inserted comments. You must remember, however, that the same comment will be printed with every row of the output, not simply once for the table. Suppose you are generating output for a report that indicates the number of orders for each day. You could label your output (see Figure 7.3) by forming the query as follows:

```
SELECT 'For ', odate, ', there are ',
    COUNT (DISTINCT onum), 'orders.'
    FROM Orders
    GROUP BY odate;
```

The grammatical incorrectness of the output for October 5 cannot be fixed without making this query much more complicated than it is. (You would have to use two queries in a UNION,

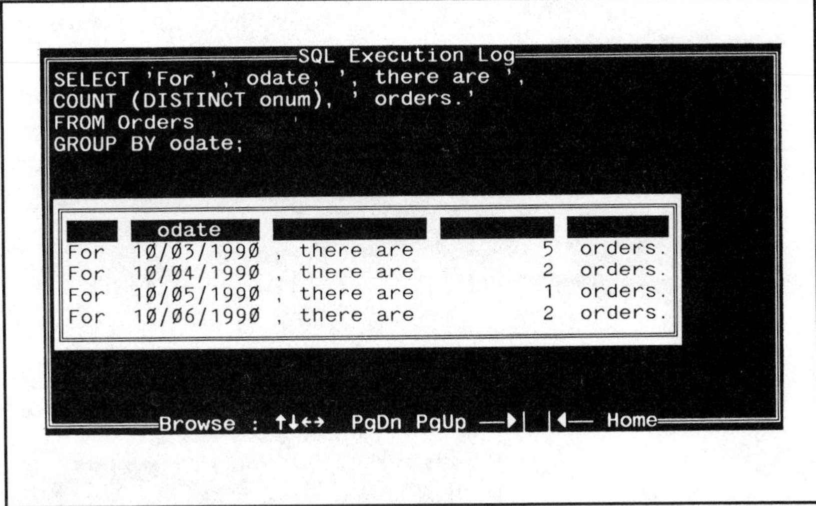

Figure 7.3: Combining text, field values, and aggregates

which we will explain in Chapter 14.) As you can see, a single unvarying comment for each row of a table can be helpful, but has limitations. It is sometimes more elegant and useful to produce a single comment for the output as a whole, or different comments for different rows.

The various programs using SQL often provide features, such as report generators, which are designed to format and refine output. Embedded SQL can also exploit the formatting capabilities of the language it is embedded in. SQL itself is primarily concerned with operating on data. Its output is essentially information, and a program using SQL can often take that information and put it in a more attractive form. This is, however, beyond the scope of SQL itself.

ORDERING OUTPUT BY FIELDS

As we have emphasized, tables are unordered sets, and the data that comes out of them does not necessarily emerge in any particular sequence. SQL uses the ORDER BY command to allow you to impose an order on your output. This command orders the query output according to the values in one or more selected columns. Multiple columns are ordered one within another, just as with GROUP BY, and you can specify ascending (ASC) or descending (DESC) for each. Ascending is the default.

Let's look at our order table arranged by customer number (notice the values in the cnum column):

```
SELECT *
    FROM Orders
    ORDER BY cnum DESC;
```

The output is shown in Figure 7.4.

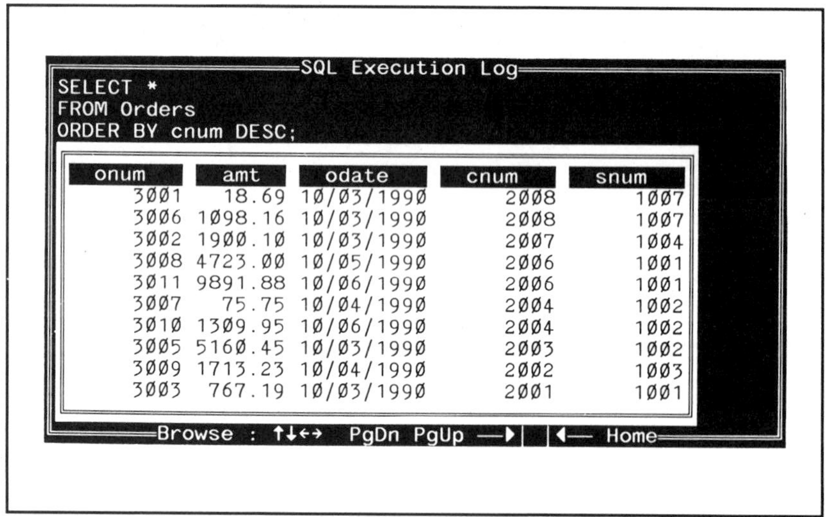

SQL Execution Log

```
SELECT *
FROM Orders
ORDER BY cnum DESC;
```

onum	amt	odate	cnum	snum
3001	18.69	10/03/1990	2008	1007
3006	1098.16	10/03/1990	2008	1007
3002	1900.10	10/03/1990	2007	1004
3008	4723.00	10/05/1990	2006	1001
3011	9891.88	10/06/1990	2006	1001
3007	75.75	10/04/1990	2004	1002
3010	1309.95	10/06/1990	2004	1002
3005	5160.45	10/03/1990	2003	1002
3009	1713.23	10/04/1990	2002	1003
3003	767.19	10/03/1990	2001	1001

Browse : ↑↓←→ PgDn PgUp —▶| |◀— Home

Figure 7.4: Ordering output by a descending field

ORDERING BY MULTIPLE COLUMNS

We could also order the table by another column, amt for example, within the cnum ordering (output shown in Figure 7.5):

```
SELECT *
    FROM Orders
    ORDER BY cnum DESC, amt DESC;
```

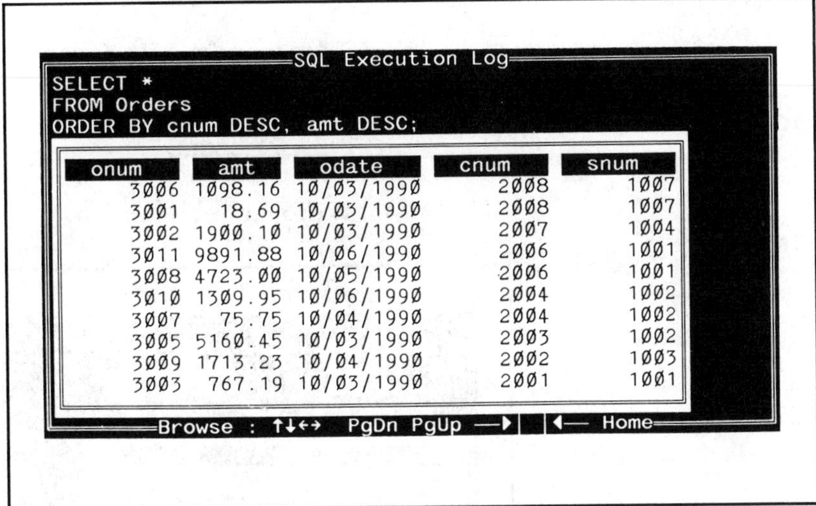

SQL Execution Log

```
SELECT *
FROM Orders
ORDER BY cnum DESC, amt DESC;
```

onum	amt	odate	cnum	snum
3006	1098.16	10/03/1990	2008	1007
3001	18.69	10/03/1990	2008	1007
3002	1900.10	10/03/1990	2007	1004
3011	9891.88	10/06/1990	2006	1001
3008	4723.00	10/05/1990	2006	1001
3010	1309.95	10/06/1990	2004	1002
3007	75.75	10/04/1990	2004	1002
3005	5160.45	10/03/1990	2003	1002
3009	1713.23	10/04/1990	2002	1003
3003	767.19	10/03/1990	2001	1001

Browse : ↑↓←→ PgDn PgUp —▶| |◀— Home

Figure 7.5: Ordering output by multiple fields

You can use ORDER BY in this manner with any number of columns at once. Notice that, in all cases, the columns being ordered are among the columns selected. This is an ANSI requirement that most, but not all, systems enforce. The following command, for instance, would be illegal:

```
SELECT cname, city
    FROM Customers
    ORDER BY cnum;
```

Since cnum was not a selected field, ORDER BY cannot find it to use for ordering the output. Even if your system does allow this, the significance of the ordering would not be evident from the output, so including all columns used in the ORDER BY clause is generally advisable.

ORDERING AGGREGATE GROUPS

ORDER BY can also be used with GROUP BY to order groups. If so, ORDER BY always comes last. Here's an example from the last chapter with an added ORDER BY clause. Before the output was grouped, but the order of the groups was arbitrary; now we force the groups to be placed in sequence:

```
SELECT snum, odate, MAX(amt)
    FROM Orders
    GROUP BY snum, odate
    ORDER BY snum;
```

The output is shown in Figure 7.6.

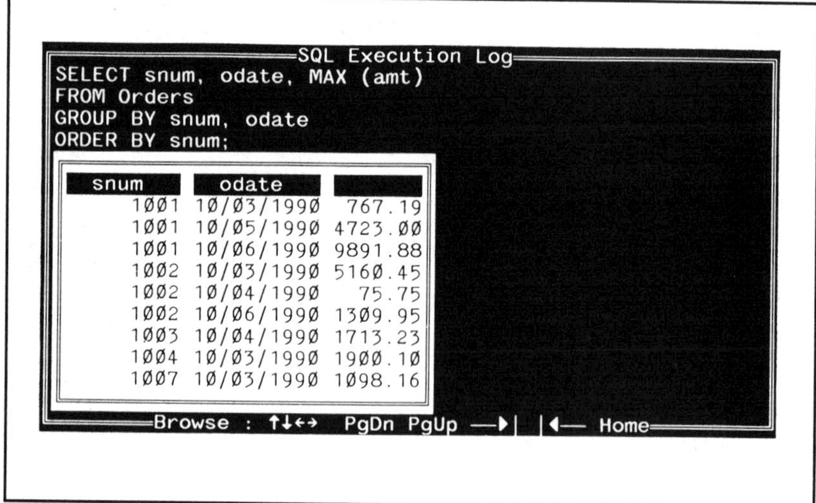

Figure 7.6: Ordering by a group

Since we did not specify ascending or descending order, ascending is used by default.

ORDERING OUTPUT BY COLUMN NUMBER

In place of column names, you can use numbers to indicate the fields being used to order the output. These numbers will refer, not to the order of the columns in the table, but to their order in the output. In other words, the first field mentioned in the SELECT clause is, for the purposes of ORDER BY, field #1, regardless of where it is found in the table. For example, you can use the following command to see certain fields of the Salespeople table, ordered in descending order of least commission (the output is shown in Figure 7.7):

```
SELECT sname, comm
    FROM Salespeople
    ORDER BY 2 DESC;
```

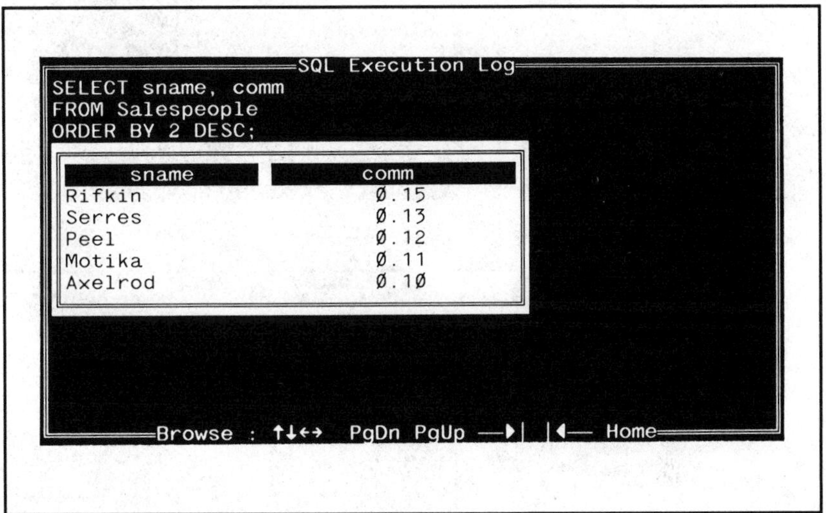

Figure 7.7: Ordering using numbers

One of the main purposes of this ORDER BY feature is to enable you to use ORDER BY with output columns as well as table columns. Columns resulting from aggregate functions, constants, or expressions in the SELECT clause of a query are perfectly usable with ORDER BY, provided that they are referred to by number. For example, let's count the orders of each of our salespeople, and output the results in descending order, as shown in Figure 7.8:

```
SELECT snum, COUNT (DISTINCT onum)
    FROM Orders
    GROUP BY snum
    ORDER BY 2 DESC;
```

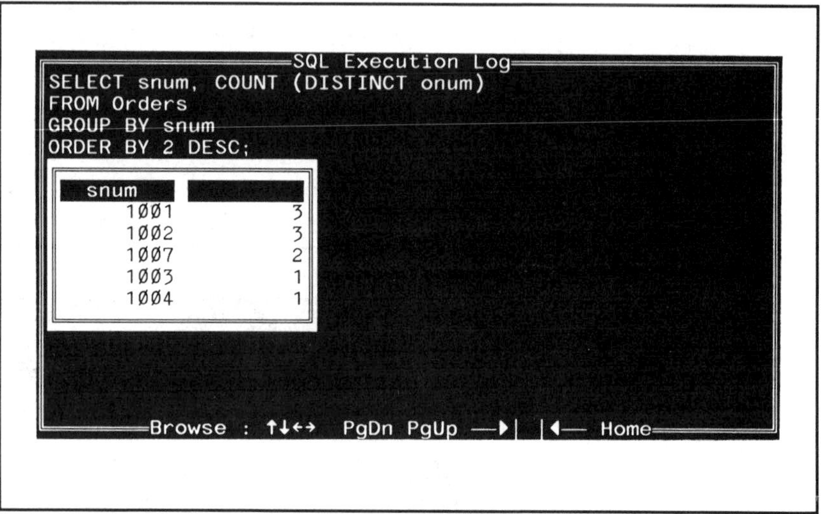

Figure 7.8: Ordering by an output column

In this case, you should use the column number, because an output column has no name; you should not use the aggregate function itself. In strict ANSI SQL, the following would not work, although some systems relax this requirement:

```
SELECT snum, COUNT (DISTINCT onum)
   FROM Orders
   GROUP BY snum
   ORDER BY COUNT (DISTINCT onum) DESC;
```

This would be rejected by many systems.

ORDER BY WITH NULLS

If there are NULL values in a field that you are using to order your output, they will either follow or precede every other value in the field. This is an option that ANSI has left up to the individual program. A given program uses one or the other form.

SUMMARY

In this chapter, you have learned how to make your queries do more than produce field values or aggregate function data from a table. You can take fields and use them in expressions: for example, you can multiply a numeric field by 10 or even multiply it by another numeric field. In addition, your ability to put constants, including characters, in your output, allows you to put text directly in a query and have it output with the table data. This enables you to label or explain your output in various ways.

You have also learned how to impose an order on your output. Even though the table itself remains unordered, the ORDER BY clause enables you to control the order of the rows of a given query's output. Query output can be in ascending or descending order, and columns can be nested one within another.

The concept of output columns was explained in this chapter. You now know that output columns may be used to order query output, but they are unnamed, and therefore must be referred to by number in the ORDER BY clause.

Now that you have seen what can be done with the output from a query based on a single table, it is time to move on to the advanced query features and learn how to query any number of tables in a single command, forging relationships between them as you do so. This will be the subject of Chapter 8.

Putting SQL to Work

1. Assume each salesperson has a 12% commission. Write a query on the Orders table that will produce the order number, the salesperson number, and the amount of the salesperson's commission for that order.
2. Write a query on the Customers table that will find the highest rating in each city. Put the output in this form:

   For the city (city), the highest rating is: (rating).

3. Write a query that lists customers in descending order of rating. Output the rating field first, followed by the customer's name and number.
4. Write a query that totals the orders for each day and places the results in descending order.

(See Appendix A for answers.)

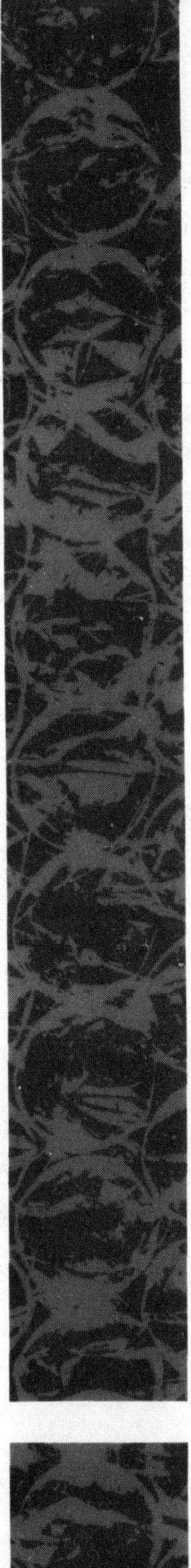

8

Querying Multiple Tables at Once

UP UNTIL NOW, EACH QUERY WE HAVE EXAMINED has been based on a single table. In this chapter, you will learn how to query any number of tables with a single command. This is an extremely powerful feature because it not only combines output from multiple tables, but defines relationships between them. You will learn about the various forms these relationships can take, as well as how to define and use them to answer specific needs.

JOINING TABLES

One of the most important features of SQL queries is their ability to define relationships between multiple tables and draw information from them in terms of these relationships, all within a single command. This kind of operation is called a *join*, which is one of the powerhouses of relational databases. As stated in Chapter 1, the strength of the relational approach is in the relationships that can be constructed between the items of data in the tables. With joins, we directly relate the information in any number of tables, and thus are able to make connections between disparate pieces of data.

In a join, the tables are listed in the FROM clause of the query, separated by commas. The predicate of the query can refer to any column of any table joined and, therefore, can be used to make connections between them. Usually, the predicate will compare the values in columns of different tables to determine whether a WHERE condition is met.

TABLE AND COLUMN NAMES

The full name of a column of a table actually consists of the table name followed by a dot and then the column name. Here are some examples:

```
Salespeople.snum
Customers.city
Orders.odate
```

Up until now, you have been able to omit the table names because you were querying only a single table at a time, and SQL is intelligent enough to assume the proper table-name prefix. Even when you query multiple tables, you will still be able to omit the table names, provided that all of the columns have different names. But this is not always the case. For example, we have two sample tables with columns called city. If we were to join them (as we will momentarily), we would have to say Salespeople.city or Customers.city, so that SQL could know which one we meant.

MAKING A JOIN

Suppose you want to match your salespeople to your customers according to what city they lived in, so that you would see all the combinations of salespeople and customers who shared a city. You would need to take each salesperson and search the customers table for all customers in the same city. You could do this by entering the following command (the output is shown in Figure 8.1):

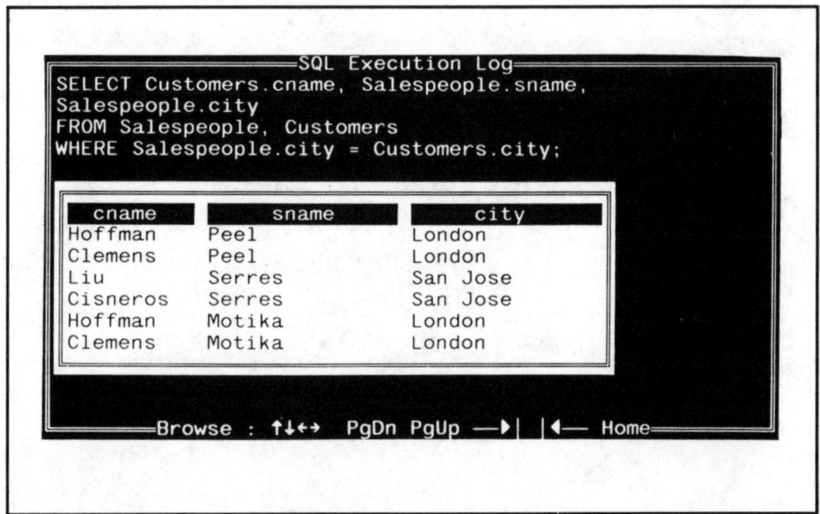

Figure 8.1: Joining two tables

```
SELECT Customers.cname, Salespeople.sname,
 Salespeople.city
    FROM Salespeople, Customers
    WHERE Salespeople.city = Customers.city;
```

Because there is a city field in both the Salespeople and Customer tables, the table names have to be used as prefixes. Although this is necessary only when two or more fields have the same name, it is often a good idea to include the table name in joins for the sake of clarity and consistency. Despite this, we will, in our examples, generally use table names only when necessary, so that it will be clear when they are needed and when they are not.

What SQL basically does in a join is examine every combination of rows possible from the two (or more) tables and test these combinations against the predicate. In the preceding example, it took the row of salesperson Peel from the Salespeople table and combined it with each row of the Customers table, one at a time. If a combination produced values that made the predicate true—in this case, if the city field of a Customer table row were London, the same as Peel's—the requested values from that combination were selected for output. The same thing was then done for every other salesperson in the Salespeople table (some of whom had no customers located in their cities).

JOINING TABLES THROUGH REFERENTIAL INTEGRITY

This feature is often used simply to exploit the relationships built into the database. In the previous example, we established a relationship between the two tables in the join. This is fine. These tables, however, are already connected through the snum field. This relationship is called the state of referential integrity, as we mentioned in Chapter 1. A common use of the join is to extract data in terms of this relationship. For example, to show the names of all customers matched with the salespeople serving them, we would use this query:

```
SELECT Customers.cname, Salespeople.sname
    FROM Customers, Salespeople
    WHERE Salespeople.snum = Customers.snum;
```

The output of this query is shown in Figure 8.2.

This is an example of a join in which the columns used to determine the predicate of the query, in this case the snum columns of both tables, have been omitted from the output. This is fine. The output shows which customers are serviced by which salespeople; the snum values that constitute the link are not, in themselves, relevant here. If you do this, however, you should either make sure the output is self-explanatory or provide some explanation of the data.

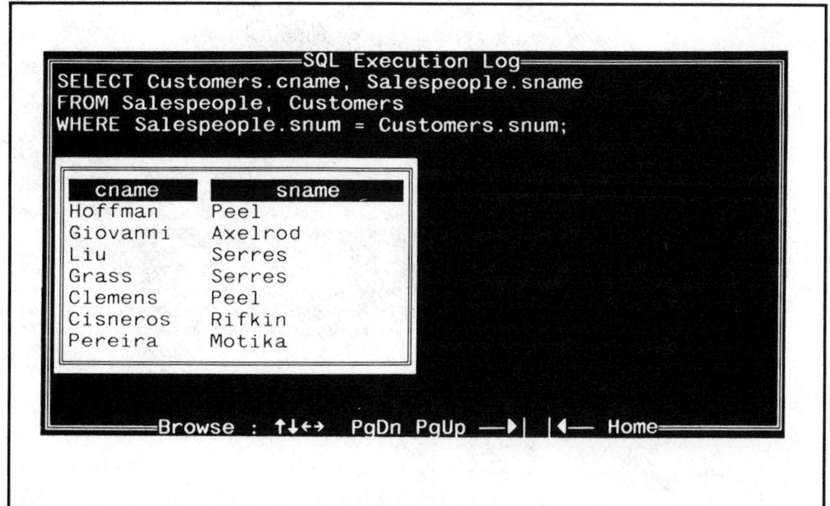

Figure 8.2: Joining salespeople to their customers

EQUIJOINS AND OTHER KINDS OF JOINS

Joins that use predicates based on equalities are called *equijoins*. Our examples in this chapter up to now have all fallen into this category because the conditions in the WHERE clauses have all been based on mathematical expressions using =. "City = 'London' " and "Salespeople.snum = Orders.snum" are examples of the types of equalities found in predicates. Equijoins are probably the most common sort of join, but there are others. You can, in fact, use any of the relational operators in a join. Here is an example of another kind of join (its output is shown in Figure 8.3):

```
SELECT sname, cname
    FROM Salespeople, Customers
    WHERE sname < cname
        AND rating < 200;
```

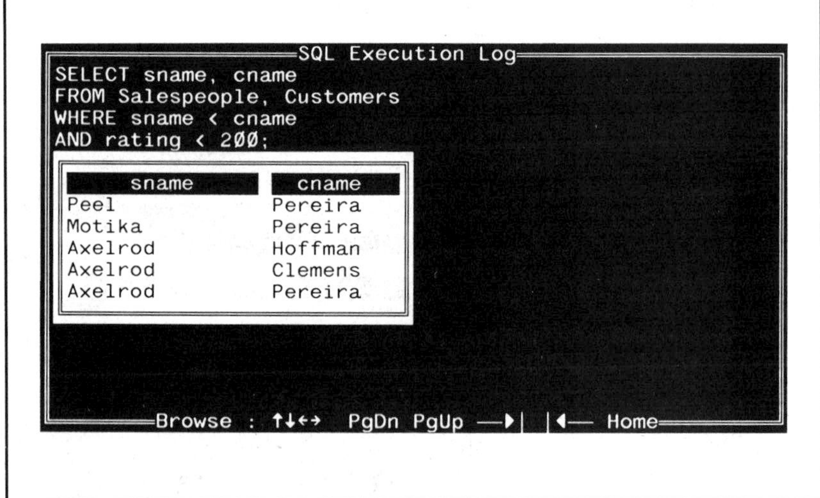

Figure 8.3: A join based on an inequality

This command is not often likely to be useful. It produces all combinations of salesperson and customer names such that the former precedes the latter alphabetically, and the latter has a rating of less than 200. Usually, you will not need to construct complex relationships like this, and, for this reason, you will probably find equijoins to be the most common, but it is good to be acquainted with the other possibilities.

JOINS OF MORE THAN TWO TABLES

You can also construct queries joining more than two tables. Suppose we wanted to find all orders by customers not located in the same cities as their salespeople. This would involve relating all three of our sample tables (the output is shown in Figure 8.4):

```
SELECT onum, cname, Orders.cnum, Orders.snum
   FROM Salespeople, Customers, Orders
   WHERE Customers.city <> Salespeople.city
      AND Orders.cnum = Customers.cnum
      AND Orders.snum = Salespeople.snum;
```

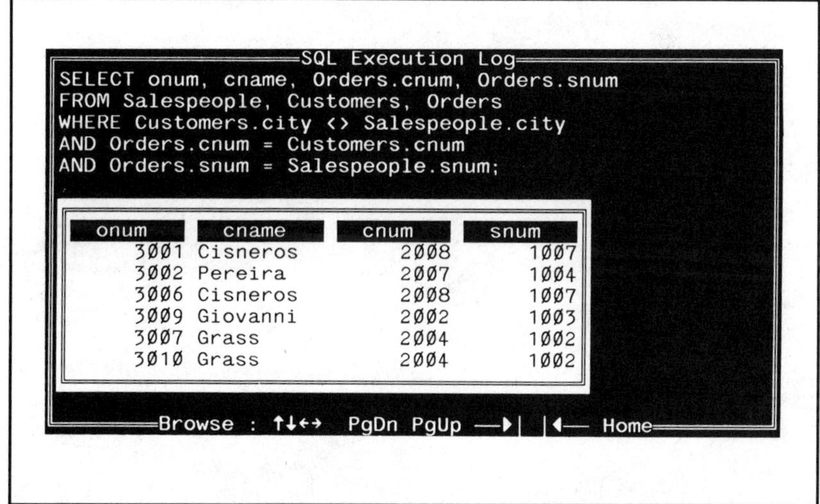

Figure 8.4: Joining three tables

Although this command looks rather complex, you can follow its logic by simply verifying that these are the customers not located in the same city as their salespeople (matching the two through the snum field), and that the orders listed are those made by these customers (matching the orders with the cnum and snum fields of the Orders table).

SUMMARY

Now you are no longer restricted to looking at one table at a time. Moreover, you can make elaborate comparisons between any of the fields of any number of tables and use the results to decide what information you want to see. In fact, this technique is so useful for constructing relationships that it is even used to construct them within a single table. That's right: you can join a table to itself, and it's a handy thing to do. This will be the subject of Chapter 9.

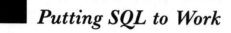

Putting SQL to Work

1. Write a query that lists each order number followed by the name of the customer who made the order.
2. Write a query that gives the names of both the salesperson and the customer for each order after the order number.
3. Write a query that produces all customers serviced by salespeople with a commission above 12%. Output the customer's name, the salesperson's name, and the salesperson's rate of commission.
4. Write a query that calculates the amount of the salesperson's commission on each order by a customer with a rating above 100.

(See Appendix A for answers.)

9

Joining a Table to Itself

IN CHAPTER 8, WE SHOWED YOU HOW TO JOIN TWO or more tables together. Interestingly enough, the same technique can be used to join together two copies of a single table. In this chapter, we will explore this process. As you will see, joining a table to itself, far from being a simple idiosyncracy, can be quite a useful way to define certain kinds of relationships between the items of data in a given table.

HOW DO YOU JOIN A TABLE TO ITSELF?

To join a table to itself means that you can take each row of the table, one at a time, and combine it with itself and with every other row of the table. You then evaluate each combination in terms of a predicate, just as in multitable joins. This allows you to easily forge certain kinds of relationships between the various items within a single table—by finding pairs of rows with a field value in common, for example.

You can picture a join of a table to itself as a join of two copies of the same table. The table is not actually copied, but SQL performs the command as though it were. In other words, the join is the same as any other join between two tables, except that in this case the two tables happen to be identical.

ALIASES

The syntax of the command for joining a table to itself is the same as that for joining multiple tables, with a single modification. When you join a table to itself, all of the column names are repeated, complete with table-name prefixes. To refer to these columns within the query, then, you must have two different names for the same table. You can do this by defining temporary names called *range variables*, *correlation variables* or simply *aliases*. You define these in the FROM clause of the query. It's quite simple: you type the name of the table, leave a space, and then type the alias for it.

Here is an example that finds all pairs of customers having the same rating (the output is shown in Figure 9.1):

```
SELECT first.cname, second.cname, first.rating
   FROM Customers first, Customers second
   WHERE first.rating = second.rating;
```

```
SQL Execution Log
Giovanni    Giovanni     200
Giovanni    Liu          200
Liu         Giovanni     200
Liu         Liu          200
Grass       Grass        300
Grass       Cisneros     300
Clemens     Hoffman      100
Clemens     Clemens      100
Clemens     Pereira      100
Cisneros    Grass        300
Cisneros    Cisneros     300
Pereira     Hoffman      100
Pereira     Clemens      100
Pereira     Pereira      100
Browse : ↑↓←→  PgDn PgUp  —▶
```

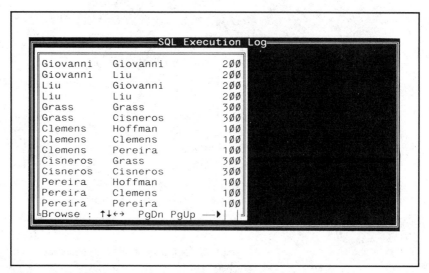

Figure 9.1: Joining a table to itself

(note that in Figure 9.1, as in some future examples, the full query cannot fit in the window with the output, and has therefore been truncated.)

In the above command, SQL behaves as though it were joining two tables called "first" and "second". Both of these are actually the Customers table, but the aliases allow them to be treated independently. The aliases first and second were found in the FROM clause of the query, immediately following the name of the table being copied. Notice that the aliases are also used in the SELECT clause, even though they are not defined until the FROM clause. This is perfectly all right. SQL will initially accept any such aliases on faith, but will reject the command if they are not defined immediately in the FROM clause of the query. The life of an alias is only as long as the command takes to execute. Once the query is finished, the aliases used in it are no longer meaningful.

Now that it has two copies of the Customers table to work with, SQL can treat this operation just as it would any other join, taking every row from one alias and matching it with each row of the other.

ELIMINATING REDUNDANCY

Notice that our output has every combination of values twice, the second time in reverse order. This is because each value shows up once in each alias, and the predicate is symmetrical. Therefore, value A in alias first is selected in combination with value B in alias second, *and* value A in alias second is selected in combination with value B in alias first. In our example, Hoffman was selected with Clemens, and then Clemens was selected with Hoffman. The same happened with Cisneros and Grass, Liu and Giovanni, and so on. Also each row was matched with itself to output rows such as Liu and Liu.

A simple way to avoid this is to impose an order on the two values, so that one will have to be less than the other or precede it in alphabetical order. This makes the predicate asymmetrical, so that the same values in reverse order will not be selected again, for example:

```
SELECT first.cname, second.cname, first.rating
   FROM Customers first, Customers second
   WHERE first.rating = second.rating
      AND first.cname < second.cname;
```

The output of this query is shown in Figure 9.2.

Hoffman precedes Periera in alphabetical order, so that combination satisfies both conditions of the predicate and appears in the output. When the same combination comes up in reverse order—when Periera in the alias first table is matched with Hoffman in the alias second table—the second condition is not met. Likewise Hoffman is not selected for having the same rating as himself because his name doesn't precede itself in alphabetical order. If you wanted to include matches of rows with themselves

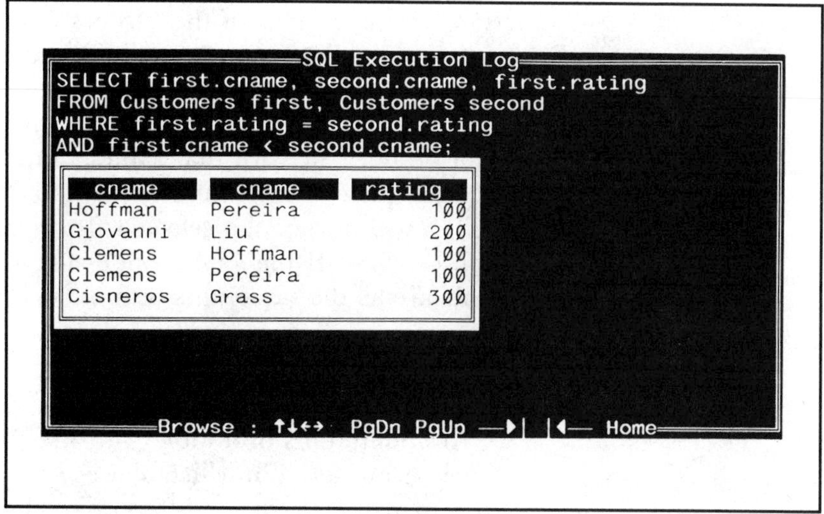

Figure 9.2: Eliminating redundant output from a self join

in queries like this, of course, you could simply use < = instead of <.

CHECKING FOR ERRORS

Another way we can use this feature of SQL is to check for certain kinds of errors. Looking at the Orders table, you can see that the cnum and snum fields should have a consistent relationship. Because each customer should be assigned to one and only one salesperson, each time a certain customer number comes up in the Orders table, it should match with the same salesperson number. The following command will locate any inconsistencies in this area:

```
SELECT first.onum, first.cnum, first.snum,
 second.onum, second.cnum, second.snum
    FROM Orders first, Orders second
    WHERE first.cnum = second.cnum
        AND first.snum <> second.snum;
```

Although it looks complicated, the logic of this command is quite straightforward. It will take the first row of the Orders table, store it under the alias first, and examine it in combination with each row of the Orders table under the alias second, one by one. If a combination of rows satisfies the predicate, it is selected for output. In this case, it will look at a row, find out that the cnum is 2008 and the snum is 1007, and then look at every other row with that same cnum value. If it finds that any of these have a different snum value, the predicate will be true, and it will output the selected fields from the current combination of rows. If the snum values for a given cnum value in our table are all the same, this command will produce no output.

MORE ON ALIASES

Although joins of a table with itself are the first situation you have encountered in which aliases are necessary, you are not limited to using them to differentiate between copies of a single table. You can use them anytime you want to create alternate names for your tables in a command. For example, if your tables had very long and complex names, you could define simple one-letter aliases, such as a and b, and use these instead of the table names in the SELECT clause and predicate. They will also be used with correlated subqueries (discussed in Chapter 11).

SOME MORE COMPLEX JOINS

You can use any number of aliases for a single table in a query, although more than two in a given SELECT clause is not common. Suppose you had not yet assigned your customers to your salespeople. Company policy is to assign each salesperson three customers initially, one at each of the three rating values. You personally are to decide which customers to assign to each salesperson, but you use the following query to see all of the possible combinations of customers you can assign (the output is shown in Figure 9.3):

```
SELECT a.cnum, b.cnum, c.cnum
    FROM Customers a, Customers b, Customers c
```

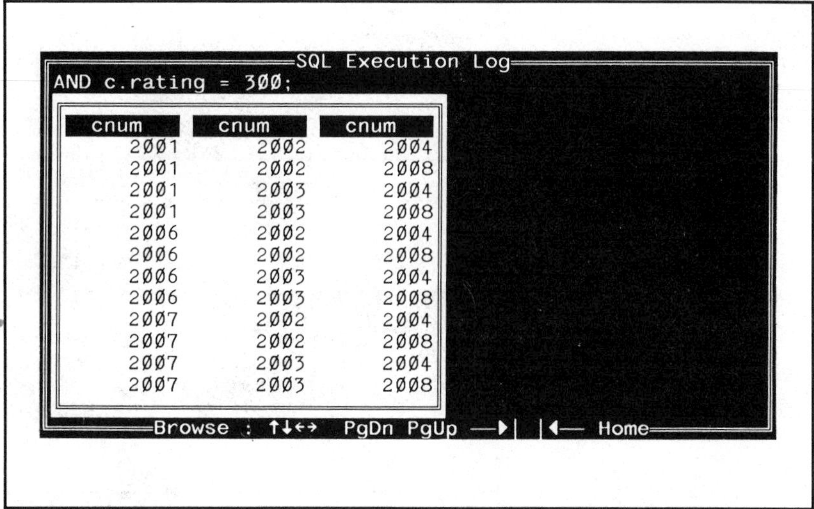

Figure 9.3: Combinations of customers with different rating values

```
WHERE a.rating = 100
    AND b.rating = 200
    AND c.rating = 300;
```

As you can see, this query finds all combinations of customers with the three rating values, so that the first column consists of customers with a 100 rating, the second of those with a 200 rating, and the last of those with a rating of 300. These are repeated in all possible combinations. This is a sort of grouping that cannot be done with GROUP BY or ORDER BY, as these compare values only in a single output column.

You should also realize that it is not always actually necessary to use every alias or table mentioned in the FROM clause of a query in the SELECT clause. Sometimes, an alias or table is queried solely so that it can be referenced in the predicate of the query. For example, the following query finds all customers located in cities where salesperson Serres (snum 1002) has customers (the output is shown in Figure 9.4):

```
SELECT b.cnum, b.cname
    FROM Customers a, Customers b
```

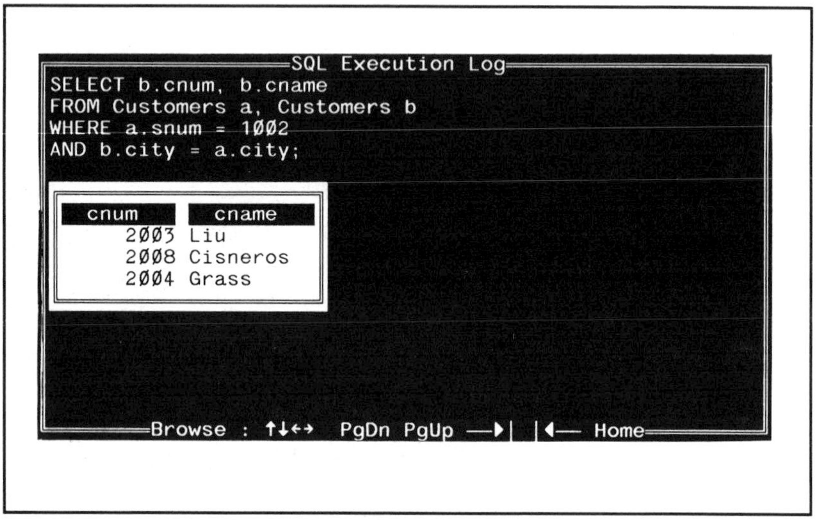

```
SQL Execution Log
SELECT b.cnum, b.cname
FROM Customers a, Customers b
WHERE a.snum = 1002
AND b.city = a.city;

  cnum     cname
  2003     Liu
  2008     Cisneros
  2004     Grass

Browse : ↑↓←→  PgDn PgUp —▸|  |◂— Home
```

Figure 9.4: Finding customers in the same cities as those of Serres

WHERE a.snum = 1002
AND b.city = a.city;

Alias a will make the predicate false except when its snum column value is 1002. So alias a eliminates all but Serres' customers. Alias b will be true for all rows with the same city value as the current city value of a; over the course of the query, a row of alias b will be true once for every time its city value is present in a. Finding these rows of alias b is the only purpose of alias a, so we did not select any columns from it. As you can see, Serres own customers are selected for being in the same city as themselves, so selecting them from alias a is not necessary. In short, alias a locates the rows of Serres customers, Liu and Grass. Alias b finds all customers located in either of their cities (San Jose and Berlin respectively) including, of course, Liu and Grass themselves.

You can also construct joins that involve both different tables *and* aliases of a single table. The following query joins the Customer table to itself to find all pairs of customers served by a single salesperson. At the same time, it joins the customer to the

Salespeople table to name that salesperson (the output is shown in Figure 9.5):

```
SELECT sname, Salespeople.snum, first.cname,
 second.cname
    FROM Customers first, Customers second, Salespeople
    WHERE first.snum = second.snum
        AND Salespeople.snum = first.snum
        AND first.cnum < second.cnum;
```

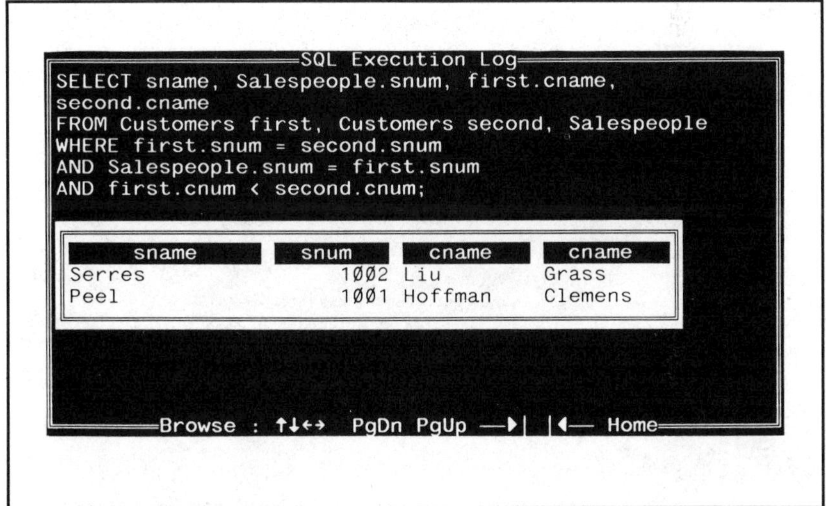

Figure 9.5: Joining a table to itself and to another table

SUMMARY

Now you understand the full power of joins and can use them to construct relationships within a table, between different tables, or both. You have been introduced to some possible uses to which these abilities can be put. You are now familiar with the terms range variables, correlation variables, and aliases (this terminology varies from product to product and writer to writer, so we decided to acquaint you with all three terms). You also understand a bit more about how queries actually work.

The next step after combining multiple tables or multiple copies of a single table in a query, is combining multiple queries, so that one query can produce output that controls what another query does. This is another powerful feature of SQL that we will introduce in Chapter 10 and elaborate on in the next several chapters.

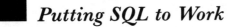

Putting SQL to Work

1. Write a query that produces all pairs of salespeople who are living in the same city. Exclude combinations of salespeople with themselves as well as duplicate rows with the order reversed.
2. Write a query that produces all pairs of orders by a given customer, names that customer, and eliminates duplicates, as above.
3. Write a query that produces the names and cities of all customers with the same rating as Hoffman. Write the query using Hoffman's cnum rather than his rating, so that it would still be usable if his rating changed.

(See Appendix A for answers.)

10

Placing Queries Inside One Another

AT THE END OF CHAPTER 9, WE SAID QUERIES could control other queries. In this chapter, you will learn that this is done (for the most part) by placing a query inside the predicate of another query, and using the inner query's output in the predicate's true or false condition. You will find out what kinds of operators can use subqueries and explore how subqueries work with features of SQL such as DISTINCT, aggregate functions, and output expressions. You will learn how to use subqueries with the HAVING clause and receive some pointers on the correct way to use subqueries.

HOW DO SUBQUERIES WORK?

With SQL you have the ability to nest queries within one another. Typically, the inner query generates values that are tested in the predicate of the outer query, determining when it will be true. For instance, suppose we knew the name but not the snum of salesperson Motika, and wanted to extract all of her orders from the Orders table. Here is one way we could do it (the output is shown in Figure 10.1):

```
SELECT *
    FROM Orders
    WHERE snum =
        (SELECT snum
            FROM Salespeople
            WHERE sname = 'Motika');
```

In order to evaluate the outer (main) query, SQL first had to evaluate the inner query (or subquery) within the WHERE clause. It does this in the same way it would have had this query been its sole task: it searched through the Salespeople table for all rows where the sname was equal to Motika, and then extracted the snum values of those rows.

The only row found, of course, was the one with the snum = 1004. Rather than simply outputting this value, however, SQL put it in the predicate of the main query in place of the subquery itself, so that the predicate read

```
WHERE snum = 1004
```

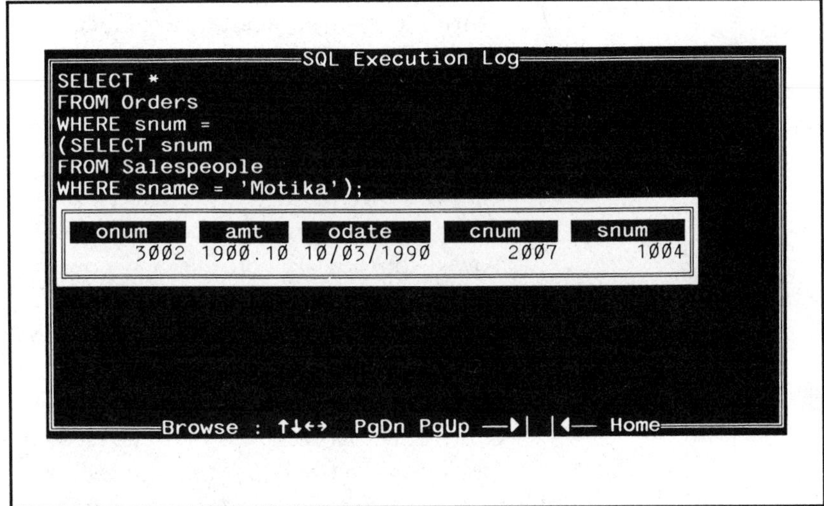

Figure 10.1: Using the subquery

The main query was then performed as usual with the above results. Naturally, the subquery must select one and only one column, and the data type of this column must match that of the value to which it is being compared in the predicate. Often, as above, the selected field and this value will have the same name (in this case, snum), but this is by no means necessary.

Of course, if we had already known Motika's salesperson number, we could have simply typed

```
WHERE snum = 1004
```

and done away with the subquery altogether, but this is much more versatile. It will continue to work even if Motika's number is changed, and, with a simple change of the name in the subquery, you could use it for anyone else.

THE VALUES THAT SUBQUERIES CAN PRODUCE

It is rather convenient that our subquery in the previous example returned one and only one value. Had it selected snums

"WHERE city = 'London' " instead of "WHERE sname = 'Motika'," there would have been several values produced. This would have made the equation in the predicate of the main query impossible to evaluate as true or false, and the command would have produced an error.

When using subqueries in predicates based on relational operators (equations or inequalities, as explained in Chapter 4), you must be sure to use a subquery that will produce one and only one row of output. If you use a subquery that produces no values at all, the command will not fail; but neither will the main query produce any output. Subqueries that produce no output (or NULL output) cause the predicate to be considered neither true nor false, but *unknown*. However, the unknown predicate has the same effect as false: no rows are selected by the main query (refer to Chapter 5 for more information on the unknown predicate).

It is not good policy to do something like the following:

```
SELECT *
   FROM Orders
   WHERE snum =
      (SELECT snum
         FROM Salespeople
         WHERE city = 'Barcelona');
```

As we have only one salesperson in Barcelona, Mr. Rifkin, the subquery would select a single snum value and therefore be accepted. But this is only a function of the current data. Most SQL databases have multiple users, and if another user had added a new salesperson in Barcelona to the table, the subquery would select two values, and your command would fail.

DISTINCT WITH SUBQUERIES

You can, in some cases, use DISTINCT to force a subquery to generate a single value. Suppose we wanted to find all orders credited to the same salesperson who services Hoffman (cnum = 2001). Here is one way to do it (the output is shown in Figure 10.2):

```
SELECT *
     FROM Orders
     WHERE snum =
          (SELECT DISTINCT snum
               FROM Orders
               WHERE cnum = 2001);
```

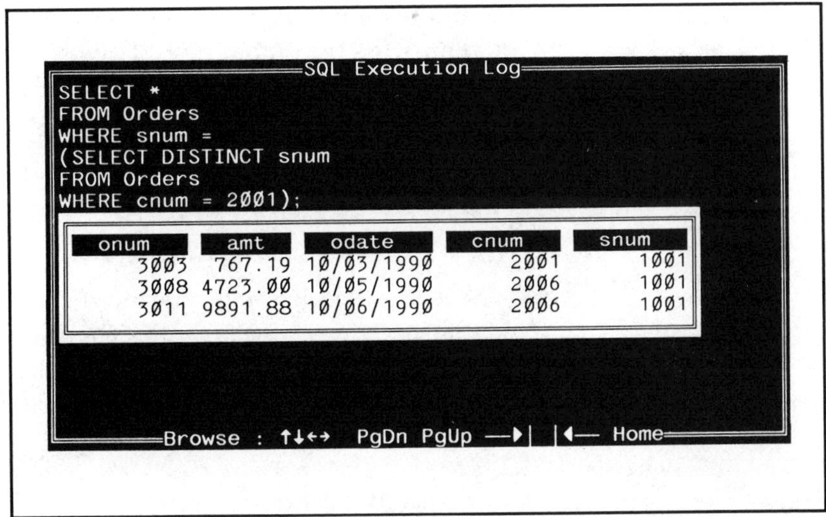

Figure 10.2: Using DISTINCT to force a single value from a subquery

The subquery ascertained that the snum matched with Hoffman is 1001, and then the main query extracted all orders with that snum (regardless of whether they were for Hoffman) from the Orders table. Since each customer is assigned to one and only one salesperson, we know that every row in the Orders table with a given cnum value should have the same snum value. However, since there can be any number of such rows, the subquery could have produced multiple (although identical) snum values for the given cnum. The DISTINCT argument prevents this. If our subquery were to still return more than one value, it would indicate an error in our data—a good thing to know about.

An alternative approach would have been to reference the Customers rather than Orders table in the subquery. As cnum is the primary key of the Customer table, a query selecting it should produce only one value. It is possible, however, that you, as a user, could have access to the Orders but not the Customers table. If this were the case, you could use the solution we presented above. (SQL has mechanisms that determine who has privileges to do what to which table. These will be explained in Chapter 22.)

Please remember, however, that the technique used in the preceding example is applicable only when you know that two different fields in a table should always match up the same, as was the case here. Although this type of situation is not uncommon in relational databases, it is the exception, not the rule.

PREDICATES WITH SUBQUERIES ARE NOT REVERSIBLE

You should also note that predicates involving subqueries use the form <*scalar expression*> <*operator*> <*subquery*>, rather than <*subquery*> <*operator*> <*scalar expression*> or <*subquery*> <*operator*><*subquery*>. In other words, you would not have written the previous example like this:

```
SELECT *
    FROM Orders
    WHERE (SELECT DISTINCT snum
            FROM Orders
            WHERE cnum = 2001)
        = snum;
```

In a strict ANSI implementation, this would fail, although some programs permit it. ANSI also prevents you from having both of the values in the comparison be produced by subqueries.

USING AGGREGATE FUNCTIONS IN SUBQUERIES

One type of function that automatically can produce a single value for any number of rows, of course, is the aggregate function. Any query using a single aggregate function without a GROUP BY clause will select a single value for use in the main predicate. For example, you might want to see all orders that are greater than the average for October 4 (the output is shown in Figure 10.3):

```
SELECT *
    FROM Orders
    WHERE amt >
        (SELECT AVG (amt)
            FROM Orders
            WHERE odate = 10/04/1990);
```

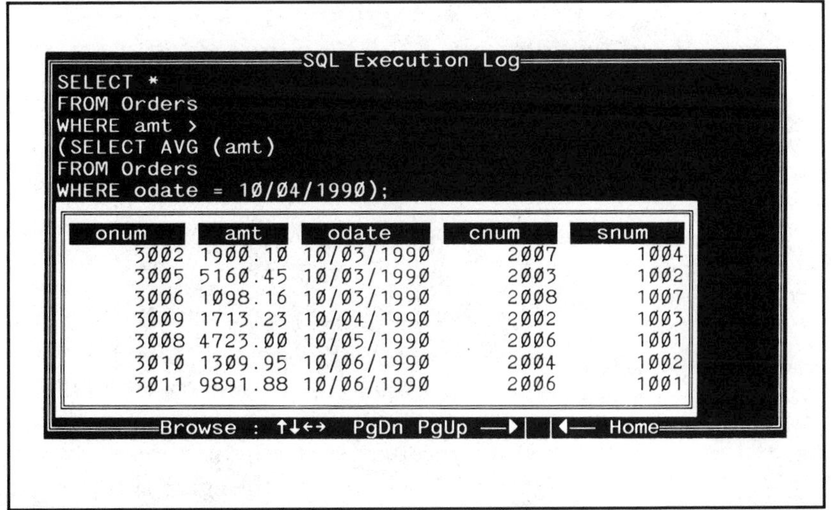

SQL Execution Log

```
SELECT *
FROM Orders
WHERE amt >
(SELECT AVG (amt)
FROM Orders
WHERE odate = 10/04/1990);
```

onum	amt	odate	cnum	snum
3002	1900.10	10/03/1990	2007	1004
3005	5160.45	10/03/1990	2003	1002
3006	1098.16	10/03/1990	2008	1007
3009	1713.23	10/04/1990	2002	1003
3008	4723.00	10/05/1990	2006	1001
3010	1309.95	10/06/1990	2004	1002
3011	9891.88	10/06/1990	2006	1001

Browse : ↑↓←→ PgDn PgUp —▶| |◀— Home

Figure 10.3: Selecting amounts greater than the average for 10/04/1990

The average amount for October 4 is 1788.98 (1713.23 + 75.75) divided by 2, which equals 894.49. Rows with amount fields greater than this were selected.

Keep in mind that grouped aggregate functions, that is aggregate functions defined in terms of a GROUP BY clause, can produce multiple values. They are, therefore, not allowed in subqueries of this nature. Even if GROUP BY and HAVING are used in such a way that only a single group is output by the subquery, the command is still rejected on principle. You should use a single aggregate function with a WHERE clause that will eliminate the undesired groups. For example, the following query to find the average commission of salespeople in London

```
SELECT AVG (comm)
     FROM Salespeople
     GROUP BY city
     HAVING city = 'London';
```

cannot be used in a subquery! This is not the best way to form the query anyway. The version you want is

```
SELECT AVG (comm)
     FROM Salespeople
     WHERE city = 'London';
```

USING SUBQUERIES THAT PRODUCE MULTIPLE ROWS WITH IN

You can use subqueries that produce any number of rows if you use the special operator IN (the operators BETWEEN, LIKE, and IS NULL cannot be used with subqueries). As you recall, IN defines a set of values, one of which must match the other term of the predicate's equation in order for the predicate to be true. When you use IN with a subquery, SQL simply builds this set from the subquery's output. We can, therefore, use IN to perform the same subquery that would not work with a relational operator, and find all Orders attributed to salespeople in London (the output is shown in Figure 10.4):

```
SELECT *
     FROM Orders
     WHERE snum IN
          (SELECT snum
               FROM Salespeople
               WHERE city = 'London');
```

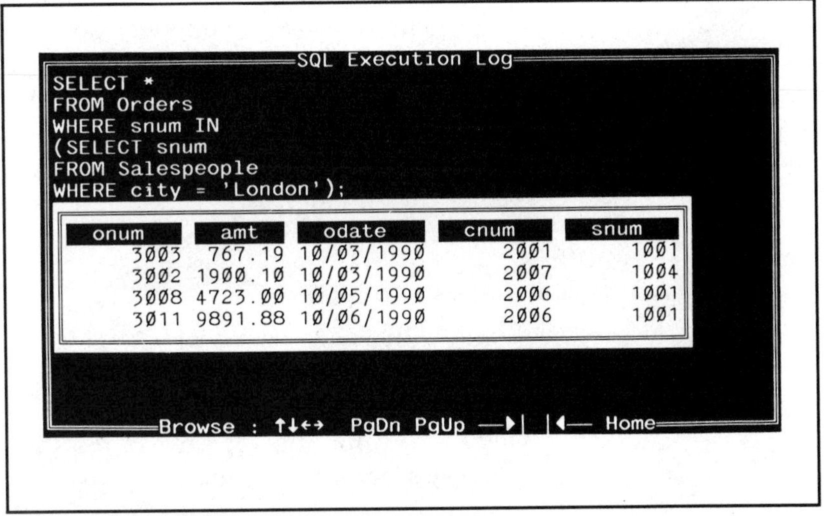

Figure 10.4: Using a subquery with IN

In a situation like this, a subquery is both easier for a user to understand and simpler (thus faster) for the computer to execute than the same problem would be if a join were used:

```
SELECT onum, amt, odate, cnum, Orders.snum
   FROM Orders, Salespeople
   WHERE Orders.snum = Salespeople.snum
      AND Salespeople.city = 'London';
```

Although this would produce the same output as the subquery example, here SQL would have to go through each possible combination of rows from the two tables and test it against the compound predicate. It is simpler and more efficient to extract from the Salespeople table the snum values where the city = 'London', and then to search for these values in the Orders table, which is what the subquery version does. The inner query gives us the snums 1001 and 1004. The outer query then gives us the rows from the Orders table where those snums are found.

Strictly speaking, whether or not the subquery version would be faster in practice depends on the *implementation*—on how the program you are using is designed. There is a part of your program called an *optimizer* that attempts to find the most efficient way to execute your queries. A good optimizer would convert the join version to a subquery anyway, but there is no easy way for you to determine if this is being done or not. It's better to write your queries with efficiency in mind than to rely entirely on the optimizer.

Of course you can also use IN, even when you are assured that the subquery will produce a single value. In any situation where you can use the relational operator equals (=), you can also use IN. Unlike relational operators, IN will not cause the command to fail if more than one value is selected by the subquery. This can be an advantage or a disadvantage. You do not directly see the output from subqueries; if you believe that a subquery is going to produce only one value, and it produces several, you may not be able to tell the difference from the main query's output. For instance, consider this command, which is similiar to a previous example:

```
SELECT onum, amt, odate
    FROM Orders
    WHERE snum =
        (SELECT DISTINCT snum
            FROM Orders
            WHERE cnum = 2001);
```

You could eliminate the need for DISTINCT by using IN instead of =, like this:

```
SELECT onum, amt, odate
    FROM Orders
    WHERE snum IN
        (SELECT snum
            FROM Orders
            WHERE cnum = 2001);
```

What happens if there is a mistake and one of the orders was credited to a different salesperson? The version using IN would give you all orders for both of the salespeople. There would be no obvious way of seeing the mistake, and reports generated or decisions made on the basis of this query would compound the error. The version using =, on the other hand, would simply fail. This, at least, lets you know there is a problem. You could then troubleshoot by executing the subquery by itself and seeing the values that it produces.

Generally speaking, if you know the subquery should, for logical reasons, produce only one value, you should use equals. IN is appropriate if the query can legitimately produce one or more values, regardless of whether you expect it to. Suppose I want to know the commissions of all salespeople servicing customers in London:

```
SELECT comm
    FROM Salespeople
    WHERE snum IN
        (SELECT snum
            FROM Customers
            WHERE city = 'London');
```

The output for this query, shown in Figure 10.5, is the commission of Peel (snum = 1001), who has both of the London customers. This is a function only of the current data, however. There is no (apparent) reason why some of the London customers could not be assigned to someone else. Therefore, IN is the most logical form to use for the query.

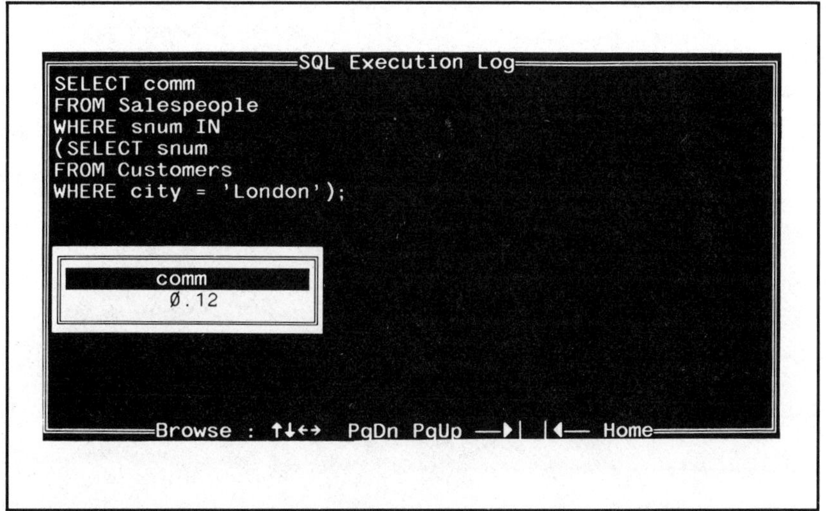

Figure 10.5: Using IN with a single-value subquery

OMITTING TABLE PREFIXES FROM SUBQUERIES By the way, a table prefix for city is not necessary in the previous example, despite the possible ambiguity between the city fields of the Salespeople and Customer tables. SQL always looks first for fields in the table(s) indicated in the FROM clause of the current (sub)query. If a field with the given name is not found there, the outer queries are checked. In the above example, "city" in the WHERE clause was meant to refer to Customers.city. Since the Customers table is named in the FROM clause of the current query, SQL's assumption was correct. This assumption can be overridden with explicit table or alias prefixes, which we will discuss further when we talk about correlated subqueries. If there is any chance of confusion, of course, it is best to use the prefixes.

SUBQUERIES TAKE SINGLE COLUMNS A common thread of all the subqueries discussed in this chapter is that they all select a single column. This is mandatory, as the select output is being compared to a single value. An implication of this is that SELECT * cannot be used in a subquery. There is an exception to this, subqueries used with the EXISTS operator, which we will introduce in Chapter 12.

USING EXPRESSIONS IN SUBQUERIES You can use an expression based on a column, rather than the column itself, in the SELECT clause of a subquery. This can be done with either relational operators or IN. For example, the following query uses the relational operator = (the output is shown in Figure 10.6):

```
SELECT *
    FROM Customers
    WHERE cnum =
        (SELECT snum + 1000
            FROM Salespeople
            WHERE sname = 'Serres');
```

This finds all customers whose cnum is 1000 above the snum of Serres. We are assuming that the sname column has no duplicate values (this can be enforced by either a UNIQUE INDEX, discussed in Chapter 17, or a UNIQUE constraint, discussed in

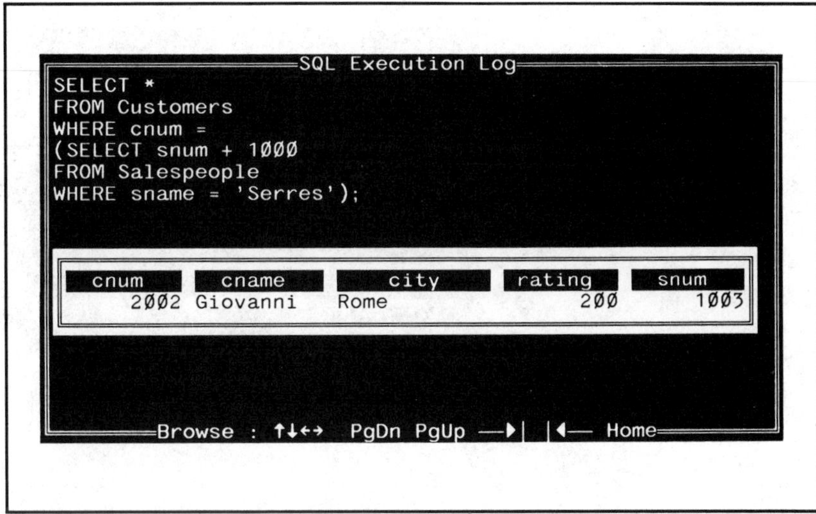

Figure 10.6: Using a subquery with an expression

Chapter 18); otherwise the subquery might produce multiple values. Unless the snum and cnum fields have meaning beyond their simple function as primary keys, which would not necessarily be a good idea, a query such as the above is probably not terribly useful, but it does illustrate the point.

SUBQUERIES IN HAVING

You can also use subqueries within the HAVING clause. These subqueries can use their own aggregate functions as long as they do not produce multiple values or use GROUP BY or HAVING themselves. The following query is an example (its output is shown in Figure 10.7):

```
SELECT rating, COUNT (DISTINCT cnum)
    FROM Customers
    GROUP by rating
    HAVING rating >
        (SELECT AVG (rating)
            FROM Customers
            WHERE city = 'San Jose';
```

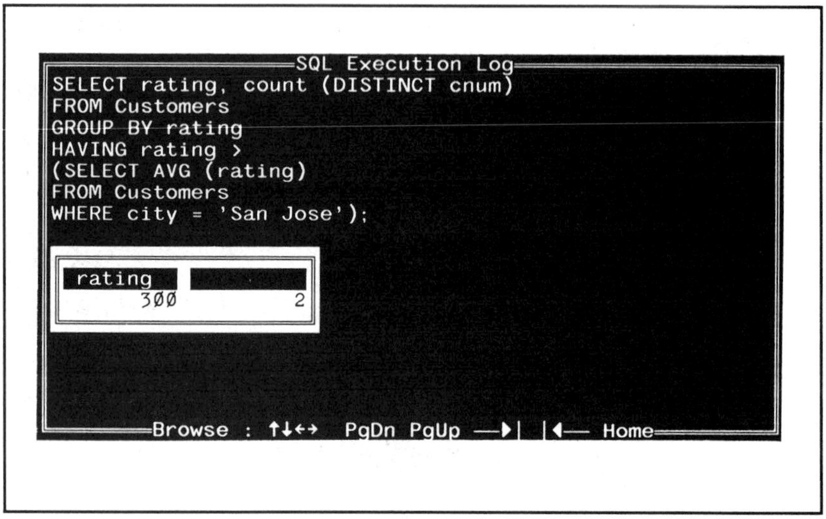

```
SQL Execution Log
SELECT rating, count (DISTINCT cnum)
FROM Customers
GROUP BY rating
HAVING rating >
(SELECT AVG (rating)
FROM Customers
WHERE city = 'San Jose');

rating
   300          2

Browse : ↑↓←→  PgDn PgUp —▶| |◀— Home
```

Figure 10.7: Finding customers with a rating above San Jose's average

This command counts the customers with ratings above San Jose's average. Had there been other ratings than 300 that qualified, each distinct rating would have been output with a count of the number of customers who had that rating.

SUMMARY

Now you are using queries in a hierarchical manner. You have seen how using the results of one query to control another extends the ease with which you can perform many functions. You now understand how to use subqueries with relational operators as well as with the special operator IN, in either the WHERE or HAVING clause of the outer query.

In the next few chapters, we will elaborate on subqueries. First in Chapter 11, we will discuss another kind of subquery, one that is executed separately for each row of the table referenced in the outer query. Then, in Chapter 12 and 13, we will introduce you to several special operators that operate on entire subqueries, as IN does, except that these operators can be used only with subqueries.

Putting SQL to Work

1. Write a query that uses a subquery to obtain all orders for the customer named Cisneros. Assume you do not know his customer number (cnum).
2. Write a query that produces the names and ratings of all customers who have above-average orders.
3. Write a query that selects the total amount in orders for each salesperson for whom this total is greater than the amount of the largest order in the table.

(See Appendix A for answers.)

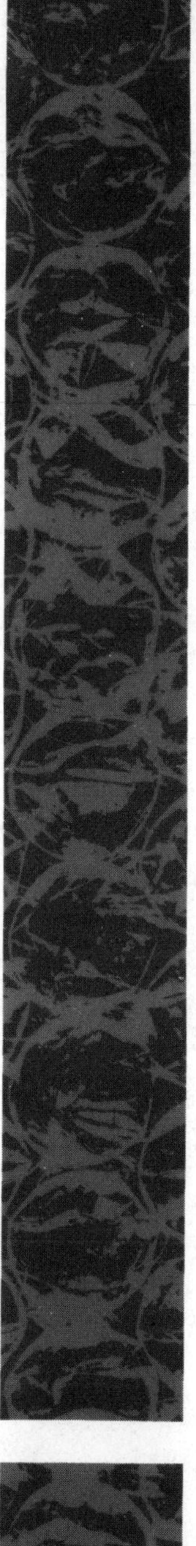

11

Correlated Subqueries

IN THIS CHAPTER, WE WILL INTRODUCE A TYPE OF subquery that we did not cover in Chapter 10—the correlated subquery. You will learn how to use correlated subqueries in the WHERE and HAVING clauses of queries. The similarities and differences between correlated subqueries and joins will be discussed, and you will sharpen your sense of aliases and table-name prefixes—when they are needed and how to use them.

HOW TO FORM A CORRELATED SUBQUERY

When you are using subqueries in SQL, you can refer in the inner query to the table in the FROM clause of the outer query, forming a *correlated subquery*. When you do this, the subquery is executed repeatedly, once for each row of the main query's table. Correlated subqueries are among the most subtle concepts in SQL because of the complexity involved in evaluating them. Once you have mastered them, however, you will find that they are quite powerful, precisely because they can perform complicated functions with such compact directions.

For example, here is one way of finding all customers with orders on October 3 (the output is shown in Figure 11.1):

```
SELECT *
    FROM Customers outer
    WHERE 10/03/1990 IN
        (SELECT odate
            FROM Orders inner
            WHERE outer.cnum = inner.cnum);
```

HOW THE CORRELATED SUBQUERY WORKS

In the above example, "inner" and "outer" are, of course, aliases, like those discussed in Chapter 9. We chose these names for the sake of clarity; they refer to values from the inner and outer queries, respectively. Because the value in the cnum field of the outer query varies, the inner query must be executed separately for each row of the outer query. The row of the outer

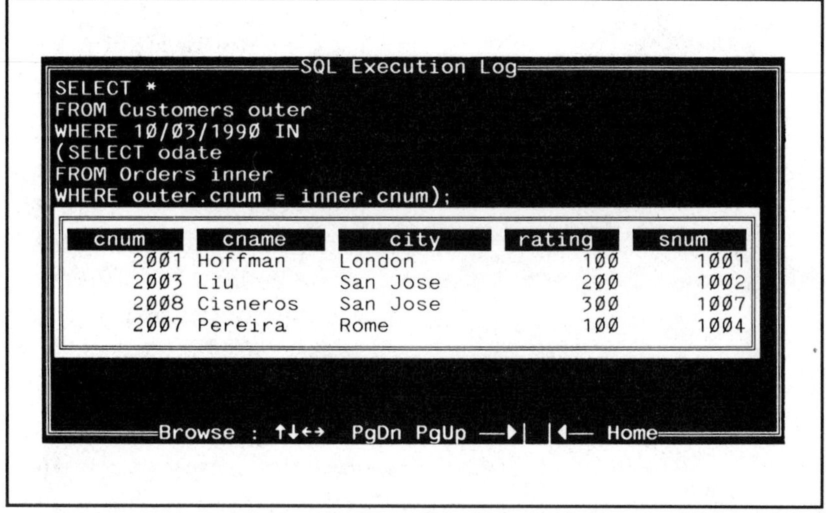

Figure 11.1: Using a correlated subquery

query for which the inner query is being executed at any time is called the current *candidate* row. Therefore, the procedure to evaluate a correlated subquery is this:

1. Select a row from the table named in the outer query. This will be the current candidate row.
2. Store the values from this candidate row in the alias named in the FROM clause of the outer query.
3. Perform the subquery. Wherever the alias given for the outer query is found (in this case "outer"), use the value for the current candidate row. The use of a value from the outer query's candidate row in a subquery is called an *outer reference*.
4. Evaluate the predicate of the outer query on the basis of the results of the subquery performed in step 3. This will determine whether the candidate row is selected for output.
5. Repeat the procedure for the next candidate row of the table, and so on until all the rows of the table have been tested.

In the above example, SQL implements the following procedure:

1. It selects the row of Hoffman from the Customers table.
2. It stores this row as the current candidate row under the alias "outer".
3. It then performs the subquery. The subquery goes through the entire Orders table to find rows where the cnum field is the same as outer.cnum, which currently is 2001, the cnum of Hoffman's row. It then extracts the odate field from each row of the Orders table for which this is true, and builds a set of the resulting odate values.
4. Having formed a set of all odate values where the cnum is 2001, it tests the predicate of the main query to see if October 3 is in this set. If it is (and it is), it selects Hoffman's row for output from the main query.
5. It repeats the entire procedure using Giovanni's row as the candidate row, and then keeps repeating until every row of the Customers table has been tested.

As you can see, the calculations that SQL performs with these simple instructions are quite complex. Of course, you could also have solved the same problem with a join, such as the following (the output for this query is shown in Figure 11.2):

```
SELECT *
    FROM Customers first, Orders second
    WHERE first.cnum = second.cnum
        AND second.odate = 10/03/1990;
```

Notice that here Cisneros was chosen twice, once for each order she had on the given date. We could have eliminated this by using SELECT DISTINCT instead of simply SELECT, of course. This is, however, not necessary with the subquery version. The IN operator, as used with the subquery version, makes no distinction between values that are selected by the subquery once and values that are selected repeatedly. Therefore DISTINCT is not needed.

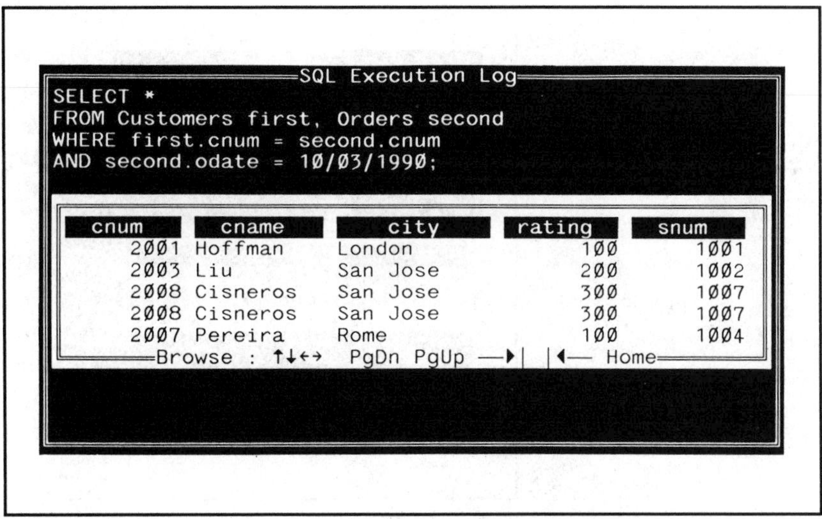
SQL Execution Log
SELECT *
FROM Customers first, Orders second
WHERE first.cnum = second.cnum
AND second.odate = 10/03/1990;

cnum	cname	city	rating	snum
2001	Hoffman	London	100	1001
2003	Liu	San Jose	200	1002
2008	Cisneros	San Jose	300	1007
2008	Cisneros	San Jose	300	1007
2007	Pereira	Rome	100	1004

Browse : ↑↓←→ PgDn PgUp —▶| |◀— Home

Figure 11.2: Using a join in place of a correlated subquery

Suppose we wanted to see the names and numbers of all salespeople who had more than one customer. The following query would accomplish this for us (the output is shown in Figure 11.3):

```
SELECT snum, sname
   FROM Salespeople main
   WHERE 1 <
      (SELECT COUNT (*)
         FROM Customers
         WHERE snum = main.snum);
```

Notice that the FROM clause of the subquery in this example makes no use of an alias. In the absence of a table-name or alias prefix, SQL will initially assume that any field is drawn from the table named in the FROM clause of the current query. If there is no field of the given name (in this case, snum) in that table, SQL will then check the outer queries. That is why table-name prefixes are usually necessary with correlated subqueries—to override this assumption. Aliases are also frequently called for to enable you to reference the same table in an inner and an outer query without ambiguity.

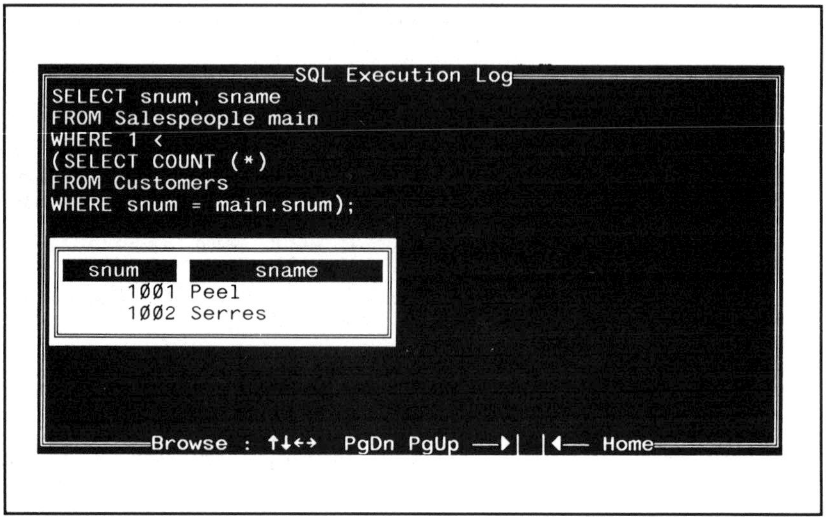

```
SQL Execution Log
SELECT snum, sname
FROM Salespeople main
WHERE 1 <
(SELECT COUNT (*)
FROM Customers
WHERE snum = main.snum);

    snum        sname
    1001 Peel
    1002 Serres

Browse : ↑↓←→  PgDn PgUp —►|  |◄— Home
```

Figure 11.3: Finding salespeople with multiple customers

USING CORRELATED SUBQUERIES TO FIND ERRORS

Sometimes it is useful to run queries that are solely designed to find errors. It is always possible for faulty information to be entered into your database, and, once entered, it can be difficult to spot. The following query should produce no output. It examines the Orders table to see if the match of snum and cnum in each row there corresponds to that in the Customers table and outputs any row where it does not. In other words, it checks to see if the correct salesperson was credited with each sale (it assumes that cnum, as the primary key of the Customers table, will have no duplicate values in that table).

```
SELECT *
    FROM Orders main
    WHERE NOT snum =
        (SELECT snum
            FROM Customers
            WHERE cnum = main.cnum);
```

Using the mechanism of referential integrity (discussed in Chapter 19), you can ensure against some errors of this kind. But this mechanism is not always available, nor is its use desirable in all cases, so error-seeking queries, such as the above, can still be useful.

CORRELATING A TABLE WITH ITSELF

You can also use correlated subqueries based on the same table as the main query. This enables you to extract certain complex forms of derived information. For example, we can find all orders with above-average amounts for their customers (the output is shown in Figure 11.4):

```
SELECT *
    FROM Orders outer
    WHERE amt >
        (SELECT AVG (amt)
            FROM Orders inner
            WHERE inner.cnum = outer.cnum);
```

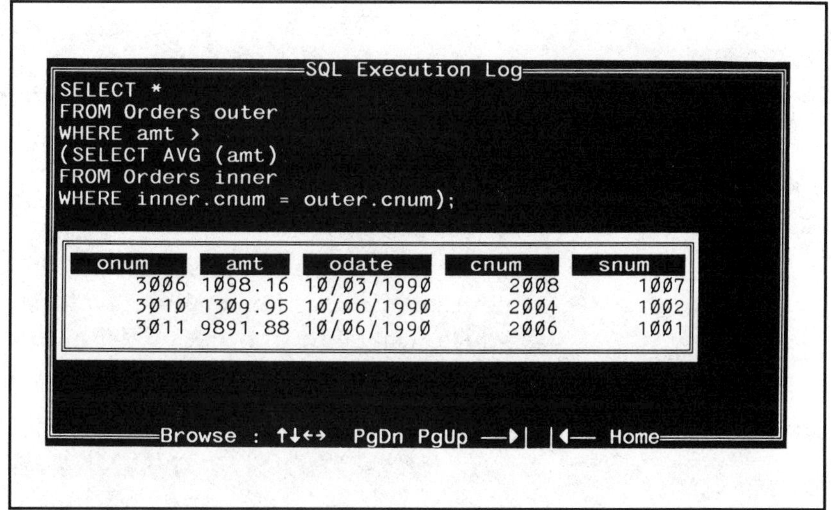

Figure 11.4: Correlating a table with itself

Of course, in our small sample table, with most customers having only one order, the majority of values are the same as the average and therefore not selected. Let's enter the command in a different way (the output is shown in Figure 11.5):

```
SELECT *
   FROM Orders outer
   WHERE amt > =
      (SELECT AVG (amt)
         FROM Orders inner
         WHERE inner.cnum = outer.cnum);
```

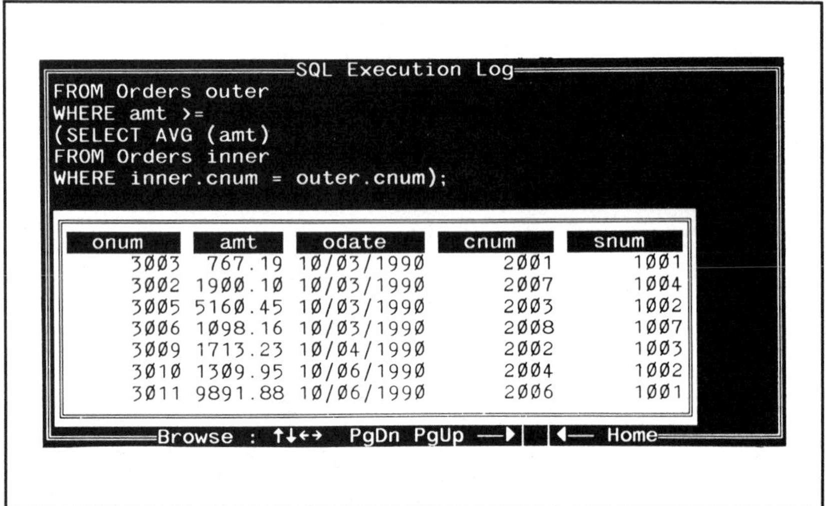

SQL Execution Log

```
FROM Orders outer
WHERE amt >=
(SELECT AVG (amt)
FROM Orders inner
WHERE inner.cnum = outer.cnum);
```

onum	amt	odate	cnum	snum
3003	767.19	10/03/1990	2001	1001
3002	1900.10	10/03/1990	2007	1004
3005	5160.45	10/03/1990	2003	1002
3006	1098.16	10/03/1990	2008	1007
3009	1713.23	10/04/1990	2002	1003
3010	1309.95	10/06/1990	2004	1002
3011	9891.88	10/06/1990	2006	1001

Browse : ↑↓←→ PgDn PgUp —▶| |◀— Home

Figure 11.5: Selecting orders > = the average amounts for their customers

The difference, of course, is that the relational operator of the main predicate here includes values that equal the average (which usually means that they are the only orders for the given customers).

CORRELATED SUBQUERIES IN HAVING

Just as the HAVING clause can take subqueries, it can take correlated subqueries. When you use a correlated subquery in a

HAVING clause, you must restrict the outer references to items that could be directly used in the HAVING clause itself. You will recall from Chapter 6 that HAVING clauses can use only aggregate functions from their SELECT clause or fields used in their GROUP BY clause. These are the only outer references you can make. This is because the predicate of the HAVING clause is evaluated for each group from the outer query, not for each row. Therefore, the subquery will be executed once for each output group from the outer query, not for each row.

Suppose you want the sums of the amounts from the Orders table, grouped by date, eliminating all those dates where the SUM was not at least 2000.00 above the MAX amount:

```
SELECT odate, SUM (amt)
    FROM Orders a
    GROUP BY odate
    HAVING SUM (amt) >
        (SELECT 2000.00 + MAX (amt)
            FROM Orders b
            WHERE a.odate = b.odate);
```

The subquery calculates the MAX value for all rows with the same date as the current aggregate group of the main query. This must be done, as above, with a WHERE clause. The subquery itself must not use a GROUP BY or HAVING clause.

CORRELATED SUBQUERIES AND JOINS

As you may have surmised, correlated subqueries are closely related to joins—both involve checking each row of one table against every row of another (or an alias of the same) table. You will find that many operations that can be performed with one of these will also work with the other.

There are differences in application between the two, however, such as the aforementioned occasional necessity for using DISTINCT with a join where it is not needed with a subquery. There are also things that each can do that the other cannot. Subqueries, for example, can employ aggregate functions in the predicate, making possible operations such as our previous example in which we extracted orders that were above the average for their customers. Joins, on the other hand, can produce rows from both of the tables being compared, whereas the output of subqueries is used only in the predicates of outer queries. As a rule of thumb, the form of query that seems most intuitive will probably be the best to use, but it is good to be cognizant of both techniques for those situations where one or the other will not work.

SUMMARY

If you are still with us, you can congratulate yourself on mastering what many consider the most abstruse concept in SQL—the correlated subquery. You have seen how the correlated subquery relates to the join, as well as how it can be used with aggregate functions and in the HAVING clause. All in all, you have now covered all types of subqueries pretty thoroughly.

The next step is the introduction of some SQL special operators. These take subqueries as arguments, as IN does, but unlike IN, they can be used *only* with subqueries. The first of these, introduced in Chapter 12, is the operator called EXISTS.

Putting SQL to Work

1. Write a SELECT command using a correlated subquery that selects the names and numbers of all customers with ratings equal to the maximum for their city.
2. Write two queries that select all salespeople (by name and number) who have customers in their cities who they do not service, one using a join and one a correlated subquery. Which solution is more elegant?

   (Hint: one way to do this is to find all customers not serviced by a given salesperson and see if any of them are in his or her city.)

(See Appendix A for answers.)

12

Using the EXISTS Operator

NOW THAT YOU ARE WELL ACQUAINTED WITH SUBqueries, we can talk about some special operators that always take subqueries as arguments. You will learn about the first of these in this chapter. The remainder will be covered in the next.

The EXISTS operator is used to base a predicate on whether a subquery produces output or not. In this chapter, you will learn how to use this operator with conventional and (more commonly) correlated subqueries. We will also discuss special considerations that come into play when you use this operator as regards aggregates, NULLS, and Booleans. In addition, you will extend your general proficiency with subqueries by examining more complex applications of them than we have been seeing up to now.

HOW DOES EXISTS WORK?

EXISTS is an operator that produces a true or false value, in other words, a Boolean expression (see Chapter 4 for review on this term). This means it can stand alone in a predicate or be combined with other Boolean expressions using the Boolean operators AND, OR, and NOT. It takes a subquery as an argument and evaluates to true if it produces any output or false if it does not. This makes it different from other predicate operators, in that it cannot be unknown. For example, we can decide to extract some data from the Customers table if and only if one or more of the customers in the Customers table are located in San Jose (the output for this query is shown in Figure 12.1):

```
SELECT cnum, cname, city
    FROM Customers
    WHERE EXISTS
        (SELECT *
            FROM Customers
            WHERE city = 'San Jose');
```

The inner query selected all data for all customers in San Jose. The EXISTS operator in the outer predicate noted that some output was produced by the subquery and, since the EXISTS expression was the entire predicate, made the predicate therefore true. The subquery (not being correlated) was performed only

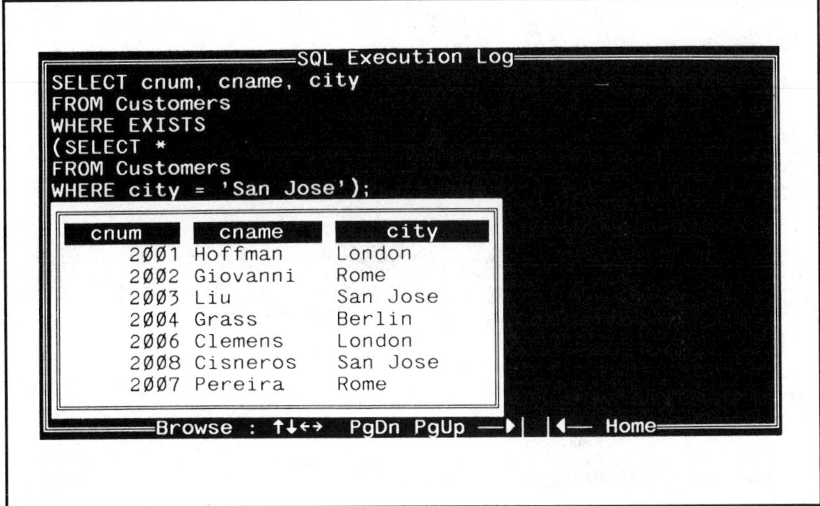
```
SQL Execution Log
SELECT cnum, cname, city
FROM Customers
WHERE EXISTS
(SELECT *
FROM Customers
WHERE city = 'San Jose');
```

cnum	cname	city
2001	Hoffman	London
2002	Giovanni	Rome
2003	Liu	San Jose
2004	Grass	Berlin
2006	Clemens	London
2008	Cisneros	San Jose
2007	Pereira	Rome

Figure 12.1: Using the EXISTS operator

once for the entire outer query, and therefore had a single value for all cases. Since EXISTS, when used in this manner, makes the predicate true or false for all rows at once, it is not terribly useful for extracting specific information.

SELECTING COLUMNS WITH EXISTS

In the above example, EXISTS could have just as easily selected a single column, instead of selecting all columns by using the star. This differs from the subqueries we have seen before that can select only a single column, as noted in Chapter 10. However, it generally makes little difference which column EXISTS selects, or if selects all columns, because it simply notes whether or not there is output from the subquery and does not use the values produced at all.

USING EXISTS WITH CORRELATED SUBQUERIES

With a correlated subquery, the EXISTS clause is evaluated separately for each row of the table referenced in the outer query, just as other predicate operators are when you use correlated subqueries. This enables you to use EXISTS as a true predicate, one that generates different answers for each row of the table referenced in the main query. Therefore information from the inner query is, in a sense, preserved, if not directly output, when you use EXISTS in this manner. For example, we can output salespeople who have multiple customers (the output for this query is shown in Figure 12.2):

```
SELECT DISTINCT snum
    FROM Customers outer
    WHERE EXISTS
        (SELECT *
            FROM Customers inner
            WHERE inner.snum = outer.snum
                AND inner.cnum <> outer.cnum);
```

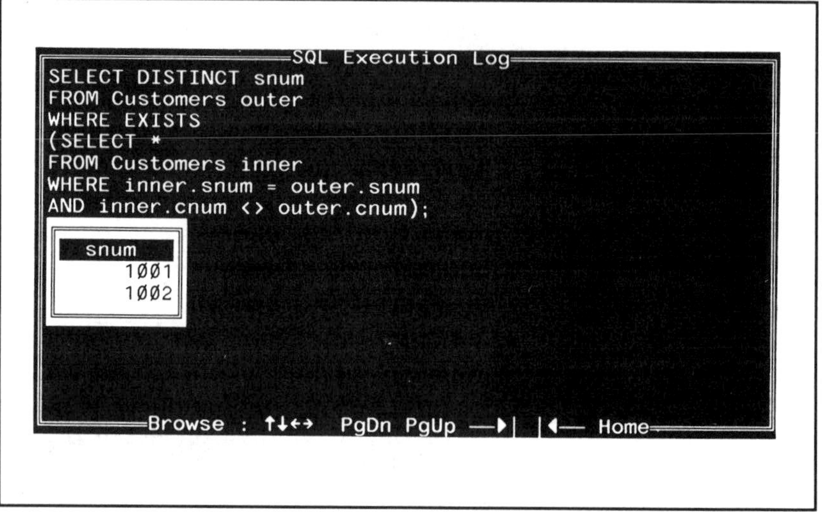

Figure 12.2: Using EXISTS with a correlated subquery

For each candidate row of the outer query (representing a customer currently being examined), the inner query found rows that matched the snum value (had the same salesperson), but not the cnum value (matched a different customer). If any such rows are found by the inner query, it implies that there are two different customers serviced by the current salesperson (that is, the salesperson of the customer in the current candidate row of the outer query). The EXISTS predicate is therefore true for the current row and the salesperson number (snum) field of the table in the outer query is output. If DISTINCT were not specified, each of these salespeople would have been selected once for each customer that she or he is assigned.

COMBINING EXISTS AND JOINS

It might be useful for us to output more information about these salespeople than their numbers, however. We can do this by joining the Customers table to the Salespeople table (the output for the query is shown in Figure 12.3):

```
SELECT DISTINCT first.snum, sname, first.city
    FROM Salespeople first, Customers second
    WHERE EXISTS
        (SELECT *
            FROM Customers third
            WHERE second.snum = third.snum
                AND second.cnum <> third.cnum)
        AND first.snum = second.snum;
```

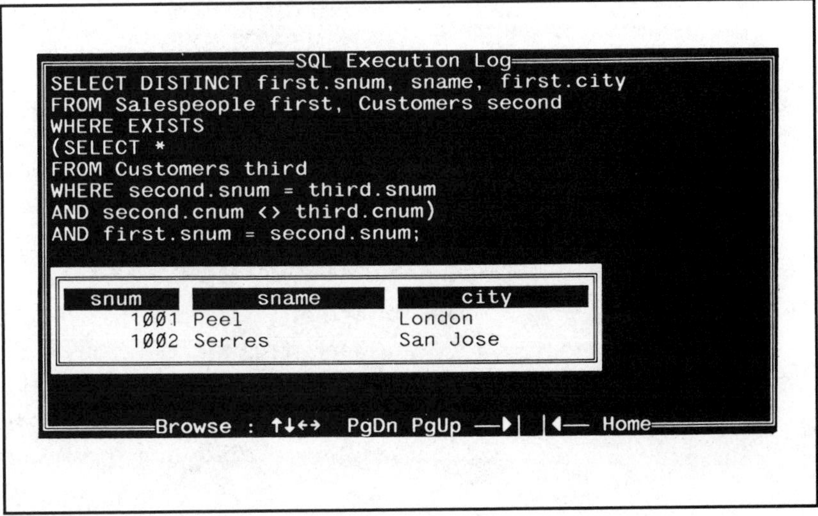

Figure 12.3: Combining EXISTS with a join

The inner query here is the same as the previous version, save for the fact that the aliases have been changed. The outer query is a join of the Salespeople and Customers tables, similar to ones we have seen before. The new clause of the main predicate (AND first.snum = second.snum) is, of course, evaluated at the same level as the EXISTS clause. It is the functional predicate of the join itself, matching the two tables from the outer query in terms of the snum field that they have in common. Because of the Boolean operator AND, both of the main predicate's conditions must be true in order for the predicate to be true. Therefore, the results of the subquery matter only in those cases where the second part of the query is true, and the join is in effect. Combining joins and subqueries in this way can be quite a powerful way of processing data.

USING NOT EXISTS

The previous example makes it clear that EXISTS can be combined with Boolean operators. Naturally, the one that is easiest to use and probably most commonly used with EXISTS is NOT. One way that we could find all salespeople with only one customer would be to reverse our previous example (the output for this query is shown in Figure 12.4):

```
SELECT DISTINCT snum
    FROM Customers outer
    WHERE NOT EXISTS
        (SELECT *
            FROM Customers inner
            WHERE inner.snum = outer.snum
                AND inner.cnum <> outer.cnum);
```

EXISTS AND AGGREGATES

One thing that EXISTS cannot do is take an aggregate function in its subquery. This makes sense. If an aggregate function finds any rows to operate on, EXISTS is true, and it does not matter what the value of the function is; if the function finds no rows, EXISTS is false. Attempting to use aggregates with EXISTS in

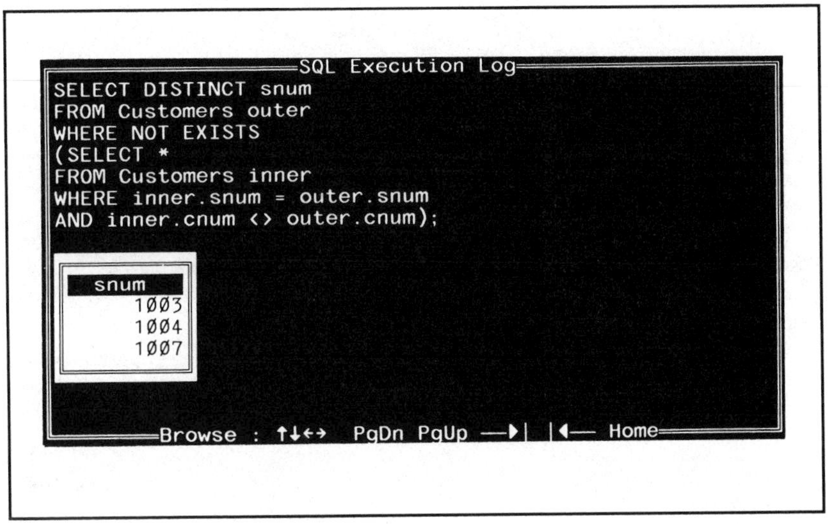

```
SQL Execution Log
SELECT DISTINCT snum
FROM Customers outer
WHERE NOT EXISTS
(SELECT *
FROM Customers inner
WHERE inner.snum = outer.snum
AND inner.cnum <> outer.cnum);

snum
1003
1004
1007

Browse : ↑↓←→ PgDn PgUp —►| |◄— Home
```

Figure 12.4: Using EXISTS with NOT

this way probably indicates that the problem has not been properly thought through.

Of course, a subquery to an EXISTS predicate may also use one or more subqueries of its own. These may be of any of the various types we have seen (or that we will see). These subqueries, and any others within them, are allowed to use aggregates, unless there is some other reason why they cannot. The next section offers an example of this.

In either case, you could have gotten the same result more easily by selecting the field that you used the aggregate function on, instead of using the function itself. In other words, the predicate EXISTS (SELECT COUNT (DISTINCT sname) FROM Salespeople) would be equivalent to EXISTS (SELECT sname FROM salespeople) were the former permissible.

A MORE ADVANCED SUBQUERY EXAMPLE

The possible applications of subqueries can get very involved. You can nest two or more of them in a single query, even inside one another. While it can take a bit of thought to figure out how these commands will work, you can do things this way in SQL that would take several commands in most other languages. Here is a query that extracts the rows of all salespeople who have customers with more than one current order. It is not necessarily the simplest solution to this problem, but is intended rather to demonstrate advanced SQL logic. Deriving this information means interrelating all three of our sample tables:

```
SELECT *
     FROM Salespeople first
     WHERE EXISTS
          (SELECT *
               FROM Customers second
               WHERE first.snum = second.snum
               AND 1 <
                    (SELECT COUNT (*)
                         FROM Orders
                         WHERE Orders.cnum =
                          second.cnum));
```

The output for this query is shown in Figure 12.5.

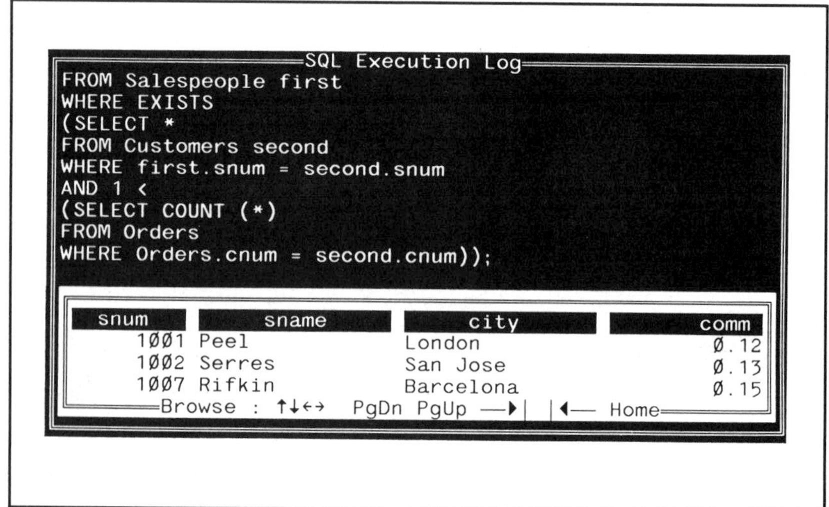

Figure 12.5: Using EXISTS with a complex subquery

We could view the evaluation of the above query like this: Take each row of the salesperson table as a candidate row (outer query) and perform the subqueries. For each candidate row from the outer query, take each row from the Customers table (middle query). If the current customer row is not matched to the current salesperson row (that is, if first.snum <> second.snum), the predicate of the middle query is false. Whenever we find a customer in the middle-query that is matched to the salesperson in the outer query, however, we must look at the innermost query to determine if our middle query predicate will be true. The innermost query counts the number of orders of the current customer (from the middle query). If this number is greater than 1, the predicate of the middle query is true, and rows are selected. This makes the EXISTS predicate of the outer query true for the current salesperson's row, meaning that at least one of the current salesperson's customers has more than one order.

If this does not seem quite intuitive to you at this point, don't worry. The complexity of this example is well beyond what you would frequently use in a business situation. The main purpose of examples such as this is to sharpen your comprehension and skills as well as to show you some advanced possibilities that may prove useful. After working with complicated situations like this, the simple queries that are most often used in SQL will seem elementary to you.

Besides, this query, even though it may seem like a convoluted way to extract information, is doing a lot of work. It is correlating three different tables to give you information that, if the tables were larger than they are here, as they are likely to be, would be difficult to derive more directly (although this is not the only, nor necessarily the best, way to do it in SQL). Perhaps you would have to see this information on a regular basis—if, for instance, you had an end-of-the-week bonus for salespeople who produced multiple orders from a single customer. In this case, it would be worth deriving the command, and keeping it to use again and again as the data changes (a good way to do this is with a view, which we will discuss in Chapter 20).

SUMMARY

EXISTS, although it seems simple, can be one of SQL's more abstruse operators. It is, however, quite flexible and powerful. In this chapter, you have seen and mastered the many possibilities that EXISTS creates for you. In the process, your comprehension of advanced subquery logic has been extended considerably.

The next step is to master three other special operators that take subqueries as arguments: ANY, ALL, and SOME. As you will see in Chapter 13, these are alternative formulations of some things you already know how to do, but, in some cases, they may be preferable.

Putting SQL to Work

1. Write a query that uses the EXISTS operator to extract all salespeople who have customers with a rating of 300.
2. How could you have solved the above problem with a join?
3. Write a query using the EXISTS operator that selects all salespeople with customers located in their cities who are not assigned to them.
4. Write a query that extracts from the Customers table every customer assigned to a salesperson who currently has at least one other customer (besides the customer being selected) with orders in the Orders table (hint: this is similar in structure to our three-level subquery example).

(See Appendix A for answers.)

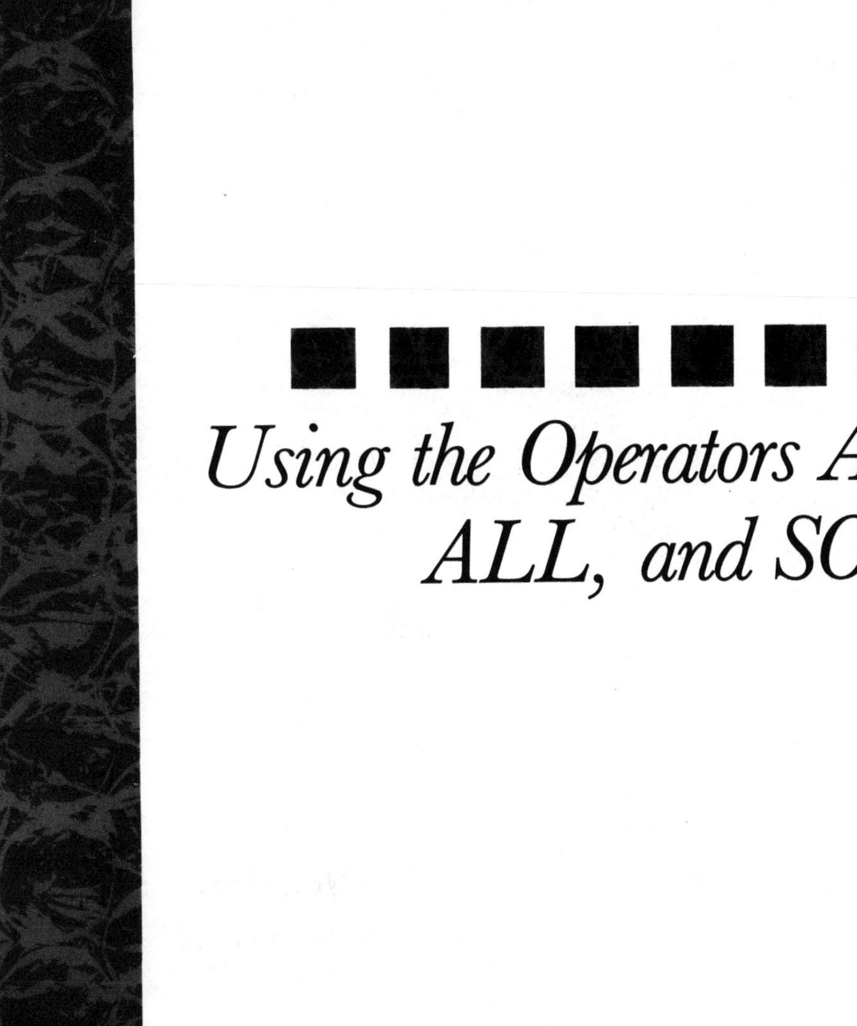

13

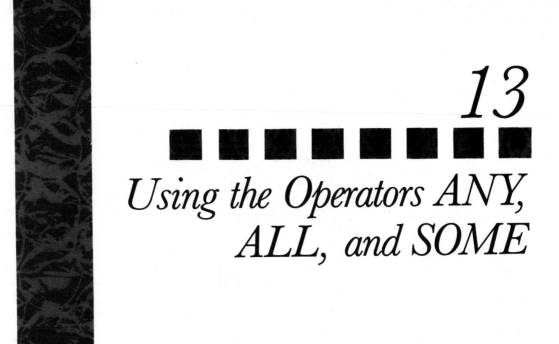

Using the Operators ANY, ALL, and SOME

NOW THAT YOU HAVE MASTERED EXISTS, YOU WILL learn about three more special operators oriented around subqueries. (Actually, there are only two, because ANY and SOME are the same.) Once you understand these operators, you will have covered all of the types of predicate subqueries used in SQL. In addition, you will be exposed to the various ways a given query can be formed using different types of predicate subqueries, and you will understand the advantages and disadvantages of each approach.

ANY, ALL, and SOME are similar to EXISTS in that they take subqueries as arguments; they differ from EXISTS, however, in that they are used in conjunction with relational operators. In this respect, they are similar to the IN operator when it is used with subqueries; they take all the values produced by the subquery and treat them as a unit. However, unlike IN, they can be used only with subqueries.

THE SPECIAL OPERATOR ANY OR SOME

Let us begin by examining the operator ANY or SOME. SOME and ANY are interchangable—wherever we use the term ANY, SOME would work just the same. The difference in terminology reflects an effort to allow people to use the term that they find more intuitive. This is somewhat problematic; as we shall see, intuitive interpretations of these operators can sometimes be misleading.

Here is a new way to find salespeople with customers located in their cities (the output for this query is shown in Figure 13.1):

```
SELECT *
    FROM Salespeople
    WHERE city = ANY
        (SELECT city
            FROM Customers);
```

The ANY operator takes all values produced by the subquery, in this case all city values in the Customers table, and evaluates to true if ANY of them equal the city value of the current row of

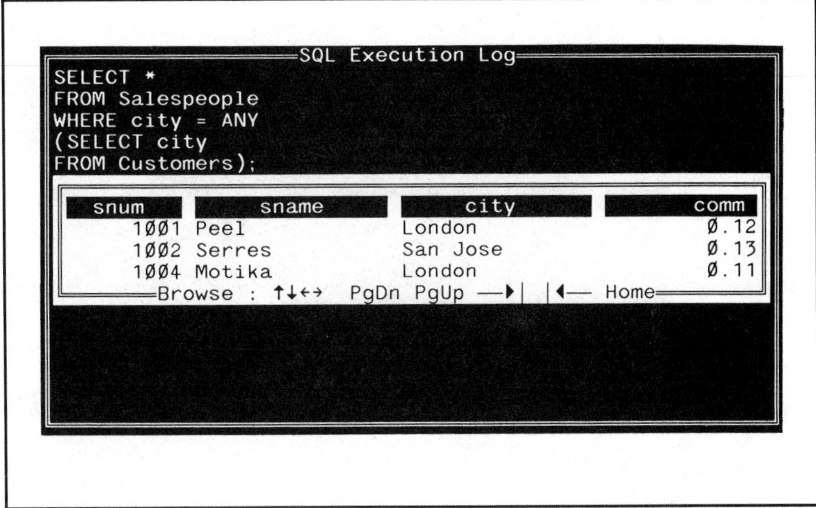

Figure 13.1: Using the ANY operator

the outer query. This means that the subquery must select values of the same type as those they are being compared to in the main predicate. This is in contrast to EXISTS, which simply determines if a subquery produces results or not and does not actually use the results.

USING IN OR EXISTS INSTEAD OF ANY

We could also have used the IN operator to construct the previous query:

```
SELECT *
    FROM Salespeople
    WHERE city IN
        (SELECT city
            FROM Customers);
```

This query will produce the output shown in Figure 13.2.

However, the ANY operator can use other relational operators besides equals, and thereby make comparisons that are beyond the capabilities of IN. For example, we could find all salespeople

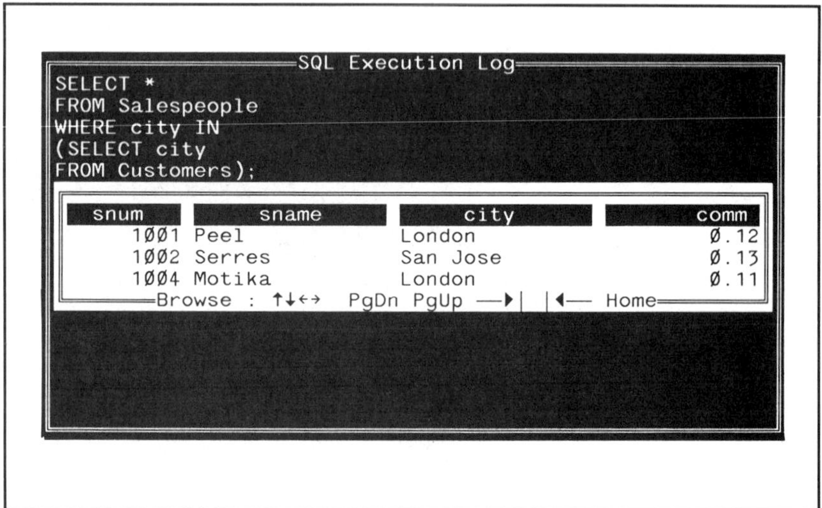

Figure 13.2: Using IN as an alternative to ANY

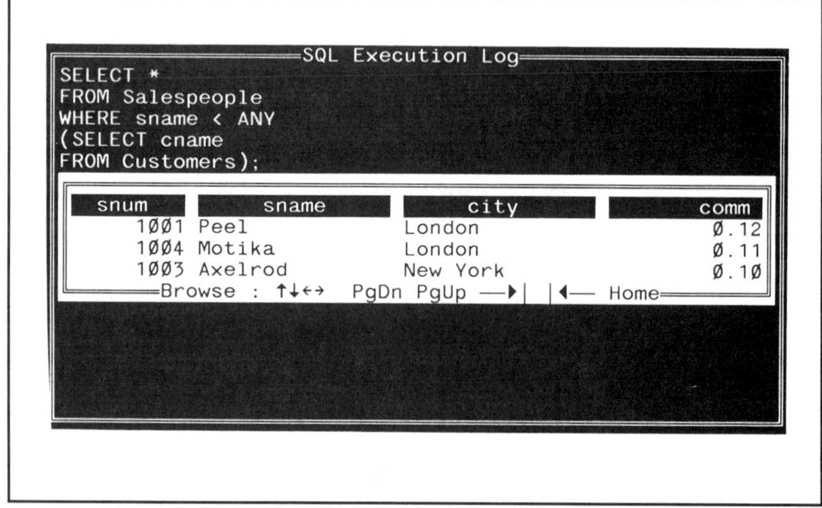

Figure 13.3: Using ANY with an inequality

for whom there are customers that follow them in alphabetical order (the output is shown in Figure 13.3):

```
SELECT *
   FROM Salespeople
```

```
WHERE sname < ANY
    (SELECT cname
        FROM Customers);
```

All rows were selected save for those of Serres and Rifkin, because there are no customers whose names follow these in alphabetical order. Notice that this is basically equivalent to the following EXISTS query, whose output is shown in Figure 13.4:

```
SELECT *
    FROM Salespeople outer
    WHERE EXISTS
        (SELECT *
            FROM Customers inner
            WHERE outer.sname < inner.cname);
```

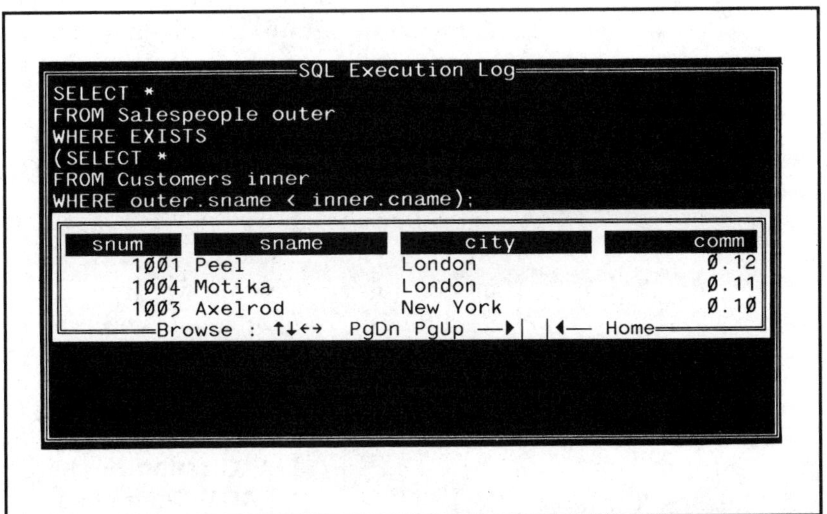

Figure 13.4: Using EXISTS as an alternative to ANY

Any query that can be formulated with ANY (or, as we shall see, ALL) could also be formulated with EXISTS, although the reverse is not true. Strictly speaking, the EXISTS versions are not quite identical to the ANY or ALL versions because of a difference in how NULLs are handled (to be discussed later in this chapter). Nonetheless, technically speaking, you could do without ANY and ALL if you became very adroit with the use of

EXISTS (and IS NULL). Many users, however, find ANY and ALL easier to use than EXISTS, which requires correlated subqueries. In addition, depending on the implementation, ANY and ALL can, at least in theory, be more efficient than EXISTS. An ANY or ALL subquery can be executed once and have its output used to determine the predicate for every row of the main query. EXISTS, on the other hand, takes a correlated subquery, which requires the entire subquery to be reexecuted for each row of the main query. SQL attempts to find the most efficient way to execute any command, so it may try to convert a less efficient formulation of a query to a more efficient one (but you can't always count on it finding the most efficient formulation).

The main reason for offering the EXISTS formulation as an alternative to ANY and ALL is that ANY and ALL can be somewhat counterintuitive, because of the way we use these terms in English, as you shall soon see. By being aware of different ways to formulate a given query, you can work around procedures that you happen to find difficult or awkward.

HOW ANY CAN BE AMBIGUOUS

As implied above, ANY is not entirely intuitive. If we construct a query to select customers who have a greater rating than any customer in Rome, we would get output that might be a little different from what we expected (as shown in Figure 13.5):

```
SELECT *
    FROM Customers
    WHERE rating > ANY
        (SELECT rating
            FROM Customers
            WHERE city = 'Rome');
```

In English, the way we would normally be inclined to interpret a rating as being "greater than *any* (where the city equals Rome)" is to say that the rating value must be higher than the rating value in *every* case where the city value equals Rome. This is not, however, the way ANY is conceived in SQL. ANY evaluates to true if the subquery finds *any* value(s) that make the condition true.

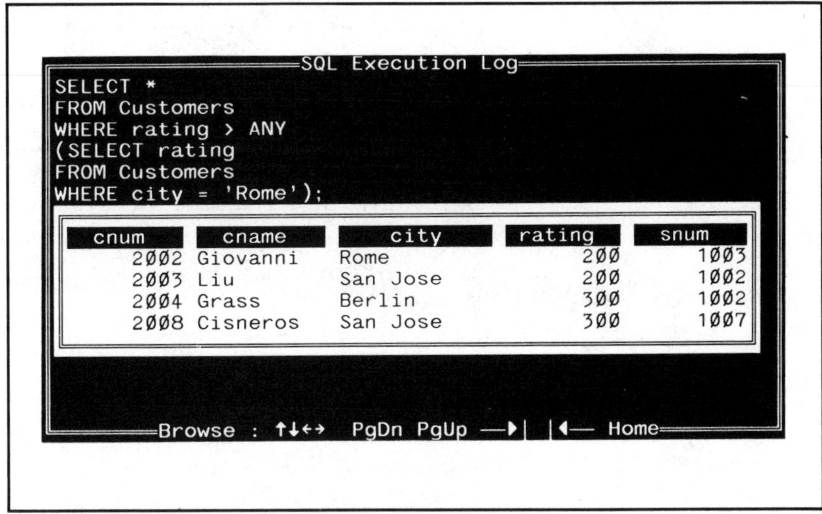
SQL Execution Log
SELECT *
FROM Customers
WHERE rating > ANY
(SELECT rating
FROM Customers
WHERE city = 'Rome');

cnum	cname	city	rating	snum
2002	Giovanni	Rome	200	1003
2003	Liu	San Jose	200	1002
2004	Grass	Berlin	300	1002
2008	Cisneros	San Jose	300	1007

Browse : ↑↓←→ PgDn PgUp —▶| |◀— Home

Figure 13.5: Greater than ANY as interpreted by SQL

If we were evaluating ANY the way we normally would in English, only the customers with a rating of 300 would beat Giovanni, who is in Rome and has a rating of 200. However, the ANY subquery also found Periera in Rome with a rating of 100. Because all the customers with a rating of 200 were higher than that, they were selected, even though there was another Rome customer (Giovanni) whose rating they did not beat (the fact that one of the customers selected is also in Rome is irrelevant). Since the subquery did produce at least one value that would make the predicate true for these rows, the rows were selected.

To give another example, suppose we were to select all orders that had amounts that were greater than at least one of the orders from October 6th:

```
SELECT *
    FROM Orders
    WHERE amt > ANY
        (SELECT amt
            FROM Orders
            WHERE odate = 10/06/1990);
```

The output for this query is shown in Figure 13.6.

Even though the highest amount in the table (9891.88) is on October 6th, the preceding rows have higher amounts than the other row for October 6th, which had an amount of 1309.95. Had the relational operator been > = instead of simply >, this row would also have been selected, because it is equal to itself.

Naturally, you can use ANY with other SQL techniques, such as joins. This query will find all orders with amounts smaller than any amount for a customer in San Jose (the output is shown in Figure 13.7):

```
SELECT *
     FROM Orders
     WHERE amt < ANY
          (SELECT amt
               FROM Orders a, Customers b
               WHERE a.cnum = b.cnum
                    AND b.city = 'San Jose');
```

Even though the smallest order in the table was for a customer in San Jose, so was the second largest; therefore almost all the rows were selected. An easy thing to remember is that < ANY means less than the largest value selected, and > ANY means

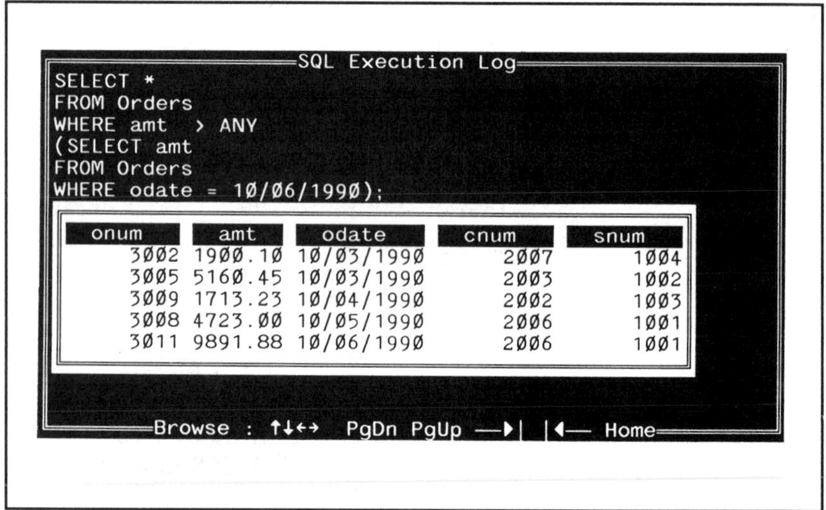

```
SQL Execution Log
SELECT *
FROM Orders
WHERE amt  > ANY
(SELECT amt
FROM Orders
WHERE odate = 10/06/1990);
```

onum	amt	odate	cnum	snum
3002	1900.10	10/03/1990	2007	1004
3005	5160.45	10/03/1990	2003	1002
3009	1713.23	10/04/1990	2002	1003
3008	4723.00	10/05/1990	2006	1001
3011	9891.88	10/06/1990	2006	1001

Browse : ↑↓←→ PgDn PgUp —▸| |◂— Home

Figure 13.6: Selecting amounts greater than ANY from Oct. 6

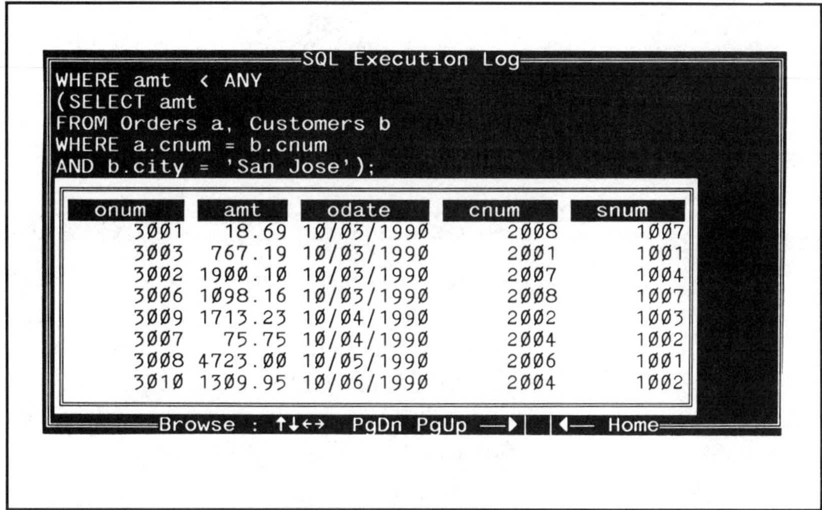

SQL Execution Log

```
WHERE amt  < ANY
(SELECT amt
FROM Orders a, Customers b
WHERE a.cnum = b.cnum
AND b.city = 'San Jose');
```

onum	amt	odate	cnum	snum
3001	18.69	10/03/1990	2008	1007
3003	767.19	10/03/1990	2001	1001
3002	1900.10	10/03/1990	2007	1004
3006	1098.16	10/03/1990	2008	1007
3009	1713.23	10/04/1990	2002	1003
3007	75.75	10/04/1990	2004	1002
3008	4723.00	10/05/1990	2006	1001
3010	1309.95	10/06/1990	2004	1002

Browse : ↑↓←→ PgDn PgUp —▶| |◀— Home

Figure 13.7: Using ANY with a join

greater than the smallest value selected. In fact, the above command could also have been given like this (the output is shown in Figure 13.8):

```
SELECT *
   FROM Orders
```

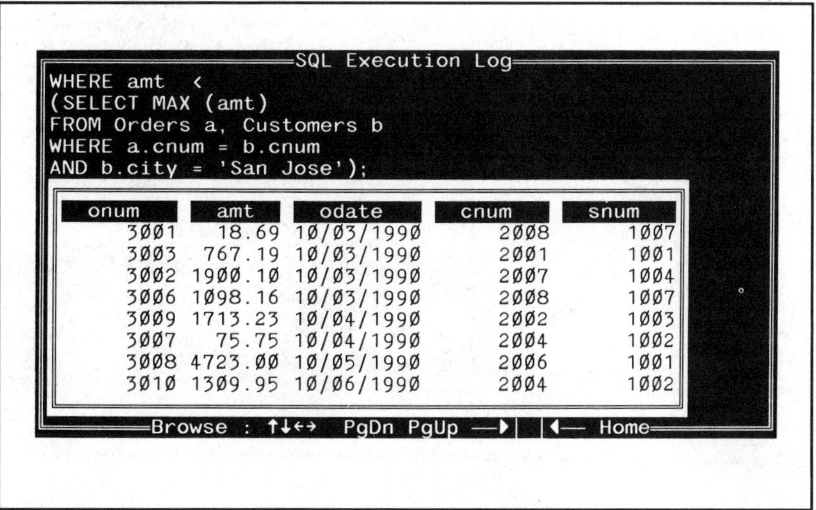

SQL Execution Log

```
WHERE amt  <
(SELECT MAX (amt)
FROM Orders a, Customers b
WHERE a.cnum = b.cnum
AND b.city = 'San Jose');
```

onum	amt	odate	cnum	snum
3001	18.69	10/03/1990	2008	1007
3003	767.19	10/03/1990	2001	1001
3002	1900.10	10/03/1990	2007	1004
3006	1098.16	10/03/1990	2008	1007
3009	1713.23	10/04/1990	2002	1003
3007	75.75	10/04/1990	2004	1002
3008	4723.00	10/05/1990	2006	1001
3010	1309.95	10/06/1990	2004	1002

Browse : ↑↓←→ PgDn PgUp —▶| |◀— Home

Figure 13.8: Using an aggregate function in place of ANY

```
WHERE amt <
    (SELECT MAX (amt)
        FROM Orders a, Customers b
        WHERE a.cnum = b.cnum
            AND b.city = 'San Jose');
```

THE SPECIAL OPERATOR ALL

With ALL, the predicate is true if *every* value selected by the subquery satisfies the condition in the predicate of the outer query. If we wanted to revise our previous example to output only those customers whose ratings are, in fact, higher than every customer in Paris, we would enter the following to produce the output shown in Figure 13.9:

```
SELECT *
    FROM Customers
    WHERE rating > ALL
        (SELECT rating
            FROM Customers
            WHERE city = 'Rome');
```

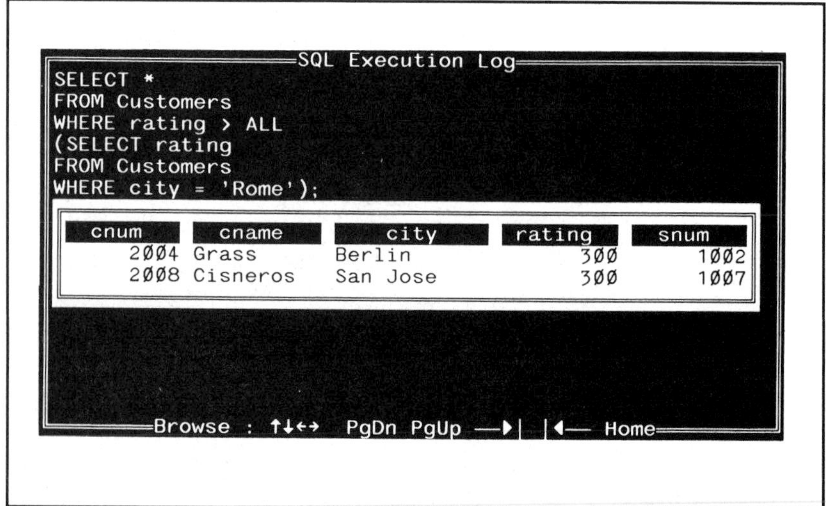

Figure 13.9: Using the ALL operator

This statement examined the rating values of all customers in Rome. It then found those customers with a higher rating than every one of the Rome customers. The highest rating in Rome is Giovanni, with a value of 200. Therefore, only those with a value higher than 200 were selected.

Just as with ANY, we can use EXISTS to produce an alternative formulation of the same query (the output is shown in Figure 13.10):

```
SELECT *
     FROM Customers outer
     WHERE NOT EXISTS
          (SELECT *
               FROM Customers inner
               WHERE outer.rating < = inner.rating
               AND inner.city = 'Rome');
```

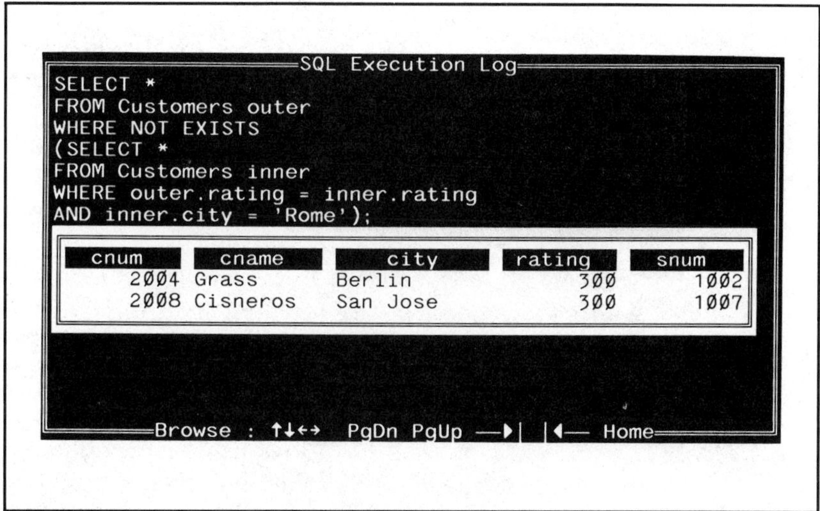

Figure 13.10: Using EXISTS as an alternative to ALL

EQUALITIES VS. INEQUALITIES

ALL is used primarily with inequalities rather than equalities because a value can be "equal to all" of the results of a subquery only if all of the said results are, in fact, identical. Examine the following query:

```
SELECT *
    FROM Customers
    WHERE rating = ALL
        (SELECT rating
            FROM Customers
            WHERE city = 'San Jose');
```

This command would be legal, but we would, with the current data, get no output. The only way output would be produced by this query is if all rating values in San Jose happened to be identical. In this case, it would be similar to saying

```
SELECT *
    FROM Customers
    WHERE rating =
        (SELECT DISTINCT rating
            FROM Customers
            WHERE city = 'San Jose');
```

The main difference is that this last command would fail if the subquery produced multiple values, whereas the ALL version would simply give no output. In general, it is not a good idea to use queries that would work only in special cases like this. Because your database will constantly be changing, it is not a good practice to make assumptions about its content.

ALL can, however, be used effectively with nonequalities, that is to say with the <> operator. To say in SQL that a value does not equal all the results of a subquery, however, is different from saying it in English. Obviously, if the subquery returns multiple distinct values, as is usually the case, no single value can be equal to all of them in the usual sense. In SQL, <> ALL really means "is not equal to any" of the subquery results. In other words, the predicate is true if the value is not found among the results of the subquery. Therefore, our previous example put in the negative looks like this (with the output shown in Figure 13.11):

```
SELECT *
    FROM Customers
    WHERE rating <> ALL
        (SELECT rating
            FROM Customers
            WHERE city = 'San Jose');
```

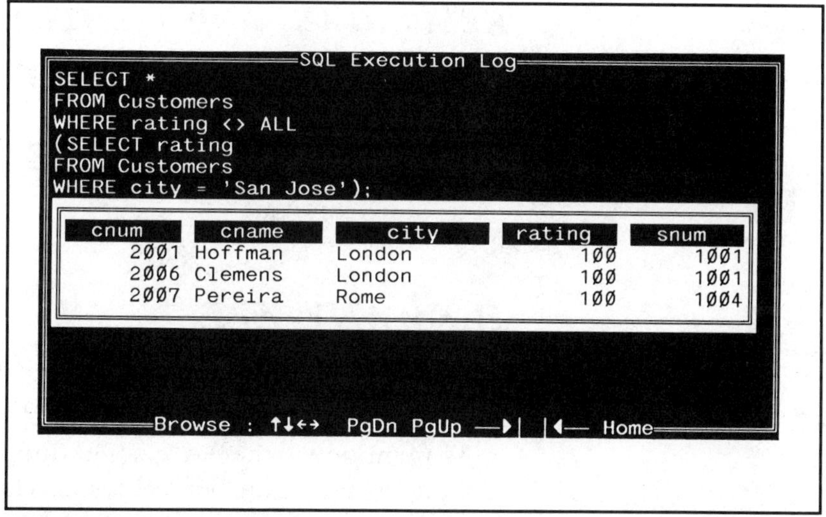

Figure 13.11: Using ALL with <>

The above subquery selected all ratings where the city was San Jose. This produced a set of two values: 200 (for Liu) and 300 (for Cisneros). The main query then selected all rows whose rating matched neither of these—that is, all rows with a rating of 100. You could have formulated the same query using NOT IN:

```
SELECT *
    FROM Customers
    WHERE rating NOT IN
        (SELECT rating
            FROM Customers
            WHERE city = 'San Jose');
```

You could also have used ANY:

```
SELECT *
    FROM Customers
```

```
WHERE NOT rating = ANY
    (SELECT rating
        FROM Customers
        WHERE city = 'San Jose');
```

The output would be the same for all three statements.

KEEPING ANY AND ALL STRAIGHT

In SQL, saying a value is greater (or less) than ANY of a set of values is the same as saying it is greater (or less) than any single one of those values. Conversely, saying a value does not equal ALL of a set of values, means that there is no value in the set to which it is equal.

HOW ANY, ALL, AND EXISTS DEAL WITH MISSING DATA AND UNKNOWNS

As mentioned, there are some differences between EXISTS and the operators introduced in this chapter with regard to how NULLs are handled. ANY and ALL also differ from each other in how they react if the subquery produces no values to use in a comparison. These differences can give your queries unexpected results if you do not account for them.

WHEN THE SUBQUERY COMES BACK EMPTY

One significant difference between ALL and ANY is the way they deal with the situation in which the subquery returns no values. Basically, whenever a legal subquery fails to produce output, ALL is automatically true, and ANY is automatically false. This means that the following query

```
SELECT *
    FROM Customers
    WHERE rating > ANY
```

```
        (SELECT rating
            FROM Customers
            WHERE city = 'Boston');
```

would produce no output, whereas this query

```
SELECT *
    FROM Customers
    WHERE rating > ALL
        (SELECT rating
            FROM Customers
            WHERE city = 'Boston');
```

would produce the entire Customers table. As there are no customers in Boston, of course, neither of these comparisons is very meaningful.

ANY AND ALL VS. EXISTS WITH NULLS

NULL values are also a bit of a problem with operators like these. When SQL compares two values in a predicate, one of which is NULL, the result is unknown (refer to Chapter 5). The unknown predicate, like false, causes a row to not be selected, but this will work out differently for some otherwise-identical queries, depending on whether they use ALL or ANY as opposed to EXISTS. Consider our previous examples:

```
SELECT *
    FROM Customers
    WHERE rating > ANY
        (SELECT rating
            FROM Customers
            WHERE city = 'Rome');
```

and:

```
SELECT *
    FROM Customers outer
    WHERE EXISTS
        (SELECT *
```

```
FROM Customers inner
WHERE outer.rating > inner.rating
AND inner.city = 'Rome');
```

In general, these two queries will behave just the same. But suppose there were a NULL value in the rating column of the customer table:

CNUM	CNAME	CITY	RATING	SNUM
2003	Liu	San Jose	NULL	1002

In the ANY version, when Mr. Liu's rating is selected by the main query, the NULL value makes the predicate unknown, and Liu's row is not selected for output. However, when the NOT EXISTS version selects this row in the main query, the NULL value is used in the predicate of the subquery, making it unknown in every case. This means the subquery will produce no values, and EXISTS will be false. This, naturally, makes NOT EXISTS true. Therefore, Mr. Liu's row is selected for output. This discrepancy stems from the fact that, unlike other types of predicates, the value of EXISTS is always true or false—never unknown.

This constitutes an argument for using the ANY formulation. We do not ordinarily think of a NULL value as being higher than a valid value. Moreover, the result would have been the same if we had been checking for a lower value.

USING COUNT IN PLACE OF EXISTS

It has been pointed out that ANY and ALL formulations can all be (imprecisely) rendered with EXISTS, while the reverse is not true. Although this is the case, it is also true that EXISTS and NOT EXISTS subqueries can be circumvented by executing the same subqueries with COUNT (*) in the subquery's SELECT clause. If more than zero rows of output are counted, it is the equivalent of EXISTS; otherwise it is the same as NOT EXISTS. The following is an example (the output is shown in Figure 13.12):

```
SELECT *
    FROM Customers outer
```

```
WHERE NOT EXISTS
    (SELECT *
        FROM Customers inner
        WHERE outer.rating < = inner.rating
            AND inner.city = 'Rome');
```

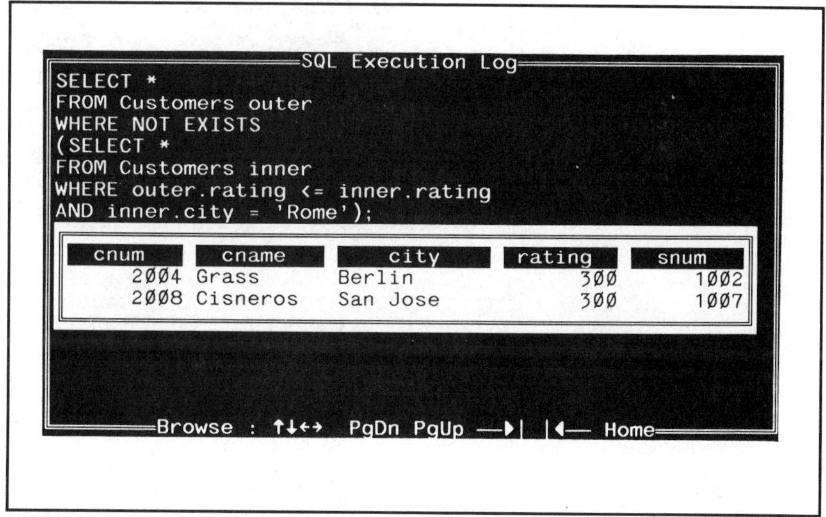

Figure 13.12: Using EXISTS with a correlated subquery

This could also be rendered as

```
SELECT *
    FROM Customers outer
    WHERE 1 >
        (SELECT COUNT (*)
            FROM Customers inner
            WHERE outer.rating < = inner.rating
                AND inner.city = 'Rome');
```

The output to this query is shown in Figure 13.13.

We are now beginning to see clearly how many ways there are of doing things in SQL. If it all seems a bit confusing at this stage, there is no need to worry. You will learn to use those techniques that best suit your needs and are most intuitive for you. At this point, we want to expose you to many different possibilities, so that you will be able to find your own best approach.

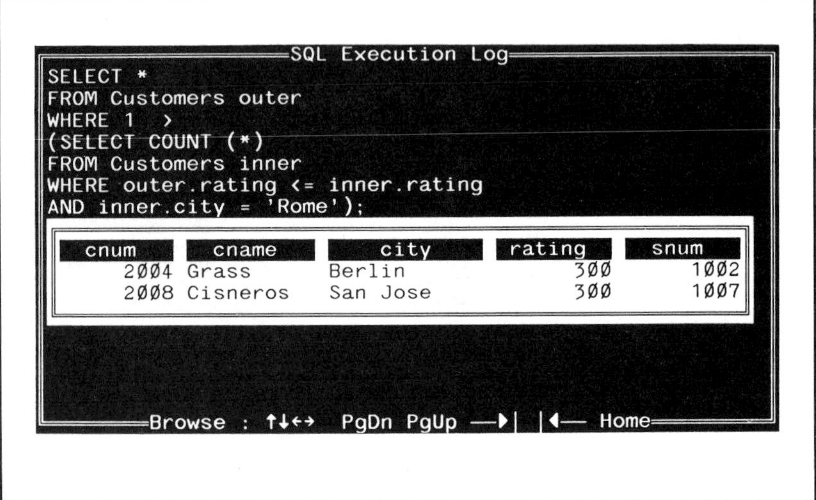

Figure 13.13: Using COUNT in place of EXISTS

SUMMARY

Well, you have covered a lot of ground in this chapter. Subqueries are not a simple topic, so we have spent this time discussing their variations and ambiguities. The mastery you now have of them is not superficial. You know several techniques for solving a given problem, so that you can choose the one that suits your purposes best. Also, you understand how different formulations will handle errors and NULL values.

Now that you have thoroughly mastered queries, the most important, and probably the most complex, aspect of SQL, the bulk of the other material will be relatively easy to understand. We have one more chapter about queries, which will show you how to combine the output from any number of queries into a single body by forming a union of multiple queries using the UNION statement.

Putting SQL to Work

1. Write a query that selects all customers whose ratings are equal to or greater than ANY (in the SQL sense) of Serres'.
2. What would be the output of the above command?
3. Write a query using ANY or ALL that will find all salespeople who have no customers located in their city.
4. Write a query that selects all orders for amounts greater than any (in the usual sense) for the customers in London.
5. Write the above query using MAX.

(See Appendix A for answers.)

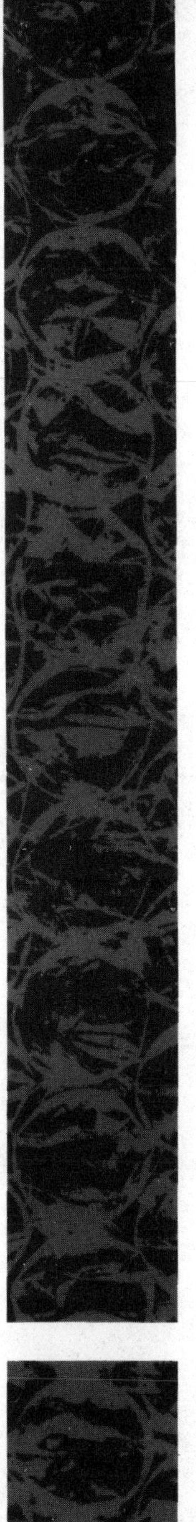

14

Using the UNION Clause

IN THE PRECEDING FEW CHAPTERS, WE DISCUSSED the various ways queries can be placed inside one another. There is another way of combining multiple queries—that is, by forming a union of them. In this chapter, you will learn about the UNION clause in SQL. *Unions* differ from subqueries in that neither of the two (or more) queries controls another. Rather, the queries are all executed independently, but their output is merged.

UNITING MULTIPLE QUERIES AS ONE

You can put multiple queries together and combine their output using the UNION clause. The UNION clause merges the output of two or more SQL queries into a single set of rows and columns. To have all salespeople and customers located in London output as a single body, for example, you could enter

```
SELECT snum, sname
     FROM Salespeople
     WHERE city = 'London'

     UNION

SELECT cnum, cname
     FROM Customers
     WHERE city = 'London';
```

to get the output shown in Figure 14.1.

As you can see, the columns selected by the two commands are output as though they were one. The column headings are omitted because no columns produced by a union are directly extracted from a single table. Therefore, these are all output columns and have no names (refer to Chapter 7 for a discussion of output columns).

Also notice that only the final query ends with a semicolon. The absence of the semicolon is what makes SQL cognizant that there is another query coming.

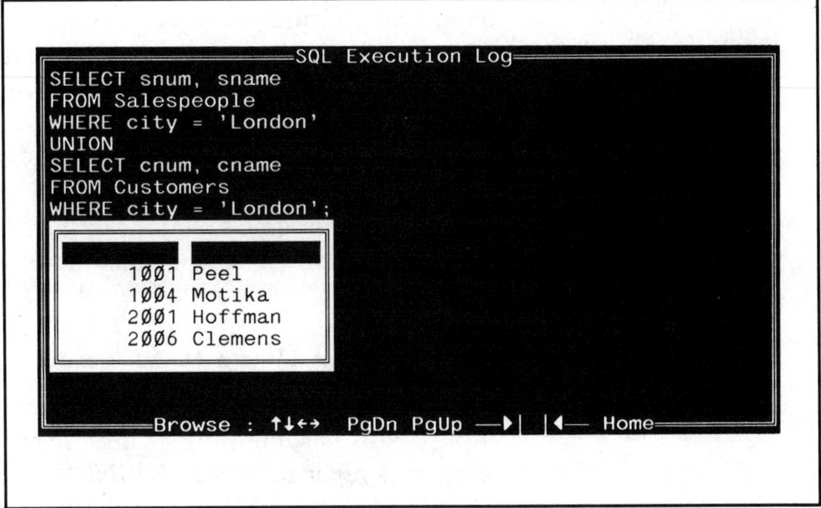

Figure 14.1: Forming a union of two queries

WHEN CAN YOU MAKE A UNION BETWEEN QUERIES?

In order for two (or more) queries to undergo a union, their output columns must be *union compatible*. This means that the queries must each specify the same number of columns and in such an order that the first, second, third, and so on, of each is of a compatible type with the first, second, third, and so on, of all the others. The meaning of compatibility of types varies. ANSI defines it very tightly, so that numeric fields must be of the exact same numeric type and size, although a few of the names ANSI uses for these types are synonyms. (Refer to Appendix B for details on the ANSI numeric types.) In addition, character fields should have the exact same number of characters (meaning the same number allotted, not necessarily the same number used).

Happily, some SQL products are more flexible than this. Non-ANSI types, such as DATE and BINARY, usually have to be matched with other columns of the same nonstandard type. Length can be a problem. Many products allows fields of varying length, but they cannot necessarily use them with UNION. On the other hand, some products (and ANSI) require character fields to be of exactly equal length. These are matters on which you should consult your own product's documentation.

Another limitation on compatibility is that, if NULLs are forbidden for any column in a union, they must also be forbidden for all corresponding columns in other queries of the union. NULLS are forbidden with the NOT NULL constraint, which is discussed in Chapter 18. Also, you cannot use UNION in subqueries, nor can you use aggregate functions in the SELECT clauses of queries in a union. (Many products relax these restrictions.)

UNION AND DUPLICATE ELIMINATION

UNION will automatically eliminate duplicate rows from the output. This is something of an idiosyncracy of SQL, since single queries must specify DISTINCT to eliminate duplicates. For example, this query, whose ouput is shown in Figure 14.2,

```
SELECT snum, city
    FROM Customers;
```

has a duplicate combination of values (1001 with London) because we did not tell SQL to eliminate duplicates. However, if

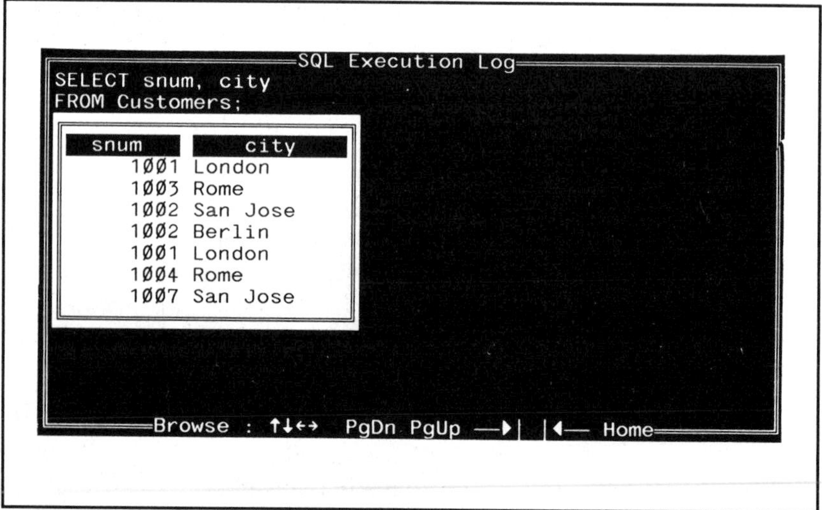

Figure 14.2: A single query with duplicated output

we use UNION to combine this query with a similar one on the Salespeople table, the same redundant combination is eliminated. Figure 14.3 shows the output of the following query.

```
SELECT snum, city
    FROM Customers

    UNION

SELECT snum, city
    FROM Salespeople;
```

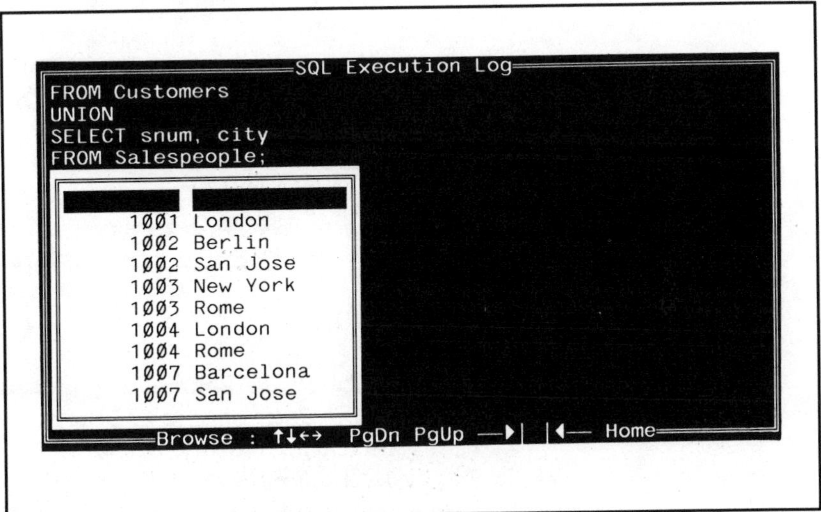

Figure 14.3: A union eliminates duplicate output

You can get around this (in some SQL products) by specifying UNION ALL in place of UNION, like this:

```
SELECT snum, city
    FROM Customers

    UNION ALL

SELECT snum, city
    FROM Salespeople;
```

USING STRINGS AND EXPRESSIONS WITH UNION

Sometimes, you can insert constants and expressions in the SELECT clauses used with UNION. This does not follow the ANSI specifications strictly, but it is a useful and not uncommonly used feature. The constants and expressions you use, however, must meet the standards of compatibility we have outlined. This feature is useful, for example, to provide comments indicating which query produced a given row.

Suppose you have to make a report of which salespeople produce the largest and smallest orders on each date. We could unite the two queries, inserting text to distinguish the two cases.

```
SELECT a.snum, sname, onum, 'Highest on', odate
    FROM Salespeople a, Orders b
    WHERE a.snum = b.snum
    AND b.amt =
        (SELECT MAX (amt)
            FROM Orders c
            WHERE c.odate = b.odate)

    UNION

SELECT a.snum, sname, onum, 'Lowest  on', odate
    FROM Salespeople a, Orders b
    WHERE a.snum = b.snum
    AND b.amt =
        (SELECT MIN (amt)
            FROM Orders c
            WHERE c.odate = b.odate);
```

The output from this command is shown in Figure 14.4.

We had to add an extra space to the 'Lowest on' string to make it match 'Highest on' for length. Note also that Peel is selected for having both the highest and lowest (in fact the only) order for October 5. Because the inserted strings of the two queries are different, the rows are not eliminated as duplicates.

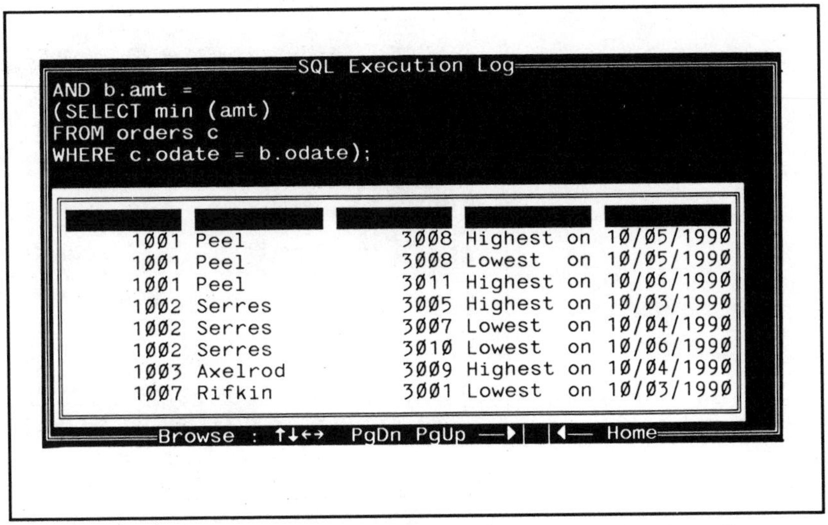

```
SQL Execution Log
AND b.amt =
(SELECT min (amt)
FROM orders c
WHERE c.odate = b.odate);

      1001 Peel              3008 Highest on 10/05/1990
      1001 Peel              3008 Lowest  on 10/05/1990
      1001 Peel              3011 Highest on 10/06/1990
      1002 Serres            3005 Highest on 10/03/1990
      1002 Serres            3007 Lowest  on 10/04/1990
      1002 Serres            3010 Lowest  on 10/06/1990
      1003 Axelrod           3009 Highest on 10/04/1990
      1007 Rifkin            3001 Lowest  on 10/03/1990

Browse : ↑↓←→  PgDn PgUp —▶| |◀— Home
```

Figure 14.4: Selecting highest and lowest orders, identified by strings

USING UNION WITH ORDER BY

Up until now, we have not been assuming that the data from the multiple queries would be output in any particular order. We have simply been showing the output first from one query and then from the other. Of course, you could not rely on the output coming in this order automatically. We just did it that way to make the examples easier to follow. You can, however, use the ORDER BY clause to order the output from a union, just as you do the output from individual queries. Let's revise our last example to order the names by order number. This will make discrepancies, such as Peel's in the last command, more obvious, as you can see from the output shown in Figure 14.5.

```
SELECT a.snum, sname, onum, 'Highest on', odate
    FROM Salespeople a, Orders b
    WHERE a.snum = b.snum
    AND b.amt =
        (SELECT MAX (amt)
            FROM Orders c
            WHERE c.odate = b.odate)
```

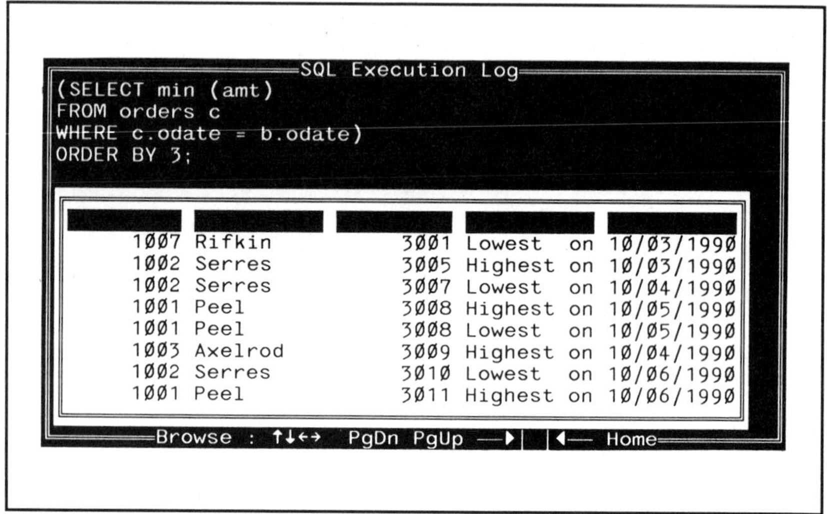

Figure 14.5: Forming a union using ORDER BY

```
    UNION

SELECT a.snum, sname, onum, 'Lowest   on', odate
    FROM Salespeople a, Orders b
    WHEREa.snum = b.snum
    AND b.amt =
        (SELECT MIN (amt)
            FROM Orders c
            WHERE c.odate = b.odate)

ORDER BY 3;
```

Since ascending is the default for ORDER BY, we did not have to specify it. We can order our output by several fields within one another and specify ASC or DESC independently for each, just as we do for single queries. Notice that the number 3 in the ORDER BY clause indicates which column in the SELECT clause to order. Because the columns of a union are output columns, they have no names and, therefore, must be referred to by number. This number indicates their placement among the other output columns. (Refer to Chapter 7 for a discussion of output columns.)

THE OUTER JOIN

An operation that is frequently useful is a union of two queries in which the second selects the rows excluded by the first. Most often, you will do this so as not to exclude rows that failed to satisfy the predicate when joining tables. This is called an *outer join*. Suppose some of your customers had not yet been assigned to salespeople. You might want to see the names and cities of all your customers, with the names of their salespeople, without leaving out those who have not yet been assigned. You can achieve this by forming a union of two queries, one of which performs the join, while the other selects customers with NULL snum values. The latter could insert blanks in the field corresponding to the sname field in the first query.

As you have seen, you can insert text strings in your output to identify the query that produced a given row. Using this technique in an outer join enables you to use predicates to classify, rather than exclude, output.

We have used the example of finding salespeople with customers located in their cities in this book before. Instead of just selecting only these rows, however, perhaps you want your output to list all of the salespeople, and indicate those who do not have customers in their cities as well as those who do. The following query, whose output is shown in Figure 14.6, will accomplish this:

```
SELECT Salespeople.snum, sname, cname, comm
    FROM Salespeople, Customers
    WHERE Salespeople.city = Customers.city.

    UNION

SELECT snum, sname, 'NO MATCH      ', comm
    FROM Salespeople
    WHERE NOT city = ANY
        (SELECT city
            FROM Customers)

    ORDER BY 2 DESC;
```

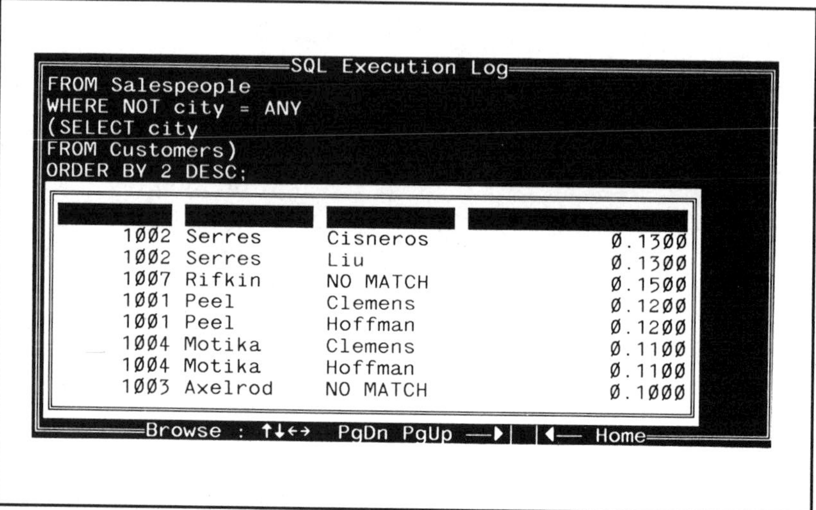

Figure 14.6: An outer join

The string 'NO MATCH' was padded with blanks, so that it would match the cname field for length (this is not necessary on all implementations of SQL). The second query selects whichever rows the first omits.

You can also add a comment or expression to your query as an extra field. If you do this, you will have to add some compatible comment or expression, at the same point among the selected fields, to every query in the union operation. Union compatibility prevents you from adding an extra field to one of the queries and not the other. Here is a query that appends strings to the selected fields, indicating whether or not a given salesperson was matched to a customer in his city:

```
SELECT a.snum, sname, a.city, 'MATCHED '
    FROM Salespeople a, Customers b
    WHERE a.city = b.city

    UNION

SELECT snum, sname, city, 'NO MATCH       '
    FROM Salespeople
```

```
WHERE NOT city = ANY
    (SELECT city
        FROM Customers)

ORDER BY 2 DESC;
```

Figure 14.7 shows this query's output.

```
SQL Execution Log
WHERE a.city = b.city
UNION
SELECT snum, sname, city, 'NO MATCH'
FROM Salespeople
WHERE NOT city = ANY
(SELECT city
FROM Customers)
ORDER BY 2 DESC;

      1002 Serres     San Jose    MATCHED
      1007 Rifkin     Barcelona   NO MATCH
      1001 Peel       London      MATCHED
      1004 Motika     London      MATCHED
      1003 Axelrod    New York    NO MATCH

Browse : ↑↓←→  PgDn PgUp —▶|  |◀— Home
```

Figure 14.7: An outer join with a comment field

This is not a full outer join, by the way, because it includes only the unmatched fields from one of the joined tables. A complete outer join would include all customers who do and do not have salespeople in their cities. This is considerably more complex, however, as you can see here (the output of the following query is shown in Figure 14.8):

```
(SELECT snum, city, 'SALESPERSON - MATCHED'
    FROM Salespeople
    WHERE city = ANY
        (SELECT city
            FROM Customers)

    UNION
```

```
SELECT snum, city, 'SALESPERSON - NO MATCH'
    FROM Salespeople
    WHERE NOT city = ANY
        (SELECT city
            FROM Customers))

    UNION

(SELECT cnum, city, 'CUSTOMER - MATCHED'
    FROM Customers
    WHERE city = ANY
        (SELECT city
            FROM Salespeople)

    UNION

SELECT cnum, city, 'CUSTOMER - NO MATCH'
    FROM Customers
    WHERE NOT city = ANY
        (SELECT city
            FROM Salespeople))

    ORDER BY 2 DESC;
```

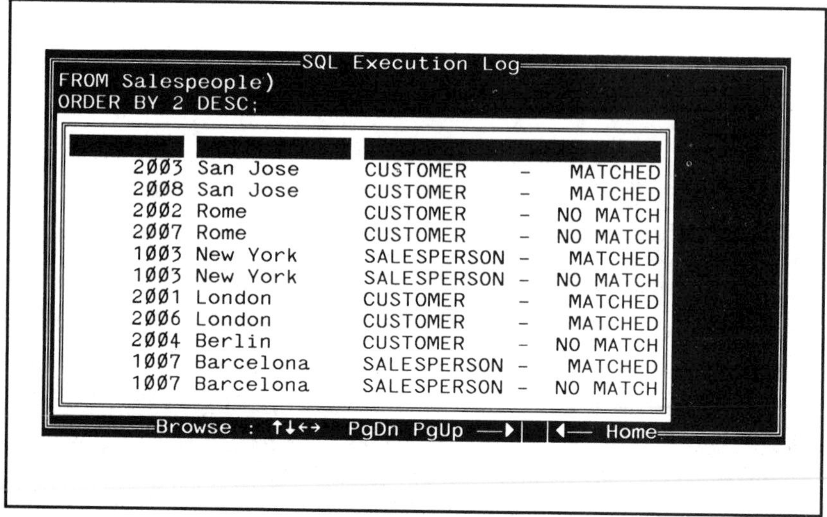

SQL Execution Log

```
FROM Salespeople)
ORDER BY 2 DESC;
```

2003	San Jose	CUSTOMER - MATCHED
2008	San Jose	CUSTOMER - MATCHED
2002	Rome	CUSTOMER - NO MATCH
2007	Rome	CUSTOMER - NO MATCH
1003	New York	SALESPERSON - MATCHED
1003	New York	SALESPERSON - NO MATCH
2001	London	CUSTOMER - MATCHED
2006	London	CUSTOMER - MATCHED
2004	Berlin	CUSTOMER - NO MATCH
1007	Barcelona	SALESPERSON - MATCHED
1007	Barcelona	SALESPERSON - NO MATCH

Browse : ↑↓←→ PgDn PgUp —▶| |◀— Home

Figure 14.8: A complete outer join

(Of course, this formulation using ANY is equivalent to the join in the previous example.)

The abbreviated outer join that we started with is probably more frequently useful than this last one. This example does, however, bring up another point. Whenever you perform a union on more than two queries, you can use parentheses to determine the order of evaluation. In other words, instead of simply saying

query X UNION _query_ Y UNION _query_ Z;

you should specify either

(_query_ X UNION _query_ Y) UNION _query_ Z;

or

query X UNION (_query_ Y UNION _query_ Z);

This is because UNION and UNION ALL can be combined to eliminate some duplicates without eliminating others. The statement

(_query_ X UNION ALL _query_ Y) UNION _query_ Z;

will not necessarily generate the same results as

query X UNION ALL (_query_ Y UNION _query_ Z);

if there are duplicate rows to eliminate.

SUMMARY

Now you know how to use the UNION clause, which enables you to combine any number of queries into a single body of output. If you have a number of similar tables—tables containing similar information but owned by different users and covering different specifics, perhaps—a union can provide an easy way to blend and order the output. Likewise, outer joins give you a new way to use conditions, not to exclude output, but to label it or to treat the parts of it that meet the condition differently from those that do not.

This concludes our chapters on queries. You now have a pretty thorough mastery of data retrieval in SQL. The next step is to deal with how the values are entered into the tables and how the tables are created in the first place. As you will see, queries are sometimes used within other types of commands, as well as by themselves.

Putting SQL to Work

1. Create a union of two queries that shows the names, cities, and ratings of all customers. Those with a rating of 200 or greater will also have the words "High Rating", while the others will have the words "Low Rating".
2. Write a command that produces the name and number of each salesperson and each customer with more than one current order. Put the results in alphabetical order.
3. Form a union of three queries. Have the first select the snums of all salespeople in San Jose; the second, the cnums of all customers in San Jose; and the third the onums of all orders on October 3. Retain duplicates between the last two queries but eliminate any redundancies between either of them and the first. (Note: in the sample tables as given, there would be no such redundancy. This is beside the point.)

(See Appendix A for answers.)

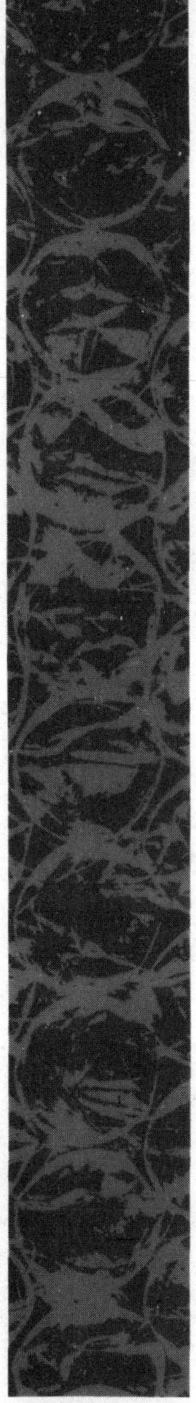

15

Entering, Deleting, and Changing Field Values

THIS CHAPTER INTRODUCES THE COMMANDS THAT control which values are present in a table at any given time. When you have finished this chapter, you will be able to place rows into a table, remove them, and change the individual values present in each row. The use of queries to generate entire groups of rows for insertion will be explored, as will the use of predicates to control the changing of values and the deletion of rows. The material in this chapter constitutes the bulk of the knowledge you need to create and manipulate the information in a database. Some more advanced ways of designing predicates will be discussed in the next chapter.

DML UPDATE COMMANDS

Values are placed in and removed from fields with three Data Manipulation Language (DML) commands: INSERT, UPDATE, and DELETE. Confusingly enough, these are all referred to in SQL as *update* commands in a generic sense. We shall simply use the lowercase "update" to indicate these commands generically and the uppercase for the keyword UPDATE, as for all keywords.

ENTERING VALUES

All rows in SQL are entered using the update command INSERT. In its simplest form, INSERT uses the following syntax:

```
INSERT INTO <table name>
    VALUES ( <value>, <value> . . .);
```

So, for example, to enter a row into the Salespeople table, you could use the following statement:

```
INSERT INTO Salespeople
    VALUES (1001, 'Peel', 'London', .12);
```

DML commands produce no output, but your program should give you some acknowledgment that data has been affected. The table name (in this case, Salespeople) must have been defined previously in a CREATE TABLE command (see Chapter 17), and each value enumerated in the values clause must match the data type of the column into which it is being inserted. In ANSI, these values may not include expressions, which means that 3 is acceptable, but 2 + 1 is not. The values, of course, are entered into the table in the order named, so that the first value named goes into column 1 automatically, the second into column 2, on so on.

INSERTING NULLS

If you have to enter a NULL, you do it just as you would a value. Suppose you did not yet have a city field for Ms. Peel. You could insert her row with a NULL in that field as follows:

```
INSERT INTO Salespeople
    VALUES (1001, 'Peel', NULL, .12);
```

Since NULL is a special marker, not a character value, it is not enclosed in single quotes.

NAMING COLUMNS FOR INSERT

You can also specify the columns you wish to insert a value into by name. This allows you to insert into them in any order. Suppose you are taking values for the customers table from a printed report, which puts them in the order: city, cname, and cnum. For simplicity's sake, you want to enter the values in that same order:

```
INSERT INTO Customers (city, cname, cnum)
    VALUES ('London', 'Hoffman', 2001);
```

You will notice that the rating and snum columns have been omitted. This means that they will be set to default values for this row automatically. The default will be either NULL or an explicitly defined default. If a constraint prevents a NULL from being accepted in a given column, and that column has no explicit default, that column must be provided with a value for any INSERT command against the table (refer to Chapter 18 for information on constraints against NULLS and on explicit defaults).

INSERTING THE RESULTS OF A QUERY

You can also use the INSERT command to take or derive values from one table and place them in another by using it with a query. To do this, you simply replace the VALUES clause with an appropriate query as in this example:

```
INSERT INTO Londonstaff
     SELECT *
          FROM Salespeople
          WHERE city = 'London';
```

This takes all values produced by the query—that is, all rows from the Salespeople table with the city values = 'London'—and places them in the table called Londonstaff. In order for this to work, the Londonstaff table must fulfill the following conditions:

- It must have already been created with a CREATE TABLE command.
- It must have four columns that match those of the Salespeople table in terms of data type; that is, the first, second, and so on, columns of each table must be of the same type (they need not have the same name).

The general rule is that the columns of the table being inserted into must match the columns output by the subquery, in this case, the entire Salespeople table.

Londonstaff is now an independent table that happens to have some of the same values as Salespeople. If the values in Salespeople change, it will not be reflected in Londonstaff (although you could create this effect by defining a view, as discussed in Chapter 20). Because either the query or the INSERT command can specify columns by name, you can, if you wish, move only selected columns as well as reorder the columns that you select.

Suppose, for example, that you decide to build a new table called Daytotals, which would simply keep track of the total dollar amount ordered each day. You are going to enter this data independently from the Orders table, but you first have to fill Daytotals with the information already present in Orders. Assuming that the Orders table covers the past fiscal year, rather than the few days in our example, you can see the advantages of using the following INSERT statement to calculate and enter the values:

```
INSERT INTO Daytotals (date, total)
    SELECT odate, SUM (amt)
        FROM Orders
        GROUP BY odate;
```

Note that, as suggested earlier, the column names of the Orders and Daytotals tables do not have to match. Also, if date and total are the only columns in the table, and they are in the given order, their names could be omitted.

REMOVING ROWS FROM TABLES

You can remove rows from a table with the update command DELETE. This can remove only entire rows, not individual field values, so no field argument is needed or accepted. To remove all the contents of Salespeople, you would enter the following statement:

```
DELETE FROM Salespeople;
```

The table would now be empty and could be destroyed with a DROP TABLE command (this is explained in Chapter 17).

Usually, you want to delete just some specific rows from a table. To determine which rows are deleted, you use a predicate, just as you do for queries. For instance, to remove salesperson Axelrod from the table, you would enter

```
DELETE FROM Salespeople
    WHERE snum = 1003;
```

We used snum instead of sname because it is the best policy to use primary keys when you want an action to affect one and only one row. That is what primary keys are for.

Of course, you can also use DELETE with a predicate that selects a group of rows, as in this example:

```
DELETE FROM Salespeople
    WHERE city = 'London';
```

CHANGING FIELD VALUES

Now that you can enter and delete rows from a table, you need to learn how to change some or all of the values in an existing row. This is done with the UPDATE command. This command has an UPDATE clause that names the table affected and a SET clause that indicates the change(s) to be made to certain column(s). For example, to change all customers' ratings to 200, you would enter

```
UPDATE Customers
    SET rating = 200;
```

UPDATING ONLY CERTAIN ROWS

Of course, you do not always want to set all rows of a table to a single value, so UPDATE, like DELETE, can take a predicate. Here's how to perform the same change on all customers of salesperson Peel (snum 1001):

```
UPDATE Customers
    SET rating = 200
    WHERE snum = 1001;
```

UPDATE WITH MULTIPLE COLUMNS

You need not, however, restrict yourself to updating a single column per UPDATE command. The SET clause can accept any number of column assignments, separated by commas. All of the said assignments will still be made to the table a single row at a time. Suppose Motika had resigned, and we wanted to reassign her number to a new salesperson:

```
UPDATE Salespeople
    SET sname = 'Gibson', city = 'Boston', comm = .10
    WHERE snum = 1004;
```

This would give Gibson all of Motika's current customers and orders, because these are linked to Motika by snum.

You cannot, however, update multiple *tables* in a single command, partly because you cannot use table prefixes with the columns being changed by the SET clause. In other words, you cannot say "SET Salespeople.sname = 'Gibson' " in an UPDATE command, you can say only "SET sname = 'Gibson'."

USING EXPRESSIONS IN UPDATE

It is possible to use scalar expressions in the SET clause of the UPDATE command, however, including expressions that employ the field being modified. This is in contrast to the VALUES clause of the INSERT command, which cannot use expressions; this is quite a useful feature. Suppose you decide to double the commission of all your salespeople. You could use the following expression:

```
UPDATE Salespeople
    SET comm = comm * 2;
```

Whenever you refer to an existing column value in the SET clause, the value produced will be that of the current row before any changes are made by UPDATE. Naturally, you can combine features to, say, double the commission of all salespeople in London with this statement:

```
UPDATE Salespeople
    SET comm = comm * 2
    WHERE city = 'London';
```

UPDATING TO NULL VALUES

The SET clause is not a predicate. It can enter NULLs just as it does values without using any special syntax (such as IS NULL). So, if you wanted to set all ratings for customers in London to NULL, you would enter the following statement:

```
UPDATE customers
    SET rating = NULL
    WHERE city = 'London';
```

This will null all the ratings of customers in London.

SUMMARY

You have now mastered the essentials of manipulating the contents of your database with three simple commands: INSERT is used to place rows in the database; DELETE, to remove them; and UPDATE, to change the values in rows previously inserted. You have learned to use predicates with UPDATE and DELETE to determine which rows will be affected by the command. Of course, predicates as such are not meaningful for INSERT, because the row in question does not exist in the table until after the INSERT command in executed. You can, however, use queries with INSERT to put entire sets of rows into a table at once. And you can do this with the columns in any order. You have learned that default values can be placed in columns if you do not explicitly state a value. You have also seen the use of the standard default value, which is NULL. In addition, you understand that UPDATE can use value expressions, whereas INSERT cannot.

The next chapter will extend your mastery of these commands by showing you how to use subqueries with them. These subqueries are similar to those with which you are already familiar, but there are some special issues and limitations when subqueries are used in DML commands, which we will discuss in Chapter 16.

Putting SQL to Work

1. Write a command that puts the following values, in their given order, into the Salespeople table: city—San Jose, name—Blanco, comm—NULL, cnum—1100.
2. Write a command that removes all orders from customer Clemens from the Orders table.
3. Write a command that increases the rating of all customers in Rome by 100.
4. Salesperson Serres has left the company. Assign her customers to Motika.

(See Appendix A for answers.)

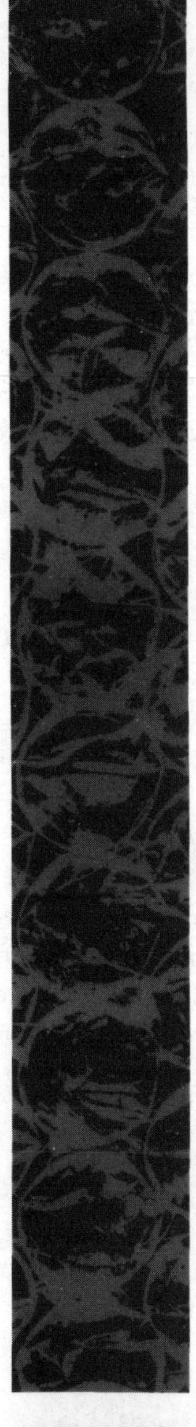

16

Using Subqueries with Update Commands

IN THIS CHAPTER, YOU WILL LEARN HOW TO USE subqueries in update commands. You will find that it is similar to something you already understand—using subqueries in queries. Knowing how subqueries are used in SELECT commands makes their usage in update commands smooth sailing, although there are differences.

Subqueries, of course, are complete SELECT commands, not predicates, so this is not the same as using simple predicates with update commands, as you have already done with UPDATE and DELETE. You have also used simple queries to produce values for INSERT, but now we will expand those queries to include subqueries.

An important principle to keep in mind with update commands is that you cannot, in the FROM clause of any subquery, reference the table being modified by the main command. This applies to all three update commands. Although there are many situations in which it would be useful to query the table you are modifying while you are modifying it, this is too ambiguous and complicated an operation to be practical, or at least that is what the designers of SQL thought. This does not (necessarily) apply to references to the current row of the table affected by the command, that is, correlated subqueries. We shall shortly elaborate on this point.

USING SUBQUERIES WITH INSERT

INSERT is our simplest case. You have already seen how to insert the results of a query into a table. You may use subqueries within any query that generates values for an INSERT command in the same way that you do for other queries—within the predicate or the HAVING clause.

Suppose we have a table called SJpeople with column definitions that match those of our Salespeople table. We have already seen how to fill a table like this with all customers in a given location, such as San Jose:

```
INSERT INTO SJpeople
    SELECT *
```

```
FROM Salespeople
WHERE city = 'San Jose';
```

Now we can use a subquery to add to the SJpeople table all salespeople who have customers in San Jose, whether the salespeople reside there or not:

```
INSERT INTO SJpeople
    SELECT *
        FROM Salespeople
        WHERE snum = ANY
            (SELECT snum
                FROM Customers
                WHERE city = 'San Jose');
```

Both queries in this command operate exactly as they would if they were not part of an INSERT expression. The subquery finds all rows for customers in San Jose and builds a set of the snum values. The outer query selects the rows from the Salespeople table where those snums are found. In our example, the rows for salespeople Rifkin and Serres, who are assigned the San Jose customers Liu and Cisneros, are inserted into table SJpeople.

(NOT) INSERTING DUPLICATE ROWS

The sequence of commands in the preceding section might be problematic. The salesperson Serres is located in San Jose, and therefore would have been inserted by the first command. The second command would attempt to insert him again, because he has a customer in San Jose. If there are any constraints on SJpeople that force values to be unique, this second insert would fail (as it should). Duplicate rows are not a good idea. (See Chapter 18 for details on constraints.)

It would be nice if you could check to see if a value were already present in the table before you attempted to insert one, by adding another subquery (using an operator such as EXISTS, IN, <>ALL, and so on) to the predicate. Unfortunately, to make this work, you would have to reference SJpeople itself in the FROM clause of this new subquery, and, as we mentioned before, you cannot reference the table being affected (as a whole) in any subquery of an update command. In the case of INSERT, this also precludes correlated subqueries based on the table you are inserting values into. This makes sense because, with INSERT, you are creating a new row in the table. The "current row" does not exist until after the INSERT is finished processing it.

USING SUBQUERIES BUILT ON OUTER QUERY TABLES

The prohibition against referring to the table being modified by an INSERT command does not prevent you from using subqueries that refer to the table(s) used in the FROM clause of an outer SELECT command. The table from which you are selecting to produce values for an INSERT is not being affected by the command; you can reference it in any of the same ways you normally would if it were in a stand-alone query.

Suppose we have a table called Samecity in which we store salespeople with customers in their home cities (our old standby). We could fill the table by using a correlated subquery:

```
INSERT INTO Samecity
    SELECT *
        FROM Salespeople outer
        WHERE city IN
            (SELECT city
                FROM Customers inner
                WHERE inner.snum = outer.snum);
```

It is the Samecity table that must not be used in the outer or inner queries of the INSERT, not the Salespeople table. For another example, suppose you have a bonus for the salesperson who has the largest order each day. You keep track of these in a table called Bonus, which contains the snums of the salespeople as well as the dates and amounts of the maximum orders. You could fill this table with the information currently in the Orders table using this command:

```
INSERT INTO Bonus
    SELECT snum, odate, amt
```

```
FROM Orders a
WHERE amt =
    (SELECT MAX (amt)
        FROM Orders b
        WHERE a.odate = b.odate);
```

Even though this command has a subquery that is based on the same table as the outer query, it doesn't reference the Bonus table, which the command will affect. It is, therefore, perfectly acceptable. The logic of the query, of course, is to traverse the Orders table and, for each row, find the maximum order amount on that given date. If that amount is the same as the current row, the current row is the largest order for that date, and its data is inserted into the Bonus table.

USING SUBQUERIES WITH DELETE

You can also use subqueries in the predicate of a DELETE command. This enables you to define some fairly sophisticated criteria for determining whether a row is to be deleted, which is important because you do not want to delete rows inadvertently. For example, if we have just closed our London office, we could use the following query to remove all customers assigned to salespeople in London:

```
DELETE
    FROM Customers
    WHERE snum = ANY
        (SELECT snum
            FROM Salespeople
            WHERE city = 'London');
```

This would remove from the Customers table the rows of Hoffman and Clemens (both assigned to Peel), and of Periera (assigned to Motika). Naturally, you would want to make sure you performed this operation before you removed or changed the rows of Peel and Motika.

This brings up an important point. Often, when we make a change in a database that will necessitate other changes, our first inclination is to make the basic change first, and then to trace down the peripheral changes. This example shows why it is often more efficient to work in the reverse manner, making the secondary changes first. If, for example, you had begun by changing the city values of your salespeople to wherever they had been reassigned, you would have made the tracing of all their customers more complicated. Since realistic databases tend to be vastly larger than our abbreviated sample tables, this might have been a serious problem. SQL can provide some help in this area with the mechanism of referential integrity (discussed in Chapter 19), but this is neither always available nor always applicable.

Although you cannot reference the table from which you are deleting in the FROM clause of a subquery, you can, in the predicate, reference the current candidate row of that table—that is, the row currently being examined in the main predicate. In other words, you can use correlated subqueries. These differ from the correlated subqueries that you can use with INSERT, in that they are actually based on candidate rows from the table being affected by the command, rather than on a query on some other table.

```
DELETE FROM Salespeople
    WHERE EXISTS
        (SELECT *
            FROM Customers
            WHERE rating = 100
            AND Salespeople.snum = Customers.snum);
```

Notice that the AND portion of the inner query's predicate refers to the Salespeople table. Naturally, this means that the entire subquery will be executed separately for each row of the Salespeople table, just as you have seen with other correlated subqueries. This command deletes all salespersons who have at least one customer with a rating of 100 from the Salespeople table. Naturally, there are other ways to achieve this. Here is one:

```
DELETE FROM Salespeople
    WHERE 100 IN
        (SELECT rating
```

```
              FROM Customers
              WHERE Salespeople.snum =
               Customers.snum);
```

This finds all the ratings for each salesperson's customers, and deletes the salesperson if 100 is among them.

Ordinary correlated subqueries—subqueries correlated with a table referenced in an outer query (rather than the DELETE clause itself)—are also perfectly usable. You could find the lowest order for each day and delete the salesperson who produced it with the following command:

```
DELETE FROM Salespeople
   WHERE snum IN
      (SELECT snum
         FROM Orders a
         WHERE amt =
            (SELECT MIN (amt)
               FROM Orders b
               WHERE a.odate = b.odate));
```

The subquery in the DELETE predicate itself takes a correlated subquery. This inner query finds the minimum order amount for the date of each row of the outer query. If this is the same as the amount of the current row, the predicate of the outer query is true, which means that the current row is the smallest order on its date. The snum of the salesperson responsible for this order is extracted and fed to the main predicate of the DELETE command itself, which then deletes all rows with this snum from the Salespeople table (since snum is the primary key of the Salespeople table, of course, there should be only one row to delete per snum output by the subquery. If there were more, however, all would be deleted.) The snum's that would be deleted are 1007, the minimum for October 3; 1002, the minimum for October 4; 1001, the minimum and only order for October 5 (this command seems rather harsh, especially since it deletes Peel for producing the only order on Oct. 5, but it does illustrate the point).

If you wanted to save Peel, of course, you could add another subquery, as this example does:

```
DELETE FROM Salespeople
    WHERE snum IN
        (SELECT snum
            FROM Orders a
            WHERE amt =
                (SELECT MIN (amt)
                    FROM Orders b
                    WHERE a.odate = b.odate)
            AND 1 <
              (SELECT COUNT (onum)
                FROM Orders b
                WHERE a.odate = b.odate));
```

Now dates on which only one order was placed would produce a count of 1 in the second correlated subquery. This would make the predicate of the outer query false, and these snum's would therefore not be fed to the main predicate.

USING SUBQUERIES WITH UPDATE

UPDATE uses subqueries in the same way as DELETE—within its optional predicate. You can use correlated subqueries of either of the forms usable with DELETE—correlated with either the table being modified or with a table referenced in an outer query). For example, with a correlated subquery on the table being updated, you can raise the commission of all salespeople who have been assigned at least two customers:

```
UPDATE Salespeople
    SET comm = comm + .01
    WHERE 2 < =
        (SELECT COUNT (cnum)
            FROM Customers
            WHERE Customers.snum =
             Salespeople.snum);
```

Now salespeople Peel and Serres, having multiple customers, will have their commissions raised.

Here is a variation on the last example from the preceding DELETE section. It reduces the commission of the salespeople who produced the smallest orders, rather than dropping them from the table:

```
UPDATE Salespeople
    SET comm = comm - .01
    WHERE snum IN
        (SELECT snum
            FROM Orders a
            WHERE amt =
                (SELECT MIN (amt)
                    FROM Orders b
                    WHERE a.odate = b.odate));
```

DEALING WITH THE LIMITATIONS OF DML COMMAND SUBQUERIES

The inability to refer to the table affected in any subquery of an update command eliminates whole categories of possible changes. For example, you cannot easily perform such an operation as deleting all customers with ratings below average. Probably the best you could do for this would be to perform the query first, obtaining the average, and then delete all rows with ratings below this number:

Step 1.

```
SELECT AVG (rating)
    FROM Customers;
```

The output is 200.

Step 2.

```
DELETE
    FROM Customers
    WHERE rating < 200;
```

SUMMARY

Now you have mastered the three commands that control the entire content of your database. There are only a few general matters regarding entry and deletion of table values left for us to explain, such as when these commands can be performed by a given user on a given table and when the changes made become permanent.

To summarize, you use the INSERT command to add rows to a table. You can either name the values for these rows in a VALUES clause (which means only one row will be added), or produce the values with a query (which means any number of rows can be added by a single command). If a query is used, it may not refer to the table into which you are inserting in any way, neither in a FROM clause, nor with an outer reference (as used in correlated subqueries). This applies as well to any subqueries within this query. The query, however, retains the liberty to use correlated subqueries or subqueries that name tables in their FROM clauses that have already been named in the FROM clauses of outer queries (this, of course, is the case for queries generally).

DELETE and UPDATE are used to remove rows from a table and to change the values in it, respectively. Both of these apply to all rows of a table, unless a predicate is used to determine which rows are to be deleted or updated. This predicate may contain subqueries, and these may be correlated with the table being deleted from or updated through the use of an outer reference. These subqueries, however, may not refer to the table being modified in any FROM clause.

It may seem odd that we have been covering SQL material in what is not the most obvious logical order. At first, we queried ready-made tables that were already filled with data. Then we showed you how you would actually put those values into the tables in the first place. But, as you can see, a thorough knowledge of queries is invaluable here. Now that we have shown you how to fill tables that have already been created (defined) with values, we shall, starting in the next chapter, explore where these tables come from in the first place.

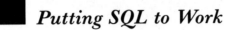

Putting SQL to Work

1. Assume there is a table called Multicust, with all of the same column definitions as Salespeople. Write a command that inserts all salespeople with more than one customer into this table.
2. Write a command that deletes all customers with no current orders.
3. Write a command that increases by twenty percent the commissions of all salespeople with total current orders above $3,000.

(See Appendix A for answers.)

17

Creating Tables

UP UNTIL NOW, WE HAVE BEEN QUERYING TABLES for data and performing update commands on them, assuming that the tables had already been created for us by someone else. Indeed, this is frequently the situation in the real world—a few people create tables that many people use. Our purpose has been to cover the information most widely needed first, progressing to more specialized needs as we go on.

In this chapter, we will discuss the creating, altering, and dropping of tables. This refers to the definitions of the tables themselves, not to the data stored in them. You may or may not need to perform these operations yourself, but a conceptual understanding of them will increase your comprehension of SQL and of the nature of the tables that you use. This puts us in the area of SQL called DDL (Data Definition Language), where SQL data objects are created.

This chapter will also discuss another kind of SQL data object: the index. Indexes are used to make retrieval more efficient and, sometimes, to force values to be different from one another. They mostly operate invisibly, but if you try to put values in a table and they are rejected because they are not unique, it means that another row has the same value for that field, and that the field has a unique index or a constraint that enforces uniqueness. The former is discussed here, the latter in Chapter 18.

THE CREATE TABLE COMMAND

Tables are defined with the CREATE TABLE command. This command creates an empty table—a table with no rows. Values are entered with the DML command INSERT (See Chapter 15). The CREATE TABLE command basically defines a table name as describing a set of named columns in a specified order. It also defines the data types and sizes of the columns. Each table must have at least one column. Here is the syntax of the CREATE TABLE command:

```
CREATE TABLE <table-name>
    (<column name> <data type>[(<size>)],
    <column name> <data type>[(<size>)] . . .);
```

As mentioned in Chapter 2, data types vary considerably between products. For the sake of compatibility with the standard, however, they should all at least support the standard ANSI types. These are enumerated in Appendix B.

Since blank spaces are used to separate parts of commands in SQL, they may not be part of a table's name (or that of any other object, such as an index). An underscore (_) is most commonly used to separate words in table names.

The meaning of the size argument varies with the data type. If you omit it, your system will assign a value automatically. For numeric values, this is usually the best course, because it will make all your fields of a given type the same size and release you from concern about union compatibility (see Chapter 14). Besides, the use of the size argument with some of the numeric types is not a simple matter. If you need to store large numbers, however, you will naturally want to ensure that the fields are large enough to contain them.

The one data type for which you should generally assign a size is CHAR. Here the size argument is an integer that specifies the maximum number of characters that the field can hold. The field's actual number of characters can range from zero (if the field is NULL) to this number. The default is 1, which means the field can contain only a single letter. This is not usually what you want.

Tables are owned by the user who creates them, and the names of all tables owned by a given user must be different from one another, as must the names of all the columns within a given table. Separate tables may use the same column names, even if they are owned by the same user. An example of this is the city column in both the Salespeople and Customers tables. Users other than the owner of a table will refer to that table by preceding its name with that of its owner followed by a dot; for example, Smith's table Employees would become Smith.Employees when referred to by another user (we are assuming that Smith is the authorization ID of said user (your authorization ID is your name as far as SQL is concerned. This issue is discussed in Chapter 2, and will come up again in Chapter 22).

This command would create the Salespeople table:

```
CREATE TABLE Salespeople
    (snum     integer,
    sname     char(10),
    city      char(10),
    comm      decimal);
```

The order of the columns in the table is determined by the order in which they are specified. The column definitions do not have to be on separate lines (that is only done for readability) but they do have to be separated by commas.

INDEXES

An *index* is an ordered (alphabetic or numeric) list of the contents of a column or group of columns in a table. Tables can have a large number of rows, and, since the rows are in no particular order, searching them for a particular value can be quite time consuming. Indexes address this problem and, at the same time, provide a way of forcing all values in a group of one or more rows to be different from one another. In Chapter 18, we will describe a more direct way to force your values to be unique. But this method did not exist in the early days of SQL. Because uniqueness is frequently needed, indexes were used to fulfill this purpose.

Indexes are a feature of SQL that has come from the marketplace, rather than from ANSI. Because of this, the ANSI standard itself does not currently support indexes, but they are quite common and useful.

When you create an index on a field, your database stores a appropriately ordered list of all the values of that field in its memory space. Suppose our Customers table had thousands of entries, and you wanted to find customer number 2999. Since the rows are not ordered, your program would normally go through the entire table, one row at a time, and check for the cnum value 2999. If there were an index on the cnum field, however, the program could go right to number 2999 in the index and get information about how to find the correct row of the table. While this can greatly improve the performance of queries, maintaining an index slows up DML update operations (such as INSERT and DELETE) somewhat, and the index itself takes up memory. Therefore, you must make a decision each time you create a table whether or not to index it.

Indexes can be of multiple fields. If more than one field is specified for a single index, the second is ordered within the first, the third within the second, and so on. If you had first and last names in two different fields of a table, you might create an index that ordered the former within the latter. This could be done regardless of the way the columns were ordered in the table.

The syntax to create an index is usually as follows (this is not ANSI standard, remember):

```
CREATE INDEX <index name> ON <table name> (<column
 name>
    [,<column name>]..);
```

The table, of course, must already have been created and must contain the column(s) named. The index name must not be used for anything else in the database (by any user). Once created, the index will be invisible to the user. SQL will decide when it is appropriate to refer to it and will do so automatically. If, for instance, the Customers table is going to be most frequently referred to by salespeople inquiring about their own clients, it would be appropriate to create an index on the snum field of the Customers table.

```
CREATE INDEX Clientgroup ON Customers (snum);
```

Now, salespeople referring to this table will be able to find their own clients quickly.

UNIQUE INDEXES

The index in the previous example (luckily) does not enforce uniqueness, even though, as we said, that is one purpose of an index. A given salesperson can still have any number of customers. However, this would not be the case if we had used the keyword UNIQUE before the keyword INDEX. The cnum field, as primary key, would be a prime candidate for a unique index:

```
CREATE UNIQUE INDEX Custid ON Customers (cnum);
```

Note: this command will be rejected if there are already identical values in the cnum field. The best way to deal with indexes is to create them immediately after the table is created and before any values are entered. Also note that, for a unique index of more than one field, it is the combination of values, not each individual value, that must be unique.

The preceding example is an indirect way of forcing cnum to function as the primary key of the Customers table. Databases are beginning to enforce primary and other keys more directly. We will discuss this issue further in Chapters 18 and 19.

DROPPING INDEXES

The main reason indexes are named is so that they can be dropped. Normally users will not be aware of the existence of an index. SQL automatically determines if it is appropriate to use an index, and will do so if it is. If you want to eliminate an index, however, you have to be able to name it. This is the syntax used to eliminate an index:

```
DROP INDEX <index name>;
```

The destruction of the index does not affect the content of the field(s).

ALTERING A TABLE ONCE IT HAS BEEN CREATED

The ALTER TABLE command is not part of the ANSI standard, but it is widely available, and its form is fairly consistent, although it capabilities vary considerably. It is used to change the definitions of extant tables. Usually, it can add columns to a table. Sometimes it can delete columns or change their sizes, and, in some programs, add or delete constraints (discussed in Chapter 18). Typically the syntax to add a column to a table is as follows:

ALTER TABLE <*table name*> ADD <*column name*> <data type> <size>;

The column will be added with NULL values for all rows currently in the table. The new column will be the last column of the table. It is generally possible to add several new columns, separated by commas, in a single command. It may be possible to drop or alter columns. Most often, altering columns will simply be a matter of increasing their size, or adding or dropping constraints. Your system should check to make sure that any modifications you make do not contradict the extant data—that is, an attempt to add a constraint to a column that already has values in violation of that constraint should be rejected. It is best to double check this, however. At least, refer to the documentation of your system to see if it guarantees that this will be the case. Because of the nonstandard nature of the ALTER TABLE command, you will have to refer to your system documentation for specifics in any case.

ALTER TABLE is invaluable when a table needs to be redefined, but you should design your database as much as possible to avoid relying on it. Changing the structure of a table already in use is full of hazards. Views of the table, which are secondary tables extracting data from other tables (see Chapter 20), may no longer function properly, and programs using embedded SQL (Chapter 25) may run incorrectly or not at all. In addition, the implications of the change will have to be made clear to all users accessing the table. For these reasons, you should try to design your tables to meet your anticipated, as well as current, needs and use ALTER TABLE only as a last resort.

If your system doesn't support ALTER TABLE, or if you want to avoid using it, you can simply create a new table, with the desired change in its definition, and use an INSERT command with a SELECT * query to transfer the old data to it. Users with access to the old table (see Chapter 22) will have to be granted access to the new table independently.

DROPPING A TABLE

You must own (have created) a table in order to drop it. So that you will not accidentally destroy your data, SQL requires you to empty a table before you eliminate it from the database. A table with rows in it cannot be dropped. Refer to Chapter 15 for details on how to remove rows from your table. The syntax to remove the definition of your table from the system once it is empty is

DROP TABLE <*table name*>;

Once this command is given, the table name is no longer recognized and no more commands can be given on that object. You should make sure that this table is not referenced by a foreign key in another table (foreign keys are discussed in Chapter 19), and that it is not used in the definition of a view (Chapter 20).

This command is actually not part of the ANSI standard, but it is generally supported (and useful). Happily, it is simpler, and therefore more consistent across implementations, than ALTER TABLE. ANSI itself simply does not specify a way to destroy or invalidate table definitions.

SUMMARY

You are now fluent in the basics of data definition. You can create, modify, and drop tables. Since only the first of these functions is part of the official SQL standard, the details of the others will vary, particularly ALTER TABLE. DROP TABLE allows you to get rid of tables that have outlived their usefulness. It drops only empty tables, and therefore does not destroy data.

You now know about indexes and how to create and drop them. SQL doesn't give you much control over how it does things, so the implementation you use pretty much determines how quickly different commands will be performed. Indexes are one tool that enables you to affect the performance of your commands in SQL directly. We have covered indexes here to keep them separate from constraints, with which they should not be confused. Constraints are the subject of Chapters 18 and 19.

Putting SQL to Work

1. Write a CREATE TABLE statement that would produce our Customers table.
2. Write a command that will enable a user to pull orders grouped by date out of the Orders table quickly.
3. If the Orders table has already been created, how can your force the onum field to be unique (assume all current values are unique)?
4. Create an index that would permit each salesperson to retrieve his or her orders grouped by date quickly.
5. Let us suppose that each salesperson is to have only one customer of a given rating, and that this is currently the case. Enter a command that enforces it.

(See Appendix A for answers.)

18

Constraining the Values of Your Data

IN CHAPTER 17, YOU LEARNED HOW TABLES ARE created. Now we will elaborate on that point to show you how you can place constraints on tables. *Constraints* are parts of a table definition that limit the values you can enter into its columns. Up until now in this book, the only restriction on the values that you could enter has been that the data types and sizes of the values entered have to be compatible with those of the columns into which the values were being placed (as defined in a CREATE TABLE or ALTER TABLE command). Constraints give you considerably more control than this, as you shall see.

You will also learn how to define default values in this chapter. A default is a value that is inserted automatically into any column of a table when a value for that column is omitted from an INSERT command to that table. NULL is the most widely used default, but this chapter will show you how to define others. Technically, defaults are not constraints, but the procedures involved in defining the two are quite similar.

CONSTRAINING TABLES

When you create a table (or, sometimes, when you alter one), you can place constraints on the values that can be entered into its fields. If you do this, SQL will reject any values that violate the criteria you define. The two basic types of constraints are column constraints and table constraints. The difference between the two is that *column constraints* apply only to individual columns, whereas *table constraints* apply to groups of one or more columns.

DECLARING CONSTRAINTS

You append column constraints to the end of column definitions after the data type and before the comma. Table constraints are placed at the end of the table definition after the last column definition, but before the closing parenthesis. The following is the syntax for the CREATE TABLE command, expanded to include constraints:

```
CREATE TABLE <table name>
    (<column name> <data type> <column constraint>,
```

<*column name*> <*data type*> <*column constraint*>. . .
<*table constraint*> (<*column name*>
[,<*column name*>. . .]). . .);

(For the sake of brevity, we have omitted the size argument, which is sometimes used with data type.) The fields given in parentheses after the table constraint(s) are the fields to which they apply. The column constraints, naturally, apply to the columns whose definitions they follow. The rest of this chapter will describe the various types of constraints and their use.

USING CONSTRAINTS TO EXCLUDE NULLS

You can use the CREATE TABLE command to prevent a field from permitting NULLS by using the NOT NULL constraint. This constraint can be only of the column variety.

You will recall that NULLs are special designations that mark a field as empty. As useful as NULLs can be, there are cases where you will want to ensure against them. Obviously, primary keys should never be NULL, as this would severely undermine their functionality. In addition, fields such as names should, in many cases, be required to have definite values. For example, you would probably want a name for every customer in the Customers table.

If you place the keywords NOT NULL immediately after the data type (including size) of a column, any attempts to put NULL values in that field will be rejected. Otherwise, SQL will assume that NULLs are permitted.

For example, let us improve our definition of the Salespeople table by not allowing NULLs in the snum or sname columns:

```
CREATE TABLE Salespeople
    (snum    integer NOT NULL,
    sname    char(10) NOT NULL,
    city     char(10),
    comm     decimal);
```

It is important to remember that any column with a NOT NULL constraint must be assigned values in every INSERT clause that affects the table. In the absence of NULLs, SQL will have no values to put in these columns unless a default value, described later in this chapter, is assigned.

If your system supports the use of ALTER TABLE to add columns to an existing table, you can probably also place column constraints, such as NOT NULL, on the new columns. If you declare a new column NOT NULL, however, the table must currently be empty.

MAKING SURE VALUES ARE UNIQUE

In Chapter 17, we discussed using unique indexes to force fields to have a different value for each row. In a sense, this practice is a leftover from the days before SQL supported the UNIQUE constraint. Uniqueness is a property of the data in a table, and is therefore more logically defined as a constraint on that data, rather than as a property of a logically distinct, but related, data object (the index).

Nonetheless, unique indexes are one of the easiest and most efficient methods of enforcing uniqueness. For this reason, some implementations of the UNIQUE constraint employ unique indexes;that is, they create an index without telling you about it. The fact remains that you are less likely to run into confusion (or incompatibility) if you enforce uniqueness with a constraint.

UNIQUE AS A COLUMN CONSTRAINT At times, you will want to make sure that all of the values entered into a column are different from one another. For example, primary keys clearly call for this. If you place the UNIQUE column constraint on a field when you create a table, the database will reject any attempt to introduce into that field a value in one row that is already present in another. This constraint can be applied only to fields that have also been declared NOT NULL, because it does not make much sense to allow one row of a table to be NULL and then exclude other NULLs as duplicates. Here is a further refinement of our definition of the Salespeople table:

```
CREATE TABLE Salespeople
    (snum     integer NOT NULL UNIQUE,
```

```
sname     char(10) NOT NULL UNIQUE,
city      char(10),
comm      decimal);
```

What you accomplish by declaring the sname field to be unique is to ensure that two Mary Smith's will be entered in different ways—Mary Smith and M. Smith, for example. While this is not necessary from a functional standpoint—the snum field as primary key provides a distinction between the two rows—it may be easier for people using the data in the tables to keep the two Smiths separate in their minds if the names are not identical. Columns (other than primary keys) whose values are required to be unique are called *candidate keys* or *unique keys*.

UNIQUE AS A TABLE CONSTRAINT You can also define a group of fields as unique with a UNIQUE table constraint. Declaring a group of fields unique differs from declaring the individual fields unique in that it is the combination of values, not each individual value, which must be unique. Group uniqueness is respective of order, so that a pair of rows with the column values 'a', 'b' and 'b', 'a' are considered to be different from one another.

Our database is structured so that each customer is assigned one and only one salesperson. This means that each combination of customer number and salesperson number in the Customers table should be unique. You can ensure this by defining the Customers table in this manner:

```
CREATE TABLE Customers
    (cnum       integer NOT NULL,
    cname       char(10) NOT NULL,
    city        char(10),
    rating      integer,
    snum        integer NOT NULL,
    UNIQUE      (cnum, snum));
```

Notice that both of the fields in the UNIQUE table constraint still use NOT NULL column constraints. If we had used the UNIQUE column constraint on cnum, this table constraint would not be necessary. If cnum field is different for each row, there cannot be two rows with identical combinations of cnum and snum. The same would apply if we had declared the snum field unique, although this would not be appropriate in this instance because salespeople can be assigned multiple customers. Therefore, the UNIQUE table constraint is most useful when you do not want to force the individual fields to be unique.

Suppose, for example, that we designed a table to keep track of the total orders per day per salesperson. Each row of this table would represent a total of any number of orders, rather than an individual order. In this case, we could eliminate some possible errors by ensuring that each day has no more than one row for a given salesperson, that is, that each combination of snum and odate is unique. Here's how we could create such a table called Salestotal:

```
CREATE TABLE Salestotal
     (snum,       integer NOT NULL,
     odate,       date NOT NULL,
     totamt,      decimal,
     UNIQUE       (snum, odate));
```

Here then, is the command you would use to put the current data into this table:

```
INSERT INTO Salestotal
     SELECT snum, odate, SUM (amt)
          FROM Orders
          GROUP BY snum, odate;
```

THE PRIMARY KEY CONSTRAINT

Up until now, we have been discussing primary keys solely as logical concepts. Although we should know, for any table, what the primary key is, and how it is to be used, we have not assumed that SQL "knows". We have therefore used UNIQUE constraints or unique indexes on primary keys to enforce their uniqueness. In earlier versions of the SQL language, this was necessary, and it still can be done this way. Now, however, SQL supports primary keys directly with the PRIMARY KEY constraint. This constraint may or may not be available on your system.

The PRIMARY KEY constraint can be of the table or column variety. It is functionally the same as the UNIQUE constraint, except that only one primary key (of any number of columns) can be defined for a given table. There is also a difference between primary keys and unique columns in the way they are used with foreign keys, which will be explained in Chapter 19. The syntax and the definition of uniqueness follow those of the UNIQUE constraint.

Primary keys cannot allow NULL values. This means that, like fields in UNIQUE constraints, any field used in a PRIMARY KEY constraint must already be declared NOT NULL. Here is an improved version of our definition of the Salespeople table:

```
CREATE TABLE Salespeople
    (snum     integer NOT NULL PRIMARY KEY,
    sname     char(10) NOT NULL UNIQUE,
    city      char(10),
    comm      decimal);
```

As you can see, UNIQUE fields can also be declared in the same table. It is best to put the PRIMARY KEY constraint on the field(s) that will constitute your unique row identifier, and save the UNIQUE constraint for fields that should be unique for logical reasons (such as phone numbers or sname above), rather than for row identification.

PRIMARY KEYS OF MORE THAN ONE FIELD The PRIMARY KEY constraint can also apply to multiple fields, forcing a unique combination of values. Suppose your primary key is a name, and you have first and last names stored in two different fields (so you could organize the data by either one). Obviously, neither the first nor last names can be forced to be unique by themselves, but we may well wish every combination of the two to be unique. We can apply the PRIMARY KEY table constraint to the pair:

```
CREATE TABLE Namefield
    (firstname      char(10) NOT NULL,
    lastname        char(10) NOT NULL,
```

```
city              char(10),
PRIMARY KEY       (firstname, lastname));
```

One problem with this approach is that we may have to force the uniqueness—by entering Mary Smith and M. Smith for example. This can easily be confusing, because your employees may not know which is which. It is usually a safer bet to define some numeric field that can distinguish one row from another, have it be the primary key, and apply the UNIQUE constraint to the two name fields.

CHECKING FIELD VALUES

Of course, there are any number of restrictions you might want to place on the data that can be entered into your tables—to see if the data is in the proper range or the correct format, for example—that SQL cannot possibly account for beforehand. For this reason, SQL provides the CHECK constraint, which allows you to define a condition that a value entered into the table has to satisfy before it can be accepted. The CHECK constraint consists of the keyword CHECK followed by a parenthesized predicate, which employs the field(s) in question. Any attempt to update to or insert field values that will make this predicate false will be rejected.

Let's look once more at the Salespeople table. The commission column is expressed as a decimal, so that it can be multiplied directly with a purchase amount to produce the right dollar figure. Someone used to thinking of it in terms of percentages, however, might be inclined to forget this. If that person were to enter 14 instead of .14 for a commission, it would be equivalent to 14.0, a legitimate decimal value, and would be accepted. To guard against this, we can impose a CHECK column constraint to make sure that the value entered is less than 1.

```
CREATE TABLE Salespeople
    (snum     integer NOT NULL UNIQUE,
     sname    char(10) NOT NULL UNIQUE,
     city     char(10),
     comm     decimal CHECK (comm < 1) );
```

USING CHECK TO PREDETERMINE VALID INPUT VALUES We can even use a CHECK constraint to restrict a field to specific values, and thereby reject mistakes. For example, suppose the only cities in which we had sales offices were London, Barcelona, San Jose, and New York. As long as we know that all of our salespeople will be operating from one of these offices, there is no need to allow other values to be entered. If nothing else, using a restriction such as this will prevent typographical and similar errors from being accepted. Here is how we would do it:

```
CREATE TABLE Salespeople
    (snum     integer NOT NULL UNIQUE,
    sname     char(10) NOT NULL UNIQUE,
    city      char(10) CHECK
    (city IN ('London', 'New York','San Jose', 'Barcelona')),
    comm      decimal CHECK (comm < 1) );
```

Of course, if you are going to do this, you should be pretty sure that your company is not opening any more sales offices soon. Changing the definition of a table once it is created is a very useful, if hazardous, feature that is not part of the ANSI standard. Most database programs do support the ALTER TABLE command (see Chapter 17) that allows you to change the definition of a table, even when it is in use. However, changing or deleting constraints is not always a feature of this command, even where it is supported. If you were using a system that cannot remove constraints, you would have to CREATE a new table and transfer the information from the old table over to it whenever you need to change a constraint. This is not something you will want to do often, and at times it may not be practical at all.

Here is a definition of the Orders table:

```
CREATE TABLE Orders
    (onum    integer NOT NULL UNIQUE,
    amt      decimal,
    odate    date NOT NULL,
    cnum     integer NOT NULL,
    snum     integer NOT NULL);
```

As we discussed in Chapter 2, the DATE type is widely supported, but is not part of the ANSI standard. What should we do if we are using a database that, following ANSI, does not recognize the DATE type? If we declare odate to be any kind of number, we cannot use either a slash (/) or a dash (-) as a delimiter. Since printable numbers are also ASCII characters, we could declare odate to be of the CHAR type. The main problem with this is that we would have to remember to use single quotes whenever we referred to odate's value in a query. There is no simple solution to this problem, which is why the DATE type has become so popular. For the purpose of illustration, let's assume that we are declaring odate to be of the CHAR type. We can at least impose our format on it with a CHECK constraint:

```
CREATE TABLE Orders
    (onum     integer NOT NULL UNIQUE,
    amt       decimal,
    odate     char (10) NOT NULL CHECK (odate LIKE
               '__/__/____'),
    cnum      integer NOT NULL,
    snum      integer NOT NULL);
```

In addition, if you wanted to, you could impose constraints ensuring that the characters entered are numerals, and that they are within sensible ranges.

CHECK CONDITIONS BASED ON MULTIPLE FIELDS

You can also use CHECK as a table constraint. This is useful for those cases where you want to involve more than one field of a row in a condition. Suppose that commissions of .15 and above were permitted only for salespeople in Barcelona. We could enforce this with the following CHECK table constraint:

```
CREATE TABLE Salespeople
    (snum     integer NOT NULL UNIQUE,
    sname     char(10) NOT NULL UNIQUE,
    city      char(10),
    comm      decimal,
    CHECK     (comm < .15 OR city = 'Barcelona') );
```

As you can see, two different fields have to be examined to determine if the predicate is true. Keep in mind, however, that they are two different fields of the *same* row. Although you can use multiple fields, SQL is not capable of checking more than one row at a time. You could not use a CHECK constraint easily to make sure that all commissions in a given city were the same, for example. To do this, SQL would have to look at the other rows of the table, whenever you update or insert a row, to see what the commission value should be for the current city. SQL is not designed to do this.

Actually, you might be able to use an elaborate CHECK constraint for the above, if you know in advance what the commissions for the various cities should be. For instance, you could define a constraint such as this:

```
CHECK ( (comm = .15 AND city = 'London')
    OR (comm = .14 AND city = 'Barcelona')
    OR (comm = 11 AND city = 'San Jose). . )
```

You get the idea. Rather than imposing a constraint this complex, however, you might consider defining a view with a WITH CHECK OPTION clause that has all of these conditions in its predicate (refer to Chapters 20 and 21 for information on views and WITH CHECK OPTION). Users could access the view instead of the table. One advantage of this would be that making a change in the constraints would not be nearly as painful or difficult. Views WITH CHECK OPTION are frequently a good alternative to CHECK constraints as will be elaborated in Chapter 21.

ASSIGNING DEFAULT VALUES

When you insert a row into a table without having a value in it for every field, SQL must have a default value to put in the excluded field(s), or the command will be rejected. The most common default value is NULL. This is the default for any column that has not been given a NOT NULL constraint or had another default assigned.

DEFAULT value assignments are defined in the CREATE TABLE command in the same way as column constraints, although, technically speaking, DEFAULT values are not constraints—they do not limit the values you can enter, but merely specify what happens if you do not enter any. Suppose you are running the New York office of your company and the vast majority of your salespeople are based in New York. You might decide to define New York as the default city value for your Salespeople table, saving the trouble of entering it each time:

```
CREATE TABLE Salespeople
    (snum     integer NOT NULL UNIQUE,
    sname     char(10) NOT NULL UNIQUE,
    city      char(10) DEFAULT = 'New York',
    comm      decimal CHECK (comm < 1) );
```

Of course, entering New York into a table each time a new salesperson is assigned is not such a great deal of trouble, and habitually omitting a field may lead to its being neglected even when it should have some other value. A default value of this type might be more advisable if, for example, you had a long office number, indicating your own office, in the Orders table. Long numeric values are error prone, so, if the vast majority (or all) of your orders will have your own office number on them, it may be advisable for that number to become the default.

Another way to use default values is as an alternative to NULLs. Since NULLs are (in effect) false in any comparison other than IS NULL, they tend to be excluded by a lot of predicates. Sometimes, you may want to see your empty field values without having to treat them in a special way. You can define a special default value, such as zero or blank, which actually functions less as a value than as an indication that there is no value present—in other words, a custom-made NULL. The difference between this and a regular NULL is that SQL will treat this the same as any other value.

Suppose that customers are not assigned ratings initially. Every six months, you raise the rating of all your lower-rated customers, including those who previously had no rating assigned, provided that all has gone well with them. If you want to select all these customers as a group, a query such as the following would exclude all customers with NULL ratings:

```
SELECT *
    FROM Customers
    WHERE rating < = 100;
```

However, if you had defined a DEFAULT of 000 for the rating field, customers without ratings would have been selected along with the others. Which method is better depends on the situation. If you were querying by the field in question, would you usually want to include the rows without values, or exclude them?

Another characteristic of defaults of this type is that they do allow you to declare the field in question NOT NULL. If you are using a default in order to avoid NULLs, this is probably good protection against mistakes.

You could also use a UNIQUE or PRIMARY KEY constraint with this field. If you do, however, keep in mind that only one row at a time may have the default value. Any row that contains the default value will have to be updated before another row with the default could be inserted. This is not how you usually want to use defaults, so UNIQUE and PRIMARY KEY constraints (especially the latter) are not usually placed on rows with default values.

SUMMARY

You have now mastered several ways of controlling the values that can be entered into your tables. You can use the NOT NULL constraint to exclude NULLS, the UNIQUE constraint to force all the values in a group of one or more columns to be different, the PRIMARY KEY constraint to do basically the same thing as UNIQUE but to a different end, and the CHECK constraint to define your own custom-made criteria that values have to meet before they can be entered. In addition, you can use a DEFAULT clause, which will automatically insert a default value into any field not named in an INSERT, just as NULLS are inserted when the DEFAULT clause is not present and there is no NOT NULL constraint.

The FOREIGN KEY or REFERENCES constraint that you will learn about in Chapter 19 is similar to these, except that it relates a group of one or more fields to another, and thereby affects the values that can be entered into either of these groups at once.

Putting SQL To Work

1. Create the Orders table so that all onum values as well as all combinations of cnum and snum are different from one another, and so that NULL values are excluded from the date field.
2. Create the Salespeople table so that the default commission is 10% with no NULLS permitted, snum is the primary key, and all names fall alphabetically between A and M, inclusive (assume all names will be uppercase).
3. Create the Orders table, making sure that the onum is greater than the cnum, and the cnum is greater than the snum. Allow no NULLS in any of these three fields.

(See Appendix A for answers.)

19

Maintaining the Integrity of Your Data

EARLY IN THIS BOOK, WE POINTED OUT CERTAIN relationships that existed among some fields of our sample tables. The snum field of the Customers table, for example, matches the snum field of the both Salespeople and the Orders tables. The cnum field of the Customers table matches the cnum field of the Orders table, as well. We called this type of relationship referential integrity; over the course of the book, you have seen some ways that this can be used.

In this chapter, you will be investigating referential integrity more closely and finding out about the constraint that you can use to maintain it. You will also see how this constraint is enforced when you use the DML update commands. As referential integrity involves relating fields or groups of fields, often in different tables, to one another, its enforcement can be somewhat more complex than that of the other constraints. For this reason, it is good to have a basic familiarity with it, even if you do not plan to create tables. Your update commands can be affected by referential-integrity constraints (as by other constraints, but referential-integrity constraints can affect other tables besides those in which they are located), and certain query functions, such as joins, are frequently structured in terms of referential-integrity relationships (as we pointed out in Chapter 8).

FOREIGN AND PARENT KEYS

When all of the values in one field of a table have to be present in a field of another table, we say that the first field *refers to* or *references* the second. It indicates a direct relationship between the meaning of the two fields. For example, the customers in the Customers table each have an snum field that indicates the salesperson he or she is assigned to in the Salespeople table. For each order in the Orders table, there is one and only one salesperson and one and only one customer. These are indicated by the snum and cnum fields in the Orders table.

When a field in a table refers to another, it is called a *foreign key*; the field to which it refers is called its *parent key*. So the snum field of the Customers table is a foreign key, and the snum field it references in the Salespeople table is its parent key. Likewise, the cnum and snum fields of the Orders table are foreign keys referring to their parent keys of the same names in the Customers and Salespeople tables. The names of foreign and parent keys do not necessarily have to be the same, by the way; this is just a convention we have followed to make the connection more clear.

MULTICOLUMN FOREIGN KEYS

In actuality, a foreign key need not consist only of a single field. Like a primary key, a foreign key can be of any number of fields, all of which are treated as a unit. A foreign key and the parent key it references must, of course, have the same number and types of fields, in the same order. Single-field foreign keys are what we have used exclusively in our sample tables; they are perhaps the most common. For the sake of keeping our discussion simple, we will often speak of a foreign key as a single column. This is not necessarily the case. Unless otherwise noted, whatever is said about a field that is a foreign key will also hold true for a group of fields that is a foreign key.

THE MEANING OF FOREIGN AND PARENT KEYS

When a field is a foreign key, it is specially linked to the table it references. You are, in effect, saying "every value in this field (the foreign key) is directly related to a value in another field (the parent key)." Each value (each row) of the foreign key should unambiguously refer to one and only one value (row) of the parent key. If this is, in fact, the case, your system is said to be in a state of referential integrity.

You can see why this is the case. The foreign key snum in the Customers table has the value 1001 for the rows of Hoffman and Clemens. Suppose we had two rows in the Salespeople table with the snum = 1001. How would we know to which of the two salespeople Hoffman and Clemens were assigned? Likewise, if there were no such rows in the Salespeople table, we would have Hoffman and Clemens assigned to a salesperson who did not exist! The implication is clear: every value in the foreign key must be present once, and only once, in the parent key.

The fact that a given foreign-key value can refer to only one parent-key value does not imply the reverse: any number of foreign keys can refer to the same parent-key value. You can see this in the sample tables. Both Hoffman and Clemens are assigned to Peel, so both of their foreign-key values match the same parent key, which is fine. A foreign-key value must refer to only a single parent-key value, but that parent-key value can be referred to by any number of foreign-key values.

For the sake of illustration, the foreign-key values from the Customers table, matched to their parent keys in the Salespeople table, are shown in Figure 19.1. We have left out unnecessary fields for readability.

THE FOREIGN KEY CONSTRAINT

SQL supports referential integrity with the FOREIGN KEY constraint. Although quite important, the FOREIGN KEY constraint is something of a new feature to SQL, so it is not yet universally supported. Moreover, some implementations of it are more sophisticated than others. Its function is to restrict the values you can enter into your database to force a foreign key and its parent key to conform to the principles of referential integrity. One effect of an enforced FOREIGN KEY constraint is to reject values for the field(s) constrained as a foreign key that are not already present in the parent key. This constraint also affects your ability to change or remove the values of the parent key (we will discuss this later in the chapter).

HOW TO DECLARE FIELDS AS FOREIGN KEYS

You use the FOREIGN KEY constraint in the CREATE TABLE (or possibly ALTER TABLE) command that contains the field you wish to declare as a foreign key. You name the parent key you are referencing within the foreign key constraint. The placement of this constraint in the command is the same as that of the other constraints discussed in the previous chapter.

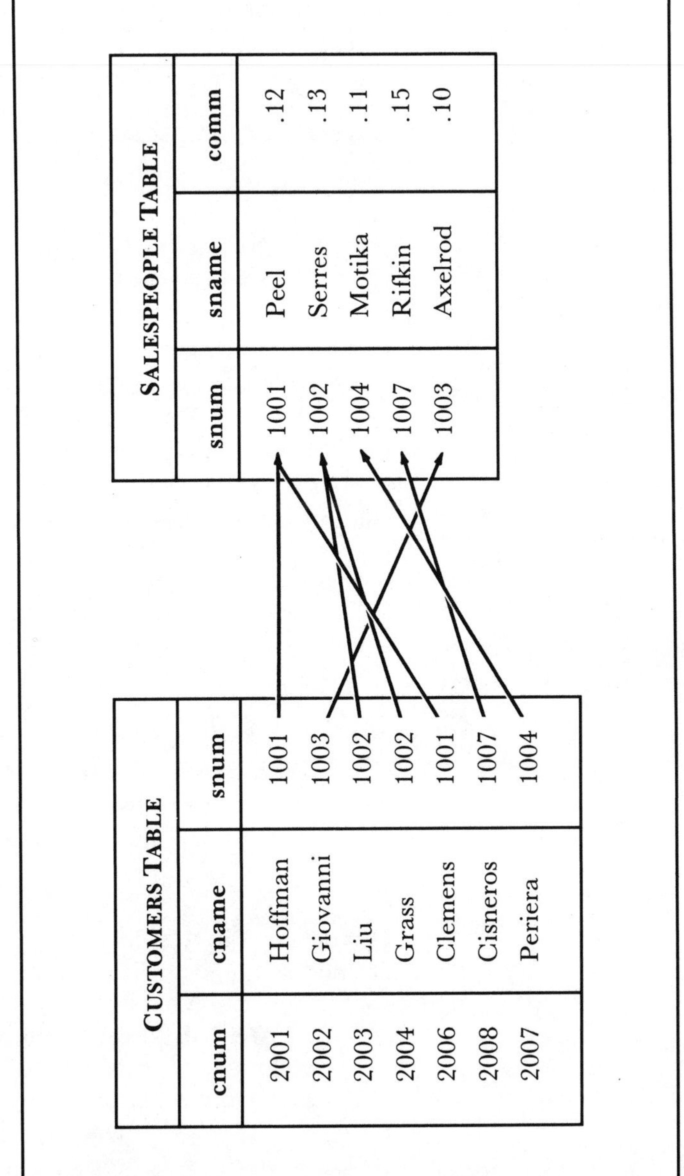

Figure 19.1: Foreign key of Customers table with parent key

Like most constraints, it can be of the table or column variety, with the table form allowing multiple fields to be used as a single foreign key.

FOREIGN KEY AS A TABLE CONSTRAINT

Here is the syntax of the FOREIGN KEY table constraint:

```
FOREIGN KEY <column list> REFERENCES <pktable>
 [<column list>]
```

The first column list is a parenthesized list of one or more columns of the table being created or altered in this command, separated by commas. The pktable is the table containing the parent key. This may be the same table that is being created or altered by the current command (more on this point later). The second column list is a parenthesized list of those columns that will constitute the parent key. The two column lists must be compatible:

- They must have the same number of columns.
- In the sequence given, the first, second, third, and so on, column of the foreign-key column list must have the same data types and sizes as the first, second, third, and so on, of the parent-key column list. The columns in the two column lists need not have the same names, although we have done it this way in our examples to make the relationship clearer.

Here is the definition of the Customers table with snum defined as a foreign key referencing the Salespeople table:

```
CREATE TABLE Customers
     (cnum      integer NOT NULL PRIMARY KEY,
     cname      char(10),
     city       char(10),
     snum       integer,
     FOREIGN KEY (snum) REFERENCES Salespeople
      (snum) );
```

An important thing to keep in mind if you are using ALTER TABLE instead of CREATE TABLE to apply the FOREIGN KEY constraint is that the values currently present in the foreign and parent keys you indicate must be in a state of referential integrity. Otherwise, the command will be rejected. Although ALTER TABLE is very useful because of the adaptability it provides, you should build structural principles, such as referential integrity, into your system from the start whenever possible.

FOREIGN KEY AS A COLUMN CONSTRAINT

The column-constraint version of the FOREIGN KEY constraint is also called the REFERENCES constraint, because it does not actually contain the words FOREIGN KEY; it simply uses the word REFERENCES, and then names the parent key, like this:

```
CREATE TABLE Customers
    (cnum     integer NOT NULL PRIMARY KEY,
    cname     char(10),
    city      char(10),
    snum      integer REFERENCES Salespeople (snum) );
```

The above defines Customers.snum as a foreign key whose parent key is Salespeople.snum. It is equivalent to this table constraint:

```
FOREIGN KEY (snum) REFERENCES Salespeople (snum)
```

OMITTING PRIMARY-KEY COLUMN LISTS

With either table or column FOREIGN KEY constraints, you may omit the column list of the parent key if the parent key has the PRIMARY KEY constraint. In case of multiple-field keys, naturally, the order of the columns in the foreign and primary keys must match, and, in any case, the principles of compatibility between the two keys still apply. For example, if we had placed the PRIMARY KEY constraint on the snum field in the Salespeople table, we could use it as a foreign key in the Customers table (similar to the previous example) with this command:

```
CREATE TABLE Customers
    (cnum     integer NOT NULL PRIMARY KEY,
    cname     char(10),
    city      char(10),
    snum      integer REFERENCES Salespeople);
```

This feature has been built into the language to encourage you to use primary keys as parent keys. The logic behind this will be outlined shortly.

HOW REFERENTIAL INTEGRITY RESTRICTS PARENT KEY VALUES

Maintaining referential integrity necessitates some restrictions on the values that can be present in fields declared as foreign and parent keys. The parent key must be structured to ensure that each foreign-key value will match one specific row. This means it must be unique and contain no NULLS. It is not sufficient for the parent key to happen to fulfill these requirements at the time the foreign key is declared. SQL must be assured that duplicate or NULL values cannot be entered into the parent key. Therefore you must make sure that all fields to be used as parent keys have either a PRIMARY KEY or a UNIQUE constraint as well as the NOT NULL constraint.

PRIMARY VS. UNIQUE PARENT KEYS

Having your foreign keys reference only primary keys, as we have done in the sample tables, is a good policy. When you use foreign keys, you are not linking them simply to the parent keys that they reference; you are linking them to the specific row of the table where that parent key is found. The parent key by itself provides no information that is not already present in the foreign key.

The significance, for example, of the snum field as a foreign key in the Customers table is the link it provides, not to the snum value that it references, but to the other information in the

Salespeople table, such as the salespeople's names, their locations, and so on. A foreign key is not simply a link between two identical values; it is a link, through those two values, between two entire rows of the tables in question. That snum field can be used to relate any information in a row from the Customers table to the referenced row of the Salespeople table—such as whether they live in the same city, who has a longer name, whether the salesperson of a given customer has any other customers, and so on.

Since the purpose of a primary key is to identify rows uniquely, it is the most logical and least ambiguous choice for a foreign key. For any foreign key that takes a unique key as a parent key, you should be able to create a foreign key that takes the primary key of that same table to the same effect. Having a foreign key that has no other purpose but to link rows, like having a primary key with no other purpose but to identify them, is a good way to keep the structure of your database clear and simple, and is therefore less likely to create difficulties.

FOREIGN KEY RESTRICTIONS

The foreign key, for its part, may contain only values that are actually present in the parent key or NULLs. Any other values you attempt to enter into that key will be rejected. You may declare foreign keys to be NOT NULL, but it is not necessary and, in many cases, not desirable. For example, suppose you enter a customer without first knowing to which salesperson he will be assigned. The best way to deal with this situation would be with a NULL that could be updated to a valid value later.

WHAT HAPPENS WHEN YOU PERFORM UPDATE COMMANDS

Let's assume that all of the foreign keys built into our sample tables are declared and enforced with FOREIGN KEY constraints, as follows:

```
CREATE TABLE Salespeople
     (snum      integer NOT NULL PRIMARY KEY,
```

```
    sname   char(10) NOT NULL,
    city    char(10),
    comm    decimal);

CREATE TABLE Customers
    (cnum   integer NOT NULL PRIMARY KEY,
    cname   char(10) NOT NULL,
    city    char(10),
    rating  integer,
    snum    integer,
    FOREIGN KEY (snum) REFERENCES Salespeople,
    UNIQUE (cnum, snum) );

CREATE TABLE Orders
    (onum   integer NOT NULL PRIMARY KEY,
    amt     decimal,
    odate   date NOT NULL,
    cnum    integer NOT NULL
    snum    integer NOT NULL
    FOREIGN KEY (cnum, snum) REFERENCES
     CUSTOMERS (cnum, snum) );
```

IMPLICATIONS OF THE TABLE DEFINITIONS

There are several attributes of these definitions that merit discussion. The reason we chose to make the cnum and snum fields of the Orders table a single foreign key is because this insures that for every customer credited with an order, the salesperson credited with that order is the same as indicated in the Customers table. In order to create this foreign key, we had to place a UNIQUE table constraint on the two fields of the Customers table, even though this is not necessary for the purposes of that table in itself. Since cnum in that table has the PRIMARY KEY constraint, it will be unique in any case, and it is therefore impossible to have a nonunique combination of cnum with any other field.

Defining the foreign key in this manner maintains the integrity of the database, even though it does prevent you from making exceptions and crediting any salesperson other than the one assigned to a customer with sales for that customer. Excluding mistakes often means also excluding the ability to make exceptions, and, of course, whether to allow exceptions is a management, not a database, decision. From the viewpoint of maintaining the integrity of the database, however, exceptions are not desirable. If you wanted to allow them and still maintain some integrity, you could declare snum and cnum in the Orders table as independent foreign keys of the same fields in the Salespeople and Customers tables, respectively.

Actually, using the snum field in the Orders table as we have done is not necessary, although it has been useful to us for deriving examples. The cnum field links each order to a customer in the Customers table, and the Orders and Customers tables could always be joined to find the correct snum for a given order (assuming no exceptions are allowed). This means we are recording a piece of information—which customer is assigned to which salesperson—twice, and extra work will have to be performed to make sure the two versions agree. If we didn't have foreign-key constraints as above, this situation would be especially problematic, because each order would have to be manually checked (with a query) to make sure the proper salesperson was credited with each sale. Having this sort of redundant information in your database is called *denormalization*; it is not desirable in an ideal relational database, although in practical situations there may be reasons for allowing it. Denormalization can make some queries execute faster, as a query on a single table will execute considerably faster than a join.

THE EFFECTS OF THE CONSTRAINTS

How do these constraints affect what you can and cannot do with DML update commands? For the fields defined as foreign keys, the answer is fairly straightforward: any values you put into these fields with an INSERT or UPDATE command must already be present in their parent keys. You may put NULLS in these fields, even though NULLS are not allowed in the parent keys, unless they have NOT NULL constraints. You may DELETE any rows with foreign keys without affecting the parent keys at all.

As far as changes to the parent-key values are concerned, the answer, as defined by ANSI, is still straightforward, but perhaps a little restrictive: any parent-key value currently referenced by a foreign-key value cannot be deleted or changed. This means, for example, that you could not remove a customer from the Customers table while he or she still has orders in the Orders table. Depending on exactly how you are using these tables, this can be either desirable or troublesome. It is certainly better, however, than a system that would allow you to remove a customer with current orders and leave the Orders table referencing nonexistent customers.

An implication of this system of enforcement is that the creator of the Orders table, by using the Customers and Salespeople tables as parent keys, is putting considerable restrictions on what can be done to them. For this reason, you cannot use a table you do not own for a parent key unless the owner of that table specifically gives you that right (this will be explained in Chapter 22).

There are some other possible effects of changing the parent key that are not part of ANSI, but can be found in some commercial products. If you want to change or remove a currently referenced parent-key value, there are essentially three possibilities:

- You can restrict, or forbid, the change (ANSI's way), which means the change on the parent key is *restricted*.
- You can make the change in the parent key and have that same change made in the foreign key automatically, which means the change *cascades*.
- You can make the change in the parent key, and set the foreign key to NULL automatically (assuming NULLS are allowed in the foreign key), which is to say the change *nulls* the foreign key.

Even within these three categories, you may not want to treat all of the update commands in the same way. INSERT, of course, is irrelevant. It puts new parent-key values in the table, so none of its values can currently be referenced. However, you may want to allow updates to cascade, but not deletions, or vice versa. The best situation, then, might be one that allows you to specify any of the three categories independently for UPDATE and DELETE commands. We shall therefore refer to *update effects* and *delete effects* that determine what happens when you perform an UPDATE or a DELETE on the parent key. These effects, as we mentioned, are RESTRICTED, CASCADES, and NULLS.

The actual capabilities of your system could be anything from a strict ANSI standard—update and delete effects both automatically restricted—to the more ideal situation outlined above. For the sake of illustration, we will show you a few examples of what you could do with a complete selection of update and delete effects. Of course, these update and delete effects, being non-standard features, lack a standard syntax. The syntax we use here is simple and descriptive and will serve to illustrate how these effects function.

For the sake of argument, let us suppose you have reason to change the snum field of the Salespeople table on occasion, perhaps when our Salespeople change divisions. (Routinely changing primary keys is actually not something we recommend in practice. This is one argument for having primary keys that have no other use or meaning than to act as primary keys: they should not need to be changed.) When you change a salesperson's number, you want him to keep all of his customers. If he is leaving the company, however, you do not want to remove his customers when you remove him from the database. Instead, you want to make sure you assign them to someone else. To achieve this, you could specify an UPDATE effect of CASCADES, and a DELETE effect of RESTRICTED.

```
CREATE TABLE Customers
    (cnum     integer NOT NULL PRIMARY KEY,
    cname     char(10) NOT NULL,
    city      char(10),
    rating    integer,
    snum      integer REFERENCES Salespeople,
    UPDATE OF Salespeople CASCADES,
    DELETE OF Salespeople RESTRICTED);
```

If you now tried to remove Peel from the Salespeople table, the command would not be accepted unless you changed the snum values of customers Hoffman and Clemens to that of another salesperson. On the other hand, you could change Peel's snum value to 1009, and Hoffman and Clemens would automatically have theirs changed as well.

The third effect is NULLS. Perhaps when salespeople leave the company their current orders are not credited to anyone. On the other hand, you want to cancel all orders automatically for customers whose accounts you remove. Changes of salesperson or customer number can simply be passed along. This is how you would create the Orders table to have these effects.

```
CREATE TABLE Orders
    (onum    integer NOT NULL PRIMARY KEY,
    amt      decimal,
    odate    date NOT NULL,
    cnum     integer NOT NULL REFERENCES Customers,
    snum     integer REFERENCES Salespeople,
    UPDATE OF Customers CASCADES,
    DELETE OF Customers CASCADES,
    UPDATE OF Salespeople CASCADES,
    DELETE OF Salespeople NULLS);
```

Of course, in order for the DELETE effect of NULLS on Salespeople to work the NOT NULL constraint had to be removed from the snum field.

FOREIGN KEYS THAT REFER BACK TO THEIR OWN TABLES

As mentioned before, the FOREIGN KEY constraint can name its own table as its parent-key table. Far from being a simple anomaly, this is a feature that can come in handy. Suppose we had an Employees table with a field called "manager". This field contains the employee number of each employee's manager. However, since each manager is also an employee, he or she will be present in this table as well. Let's create the table, declaring empno (employee number) as the primary key, and manager as a foreign key referencing it:

```
CREATE TABLE Employees
    (empno      integer NOT NULL PRIMARY KEY,
    name        char(10) NOT NULL UNIQUE,
    manager     integer REFERENCES Employees);
```

(Since the foreign key is referencing the primary key of the table, the column list can naturally be omitted.) Here are some possible contents of this table:

EMPNO	*NAME*	*MANAGER*
1003	Terrence	2007
2007	Atali	NULL
1688	McKenna	1003
2002	Collier	2007

As you can see, everybody but Atali references another employee in the table as his or her manager. Atali, being the highest in the table, has to have his value set to NULL. This brings up another principle of referential integrity. A foreign key that refers back to its own table must allow NULLs. If it did not, how could you insert the first row? Even if this first row referred to itself, the parent-key value is supposed to be already present when the foreign-key value is entered.

This principle holds true even if a foreign key refers back to its own table indirectly—that is, by referring to another table that then refers back to the foreign key's table. For example, suppose our Salespeople table had an additional field that referenced the Customers table, so that each table referred to the other, as shown in the following CREATE TABLE statement:

```
CREATE TABLE Salespeople
    (snum     integer NOT NULL PRIMARY KEY,
    sname     char(10) NOT NULL,
    city      char(10),
    comm      decimal,
    cnum      integer REFERENCES Customers);
```

```
CREATE TABLE Customers
    (cnum     integer NOT NULL PRIMARY KEY,
    cname     char(10) NOT NULL,
    city      char(10),
    rating    integer,
    snum      integer REFERENCES Salespeople);
```

This is called *circularity* or *cross referencing*. SQL supports it theoretically, but it can present problems in practice. Whichever table of the two is created first will be referencing a table that does not yet exist, for one thing. In the interest of supporting circularity, SQL will actually allow this, but neither table is usable until both are created. On the other hand, if these two tables are created by different users, the problems become more difficult. Circularity can be a useful tool, but it is not without its ambiguities and hazards. The preceding example, for instance, is not very usable: it restricts salespeople to a single customer, and needn't be circular, even to achieve that. We recommend that you be very careful how you use it and study closely exactly how your system handles update and delete effects as well as privileges and transaction processing before you create a circular system of referential integrity. (Privileges and transaction processing will be discussed in Chapters 22 and 23, respectively.)

SUMMARY

Now you have a pretty good handle on referential integrity. The basic idea is that all foreign-key values refer to a specific row of the parent key. This means that each foreign-key value must be present once and only once in the parent key. Whenever a value is placed in a foreign key, the parent key is checked to make sure that value is present; otherwise, the command is rejected. The parent key must have a PRIMARY KEY or UNIQUE constraint to ensure that a value will not be present more than once. Attempts to change a parent-key value that is currently present in the foreign key will generally be rejected. Your system may, however, offer you the option to have the foreign-key value set to NULL or to the new parent-key value, and to specify which of these will happen independently for UPDATE and for DELETE commands. This completes our discussion of the CREATE TABLE command. Next we will introduce you to another type of CREATE command.

In Chapter 20, you will learn about views, data objects that look and act like tables, but are actually the results of queries. Some of the functions of constraints can also be fulfilled by views, so you will be better able to evaluate your need for constraints after you have read the next three chapters.

Putting SQL to Work

1. Create a table called Cityorders. This will contain the same onum, amt, and snum fields as the Orders table, and the same cnum and city fields as the Customers table, so that each customer's order will be entered into this table along with his or her city. Onum will be the primary key of Cityorders. All of the fields in Cityorders will be constrained to match the Customers and Orders tables. Assume the parent keys in these tables already have the proper constraints.
2. Here is an advanced problem. Redefine the Orders table as follows: add a new column called prev, which will identify, for each order, the onum of the previous order for that current customer. Implement this with a foreign key referring to the Orders table itself. The foreign key should refer as well to the cnum of the customer, providing a definite enforced link between the current order and the one referenced.

(See Appendix A for answers.)

20

Introducing: Views

A VIEW IS A DATA OBJECT THAT CONTAINS NO DATA of its own. It is a kind of table whose contents are taken from other tables through the execution of a query. As the values in those tables change, so, automatically, will the values the view exhibits.

In this chapter, you will learn what views are, how they are created, and a bit about their limitations and restrictions. The use of views based on advanced query features, such as joins and subqueries, will be elaborated, as will some special considerations that come into play with queries made against views.

WHAT ARE VIEWS?

The kinds of tables that you have been dealing with up until now are called *base tables*. These are tables that contain data. There is another kind of table, however: the view. *Views* are tables whose contents are taken or derived from other tables. They are operated on in queries and DML statements just as base tables are, but they contain no data of their own. Views are like windows through which you view information (as is, or in a derived form, as you will see) that is actually stored in a base table. A view is actually a query that is executed whenever the view is the subject of a command. The output of the query becomes the content of the view at that moment.

THE CREATE VIEW COMMAND

You define views with the CREATE VIEW command. This consists of the words CREATE VIEW, the name of the view to be created, the word AS, and then a query, as in the following example:

```
CREATE VIEW Londonstaff
    AS SELECT *
        FROM Salespeople
        WHERE city = 'London';
```

You now own a view called Londonstaff. You can use this view just like any other table. It can be queried, updated, inserted into, deleted from, and joined with other tables and views. Let's query this view (shown in Figure 20.1):

```
SELECT *
   FROM Londonstaff;
```

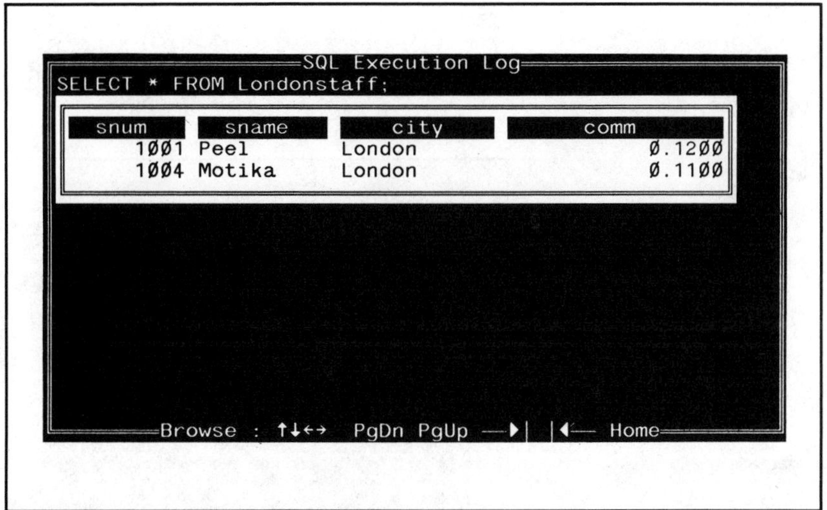

Figure 20.1: The Londonstaff view

When you told SQL to SELECT all rows from the view, it executed the query contained in the definition of Londonstaff, and returned all of its output. Had there been a predicate in the query of the view, only those rows of the view that satisfied it would have been output.

You may remember that in Chapter 15, you had a table called Londonstaff, into which you inserted these same contents (of course, we are assuming that table is no longer extant. If it were, you would have to pick another name for your view). The advantage of using a view, instead of a base table, is that the view will be updated automatically whenever the underlying table changes. The contents of the view are not fixed, but are reevaluated each time you reference the view in a command. If you added another London-based salesperson tomorrow, she would automatically appear in the view.

Views greatly extend the control you have over your data. They are an excellent way to give people access to some but not all of the information in a table. If you wanted your salespeople to be able to look at the Salespeople table, but not to see each other's commissions, you could create a view for their use (shown in Figure 20.2) with the following statement:

```
CREATE VIEW Salesown
    AS SELECT snum, sname, city
        FROM Salespeople;
```

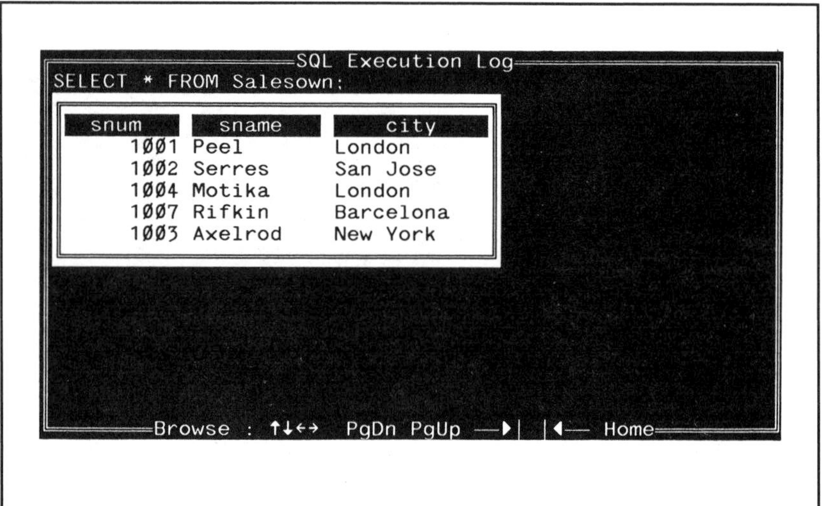

Figure 20.2: The Salesown view

In other words, this view is the same as the Salespeople table, except that the comm field was not named in the query, and is therefore not included in the view.

UPDATING VIEWS

This view can now be modified by DML update commands, but the modifications will not affect the view itself. They will be passed along to the underlying table:

```
UPDATE Salesown
    SET city = 'Palo Alto'
    WHERE snum = 1004;
```

The effect of this is identical to performing the same command on the Salespeople table. However, if a salesperson tried to UPDATE his commission

```
UPDATE Salesown
    SET comm = .20
    WHERE snum = 1004;
```

it would be rejected, because there is no comm field in the Salesown view. It is important to note that not all views can be updated. We will explore the issue of updating views thoroughly in Chapter 21.

NAMING COLUMNS

In our examples so far, the fields of our views have had their names taken directly from the names of the fields in the underlying table. This is the easiest course. However, sometimes you will have to provide new names for your columns:

- When some of the columns are output columns, and therefore unnamed.
- When two or more columns in a join have the same name in their respective tables.

The names that will become the names of the fields are given in parentheses after the table name. It does not matter if they match the field names of the table being queried. Their data types and sizes are still derived from the fields of the query that are "piped" into them. Often you do not have to specify new field names, but if you do, you will have to do so for every field in the view.

COMBINING THE PREDICATES OF VIEWS AND QUERIES BASED ON VIEWS

When you query a view you are, in a sense, querying a query. The main way SQL deals with this is to combine the predicates of the two queries into one. Let's look again at our view named Londonstaff:

```
CREATE VIEW Londonstaff
    AS SELECT *
        FROM Salespeople
            WHERE city = 'London';
```

If we perform the following query on this view

```
SELECT *
    FROM Londonstaff
    WHERE comm > .12;
```

it is as though we performed this next on the Salespeople table:

```
SELECT *
    FROM Salespeople
    WHERE  city = 'London'
    AND comm > .12;
```

This is fine, except that it does bring up a possible problem with views. It is quite possible to combine two perfectly acceptable predicates and get a predicate that will not work. For example, suppose we CREATE the following view:

```
CREATE VIEW Ratingcount (rating, number)
    AS SELECT rating, COUNT (*)
        FROM Customers
        GROUP BY rating;
```

This will give us a count of how many customers we have at each level of rating. You could then query this view to find out if there are any ratings currently assigned to three customers:

```
SELECT *
    FROM Ratingcount
    WHERE number = 3;
```

Look what happens when we combine the two predicates:

```
SELECT rating, COUNT (*)
    FROM Customers
    WHERE COUNT (*) = 3
    GROUP BY rating;
```

This is not a legal query. Aggregate functions, such as COUNT, cannot be used in a predicate.

The proper way to form the above query, of course, would be

```
SELECT rating, COUNT (*)
    FROM Customers
    GROUP BY rating;
    HAVING COUNT (*) = 3;
```

But SQL will not perform the conversion. Will the equivalent query against Ratingcount therefore fail? It may. This is an ambiguous area of SQL where the technique for implementing views may well affect the results. The best thing to do in a case like this, which your system documentation may not address, is try it and see. If the command is accepted, you may be able to use views to get around some of SQL's restrictions on query syntax.

GROUPED VIEWS

Grouped views are views, like Ratingcount in the previous example, that contain a GROUP BY clause, or that are based on other grouped views.

Grouped views can be an excellent way to process derived information continuously. Suppose each day you have to keep track of the number of customers ordering, the number of salespeople taking orders, the number of orders, the average amount ordered, and the total amount ordered. Rather than constructing a complex query repeatedly, you can simply create the following view:

```
CREATE VIEW Totalforday
    AS SELECT odate, COUNT (DISTINCT cnum), COUNT
                (DISTINCT snum), COUNT (onum), AVG
                (amt), SUM (amt)
        FROM Orders
        GROUP BY odate;
```

Now you can see all this information with a simple query:

```
SELECT *
    FROM Totalforday;
```

As we have seen, SQL queries can get quite complex, so views provide you with an extremely flexible and powerful tool to determine just how your data will be used. They can also make your life easier by reformatting data in useful ways and eliminating repetitive work.

VIEWS AND JOINS

Views need not be drawn from a single base table. Because almost any valid SQL query can be used in a view, they can distill information from any number of base tables, or other views. We can, for example, define a view that shows, for each order, the salesperson and the customer by name:

```
CREATE VIEW Nameorders
    AS SELECT onum, amt, a.snum, sname, cname
        FROM Orders a, Customers b, Salespeople c
        WHERE a.cnum = b.cnum
            AND a.snum = c.snum;
```

Now you can SELECT all orders by customer or by salesperson, or you can see this information for any order. For example, to see all of salesperson Rifkin's orders, you would enter the following query (the output is shown in Figure 20.3):

```
SELECT *
    FROM Nameorders
    WHERE sname = 'Rifkin';
```

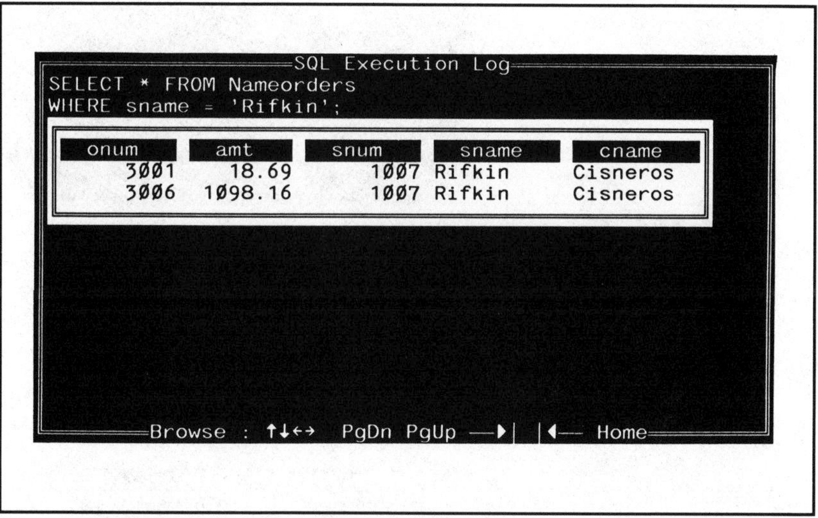

Figure 20.3: Rifkin's orders as seen in Nameorders

You can also join views with other tables, either base tables or views, so that you can see all of Axelrod's orders and her commission on each one:

```
SELECT a.sname, cname, amt * comm
    FROM Nameorders a, Salespeople b
    WHERE a.sname = 'Axelrod'
        AND b.snum = a.snum;
```

The output for this query is shown in Figure 20.4.

In the predicate, we could have said " WHERE a.sname = 'Axelrod' AND b.sname = 'Axelrod' ", but the predicate we used is more general. All we have to change to make it apply to anyone else is the name. Besides, snum is the primary key of Salespeople, and therefore should definitely be unique. If there

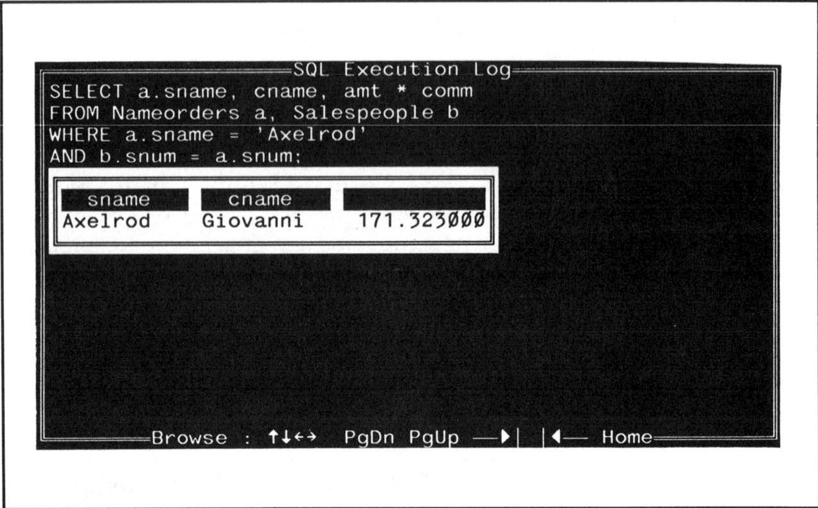
SQL Execution Log
SELECT a.sname, cname, amt * comm
FROM Nameorders a, Salespeople b
WHERE a.sname = 'Axelrod'
AND b.snum = a.snum;

sname	cname	
Axelrod	Giovanni	171.323000

Figure 20.4: A join of a base table to a view

were two Axelrod's, the name version would combine their data. The preferred version would use the snum to keep them separate.

VIEWS AND SUBQUERIES

Views can also use subqueries, including correlated subqueries. Perhaps your company provides a bonus for the salesperson who has the customer with the highest order on any given date. You could track that information with this view:

```
CREATE VIEW Elitesalesforce
    AS SELECT b.odate, a.snum, a.sname,
        FROM Salespeople a, Orders b
        WHERE a.snum = b.snum
            AND b.amt =
                (SELECT MAX (amt)
                    FROM Orders c
                    WHERE c.odate = b.odate);
```

If, on the other hand, the bonus will go only to salespeople when they have had the highest order at least ten times, you might track them in another view based on the first:

```
CREATE VIEW Bonus
    AS SELECT DISTINCT snum, sname
        FROM Elitesalesforce a
        WHERE 10 < =
            (SELECT-COUNT (*)
                FROM Elitesalesforce b
                WHERE a.snum = b.snum);
```

Extracting from this table the salespeople who will receive bonuses is simply a matter of entering the following:

```
SELECT *
    FROM Bonus;
```

Now we are seeing the true power of SQL. Extracting this derived information with an RPG or COBOL program would have been a much lengthier procedure. In SQL, it is just a matter of two somewhat complex commands stored as view definitions along with simple query. The query itself is all we would have to be concerned with on a day-to-day basis, because the information it extracts is continuously changed to reflect the current state of the database.

WHAT VIEWS CANNOT DO

There are many types of views (including many of our examples in this chapter) that are read only. This means that they can be queried, but they cannot be subjected to update commands. (We will explore this topic in Chapter 21.)

There are also some aspects of queries that are not permissible in view definitions. A single view must be based on a single query; UNION and UNION ALL are not allowed. Neither is ORDER BY to be used in the definition of a view. The output of the query forms the content of the view, which like a base table, is by definition unordered.

DROPPING VIEWS

The syntax to eliminate a view from the database is similar to that for removing base tables:

DROP VIEW <*view name*>

There is no need, however, to first delete all the contents as there is with base tables, because the contents of a view are never defined, save for the duration of a particular command. The underlying table(s) from which the view is drawn are not affected when it is dropped. Remember, you must own the view in order to drop it.

SUMMARY

Now that you can use views, your ability to track and process the content of your database easily is greatly enhanced. Almost anything you can create spontaneously with a query, you can define permanently as a view. Queries against these views are, in effect, queries on queries. The use of views for both convenience and security, as well as many of the capabilities of views for formatting and deriving values from the ever-changing content of your database, have been explored. There is one major issue regarding views, updatability, that we chose to defer until Chapter 21. As indicated, you can update views as you would base tables, with the changes applied to the table(s) from which the view is derived, but this is not possible in all cases.

Putting SQL to Work

1. Create a view that shows all of the customers who have the highest ratings.
2. Create a view that shows the number of salespeople in each city.
3. Create a view that shows the average and total orders for each salesperson after his or her name. Assume all names are unique.
4. Create a view that shows each salesperson with multiple customers.

(See Appendix A for answers.)

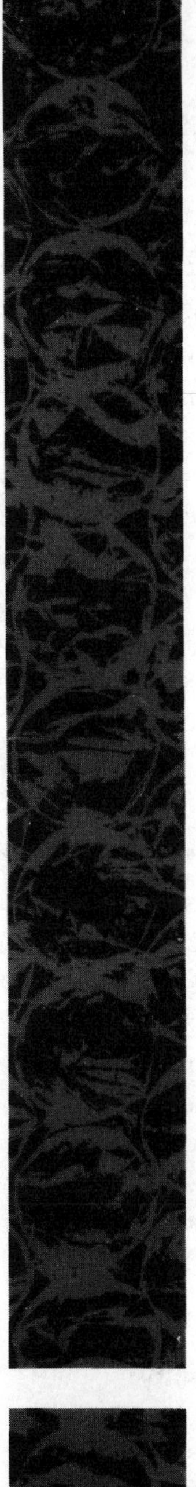

21

Changing Values Through Views

THIS CHAPTER TALKS ABOUT THE DML UPDATE commands—INSERT, UPDATE, and DELETE—when they are applied to views. As mentioned in the previous chapter, using update commands on views is an indirect way of using them on the tables referenced by the queries of the views. However, not all views can be updated. In this chapter, we will discuss the rules for determining whether or not a view is updatable and explore their implications. In addition, you will learn to use the clause WITH CHECK OPTION, which controls the specific values that can enter a table through a view. As mentioned in Chapter 18, this can, in some cases, be a desirable alternative to constraining a table directly.

UPDATING VIEWS

One of the most difficult and ambiguous aspects of views is the implication of their usage with the DML update commands. As mentioned in the previous chapter, these commands actually affect the values in the underlying base tables of the view. This is something of a contradiction. A view consists of the results of a query, and when you update a view, you are updating a set of query results. But the update is not to affect the query per se; it is to affect the values in the table(s) on which the query was made, and thereby change the output of the query. This is not necessarily a simple matter. The following statement will create the view shown in Figure 21.1:

```
CREATE VIEW Citymatch (custcity, salescity)
    AS SELECT DISTINCT a.city, b.city
        FROM Customers a, Salespeople b
        WHERE a.snum = b.snum;
```

This view shows all matches of customers with salespeople such that there is at least one customer in custcity served by a salesperson in salescity.

For example, one row of this table—London London—indicates that there is at least one customer in London served by a salesperson in London. This row could have been produced by the match of Hoffman with her salesperson Peel, both in London.

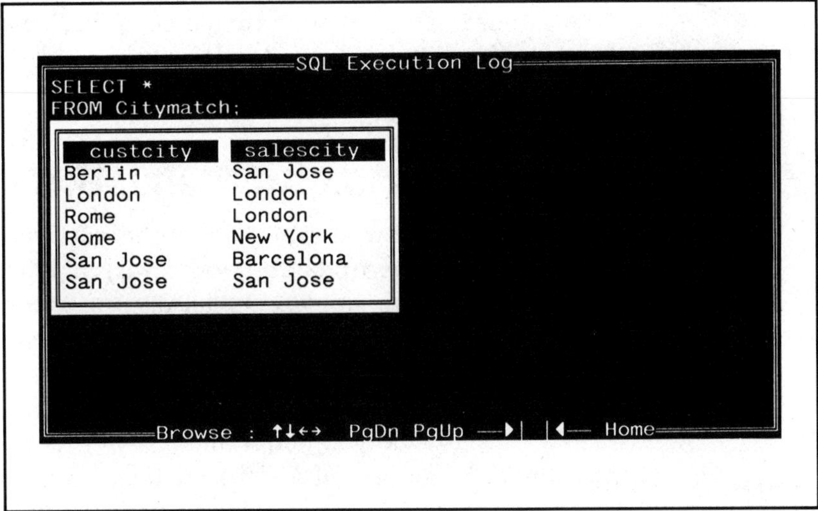

Figure 21.1: The Citymatch View

The same value, however, would be produced by matching Clemens, also in London, with his salesperson, who also happens to be Peel. Since distinct city combinations were specifically selected, only one compound row with these values was produced. But which match of underlying table values does it represent?

Even if you hadn't selected using distinct, you would still be in the same boat, because you would then have two rows in the view with identical values, that is, with both columns equal to London. These two rows of the view would be indistinguishable from one another, so you still would not be able to tell which row of the view came from which input values of the base tables (keep in mind that queries that omit the ORDER BY clause produce output in an arbitrary order. This applies as well to queries used within views, which cannot use ORDER BY. So the order of the two rows cannot be used to distinguish them). This means that we would again be faced with output rows that could not be definitely linked to specific rows of the tables queried.

What if you tried to delete the row London London from the view? Would it mean deleting Hoffman from the Customers table, Clemens, or both? Should SQL also delete Peel from the Salespeople table? Such questions are impossible to answer definitively, so deletions are not permitted on views of this nature. The view Citymatch is an example of a read-only view, one that can be queried, but not changed.

DETERMINING IF A VIEW IS UPDATABLE

If update commands can be performed on a view, the view is said to be updatable; otherwise it is read-only. Consistent with this terminology, we shall use the expression "updating a view" to mean executing on the view any of the three DML update commands (INSERT, UPDATE and DELETE) that can change its values.

How do you determine if a view is updatable? In database theory, this is still a debated topic. The basic principle is that an updatable view is one on which an update command can be performed, altering one and only one row of the underlying table at a time without affecting any other rows of any table. Putting this principle into practice, however, can be difficult. Moreover, some views that are updatable in theory are not really updatable in SQL. The criteria that determine whether or not a view is updatable in SQL are as follows:

- It must be drawn on one and only one underlying table.
- It must include the primary key of that table (this is not technically enforced by the ANSI standard, but you would be well-advised to stick to it).
- It must have no fields that are aggregate functions.
- It must not specify DISTINCT in its definition.
- It must not use GROUP BY or HAVING in its definition.
- It must not use subqueries (this is an ANSI restriction that is not enforced in some implementations).
- It may be defined on another view, but that view must also be updatable.

- It must not use constants, strings, or value expressions (for example: comm * 100) among the selected output fields.
- For INSERT, it must include any fields of the underlying table that have the NOT NULL constraint, unless another default has been specified.

UPDATABLE VS. READ-ONLY VIEWS

One implication of these restrictions is that updatable views are, in effect, like windows on the underlying tables. They show some, but not necessarily all, of a table's contents. They can be restricted to certain rows (by the use of predicates), or to specifically named columns (with exceptions), but they present the values directly and do not derive information from them, such as by using aggregate functions and expressions. They also do not compare table rows to one another (as in joins and subqueries, and as with DISTINCT).

The differences between updatable and read-only views are not merely incidental. The purposes for which you use them are frequently different. Updatable views are generally used just like base tables. In fact, users may not even be aware of whether the object they are querying is a base table or a view. They are an excellent security mechanism for concealing parts of a table that are confidential or are superfluous to a given user's needs. (In Chapter 22, we shall show you how to allow users to access a view, but not the underlying table).

Read-only views, on the other hand, allow you to derive and reformat data extensively. They give you a library of complex queries that you can execute and reexecute, keeping your derived information strictly up to the minute. In addition, having the results of these queries in tables that can then be used in queries themselves (for example, in joins) has advantages over simply executing the queries. Read-only views can also have security applications. For instance, you may want some users to see aggregate data, such as the average salesperson's commission, without being able to see individual commission values.

TELLING WHICH ARE UPDATABLE VIEWS

Here are some examples of updatable and read-only views:

```
CREATE VIEW Dateorders (odate, ocount)
    AS SELECT odate, COUNT (*)
        FROM Orders
        GROUP BY odate;
```

This is a read-only view because of the presence of an aggregate function and GROUP BY.

```
CREATE VIEW Londoncust
    AS SELECT *
        FROM Customers
        WHERE city = 'London';
```

This is an updatable view.

```
CREATE VIEW SJsales (name, number, percentage)
    AS SELECT sname, snum, comm * 100
        FROM Salespeople
        WHERE city = 'San Jose';
```

This is a read-only view because of the expression "comm * 100." The reordering and renaming of the fields is permissable, however. Some programs would allow deletions on this view or ordates on the snum and sname columns.

```
CREATE VIEW Salesonthird
    AS SELECT *
        FROM Salespeople
        WHERE snum IN
            (SELECT snum
                FROM Orders
                WHERE odate = 10/03/1990);
```

This is a read-only view in ANSI because of the subquery. In some programs, it might be acceptable.

```
CREATE VIEW Someorders
    AS SELECT snum, onum, cnum
        FROM Orders
        WHERE odate IN (10/03/1990, 10/05/1990);
```

This is updatable.

CHECKING THE VALUES PLACED IN VIEWS

Another issue involving updates of views is that you can enter values that get "swallowed" in the underlying table. Consider this view:

```
CREATE VIEW Highratings
    AS SELECT cnum, rating
        FROM Customers
        WHERE rating = 300;
```

This is an updatable view. It simply restricts your access to the table to certain rows and columns. Suppose, then, you INSERT the following row:

```
INSERT INTO Highratings
    VALUES (2018, 200);
```

This is a legal INSERT command on this view. The row would be inserted, through the Highratings view, into the Customers table. Once it was there, however, it would disappear from the view, as its rating value is not 300. This is usually a problem. The 200 value might have been a simple typo, but now the row is in the Customers table where you cannot even see it. A user may not be aware that she has entered a row she cannot see, and would be unable to delete it in any case.

You can ensure against modifications of this sort by including WITH CHECK OPTION in the definition of the view. Had we used WITH CHECK OPTION in the definition of the Highratings view

```
CREATE VIEW Highratings
    AS SELECT cnum, rating
        FROM Customers
        WHERE rating = 300
        WITH CHECK OPTION;
```

the above insertion would have been rejected.

WITH CHECK OPTION is a kind of all-or-nothing affair. You put it in the definition of the view, not in a DML command, so either all update commands against the view will be checked, or none will. Usually you do want to employ the check option, so having it in the definition of the view may be a convenience. Generally, you should use this option unless you have a specific reason for allowing a view to put into a table values it will not itself contain.

PREDICATES AND EXCLUDED FIELDS

A related problem that you should be aware of involves inserting rows into a view with a predicate based on one or more excluded fields. For instance, it might seem sensible to define Londonstaff like this:

```
CREATE VIEW Londonstaff
    AS SELECT snum, sname, comm
        FROM Salespeople
        WHERE city = 'London';
```

After all, why include the city value when all the city values will be the same, and the name of the view tells us which city this view is for? But picture what happens whenever we try to insert a row. Since we cannot specify a city value, a default value, probably NULL, would be entered in the city field (NULL would be used unless another default were explicitly defined. See Chapter 18 for details). Since the city field would not then equal London, the inserted row would be excluded from the view. This would be true for any row that you tried to insert into Londonstaff. They would all be entered through the Londonstaff view into the Salespeople table, and then be excluded from the view itself (unless the explicitly defined default were 'London', a special case). A user would be unable to enter rows into this view, yet, perhaps unknowingly, could enter rows into the underlying table. Even if we add WITH CHECK OPTION to the definition of the view

```
CREATE VIEW Londonstaff
    AS SELECT snum, sname, comm
        FROM Salespeople
        WHERE city = 'London'
        WITH CHECK OPTION;
```

the problem would not necessarily be solved. The effect of this would be to give us a view that we could update or delete from, but not insert into. In some cases, this may be fine; perhaps there is no reason for users with access to this view to be able to add rows. But you should definitely determine that this is the case before you create such a view.

Even though they may not always provide useful information, it is frequently a good idea to include, in your view, all fields referenced in its predicate. If you do not want these fields in your output, you can always omit them from a query *on* the view, as opposed to the query *within* the view. In other words, you could define the Londonstaff view like this:

```
CREATE VIEW Londonstaff
    AS SELECT *
        FROM Salespeople
        WHERE city = 'London'
        WITH CHECK OPTION;
```

This would fill the view with identical city values that you could simply omit from the output with a query along these lines:

```
SELECT snum, sname, comm
    FROM Londonstaff;
```

CHECKING VIEWS THAT ARE BASED ON OTHER VIEWS

One more thing should be mentioned about WITH CHECK OPTION in ANSI: it does not *cascade up*: It applies only to the view in which it is defined, not to other views based on that view. For instance, in a previous example

```
CREATE VIEW Highratings
    AS SELECT cnum, rating
        FROM Customers
        WHERE rating = 300
        WITH CHECK OPTION;
```

attempts to insert or update to rating values other than 300 will fail. However, we could create a second view (with identical content) based on the first:

```
CREATE VIEW Myratings
    AS SELECT *
        FROM Highratings;
```

We could then update to a rating other than 300:

```
UPDATE Myratings
    SET rating = 200
    WHERE cnum = 2004;
```

This command, which would have the same effect as if it were performed on the first view, could be accepted.

The WITH CHECK OPTION clause merely ensures that any update to the view it's in produces values that satisfy the predicate of that view. Updates to other views based on the current one are all still legal, unless prevented by WITH CHECK OPTION clauses within those views. Even if such clauses are present, they check only the predicates of views in which they are contained. So, even if Myratings were defined as follows

```
CREATE VIEW Myratings
    AS SELECT *
        FROM Highratings
        WITH CHECK OPTION;
```

the problem would not be solved. This WITH CHECK OPTION would only examine the predicate of the Myratings view. Since Myratings, in fact, has no predicate, the WITH CHECK OPTION would do nothing. If there were a predicate used, it would be checked whenever Myratings were updated, but the predicate of Highratings would still be ignored.

This is a flaw in the ANSI standard that many products have corrected. You might want to try using a view definition like the last example and see if your system avoids this pitfall. (Trying something out can sometimes be considerably easier and more dependable than trying to extract the answer from system documentation.)

SUMMARY

You have now mastered views pretty thoroughly. In addition to a checklist of rules to determine if a given view is updatable in SQL, you know the basic concepts on which the rules are based—updates to views are permissible only if SQL can unambiguously determine which values of the underlying table to change. This means that the update command, when performed, must not require changes to multiple rows at once, nor comparisons between multiple rows of either the base table or the query output. Since joins involve comparing rows, they are prohibited. You also understand the differences between some of the ways that updatable and read-only views are used.

You have learned to think of updatable views as windows, showing the data of a single table, but optionally omitting or rearranging its columns as well as selecting only certain rows according to a predicate criteria.

Read-only views, on the other hand, can contain most valid SQL queries; they can therefore be a way of keeping queries you need to execute frequently in a permanent form. In addition, having a query whose output is treated as a data object enables you to have the clarity and convenience of making queries on the output of queries.

You now can prevent update commands on a view from producing rows in the underlying table that are not present in the view itself by using the WITH CHECK OPTION clause in the view definition. You can also use WITH CHECK OPTION as an alternative to a constraint on the underlying table.

In stand-alone queries, you can usually use one or more columns in a predicate that are not present among the selected output without causing a problem. If these queries are used in updatable views, however, they are problematic because they produce views that cannot have rows inserted into them (although, in the absence of WITH CHECK OPTION, the rows may end up in the underlying table). You have seen the implications of, and some approaches to, this problem.

In Chapters 20 and 21, we have mentioned that views have security applications. You can allow users to access views without allowing them to access the tables on which the views are based directly. Chapter 22 will explore the question of access to data objects in SQL.

Putting SQL to Work

1. Which of these views are updatable?

```
#1 CREATE VIEW Dailyorders
        AS SELECT DISTINCT cnum, snum, onum,
         odate
           FROM Orders;

#2 CREATE VIEW Custotals
        AS SELECT cname, SUM (amt)
           FROM Orders, Customers
           WHERE Orders.cnum = customer.cnum
           GROUP BY cname;

#3 CREATE VIEW Thirdorders
        AS SELECT *
           FROM Dailyorders
           WHERE odate = 10/03/1990;

#4 CREATE VIEW Nullcities
        AS SELECT snum, sname, city
           FROM Salespeople
           WHERE city IS NULL
              OR sname BETWEEN 'A' AND 'MZ';
```

2. Create a view of the Salespeople table called Commissions. This view will include only the snum and comm fields. Through this view, someone could enter or change commissions, but only to values between .10 and .20.
3. Some SQL implementations have a built-in constant representing the current date, sometimes called "CURDATE". The word CURDATE can therefore be used in a SQL statement, and be replaced by the current date when the value is accessed by commands such as SELECT or INSERT. We will use a view of the Orders table called

Entryorders to insert rows into the Orders table. Create the Orders table, so that CURDATE is automatically inserted for odate if no value is given. Then create the Entryorders view so that no values can be given.

(See Appendix A for answers.)

22

Determining Who Can Do What

IN THIS CHAPTER, YOU WILL LEARN ABOUT PRIVILEGES. As mentioned in Chapter 2, SQL is used mostly in environments that require it to recognize and differentiate between the various users of the system. Generally speaking, those in charge of administering the database create the other users and give them privileges. Users who create tables, on the other hand, have control over those tables. *Privileges* are what determines whether or not a particular user can perform a given command. There are several types of privileges corresponding to several types of operations. Privileges are given and taken away with two SQL commands—GRANT and REVOKE. This chapter will show you how these commands are used.

USERS

Each user in a SQL environment has a specific identifying name or number. The specific terminology varies, but we have chosen (following ANSI) to refer to this name or number as an authorization ID. Commands given to the database are associated with a particular user; that is, a specific authorization ID. As far as the SQL database is concerned, the authorization ID is the name of the user, and SQL can use the special keyword USER, which refers to the Authorization ID associated with the current command. Commands are interpreted and permitted (or prohibited) on the basis of information associated with the authorization ID of the user issuing the command.

LOGGING ON

In systems with multiple users, there is generally some kind of log-on procedure that a user has to go through when gaining access to the computer system. This procedure determines which authorization ID will be associated with the current user. Normally, each person using the database will have his own authorization ID, so that the users as conceived by SQL will correspond to actual users. However, often users with multiple functions can log on to various authorization IDs, or an ID can be used by several users. SQL generally has no way of making distinctions between these cases; it simply sees the user as the authorization ID.

A SQL database may use a log-on procedure of its own, or it may allow another program, such as the operating system (the main program that runs your computer), to handle log ons and obtain its authorization IDs from that program. One way or another SQL, will have an authorization ID to associate with your actions, and this will be the value of the keyword USER for you.

GRANTING PRIVILEGES

Each user in a SQL database has a set of privileges. These are things that the user is permitted to do (one of which, presumably, is log on, which can be considered a minimal privilege). These privileges can change over time—new ones can be added, old ones taken away. Some of these privileges are defined in ANSI SQL, but there are additional ones that are necessary as well. The SQL privileges as defined by ANSI are not sufficient for the needs of many real-life situations. On the other hand, the types of privileges that are needed may vary with the kind of system you are running—something about which ANSI could make no assumptions. Privileges that are not part of standard SQL will still use a syntax similar, though not identical, to the standard, for the sake of consistency.

THE STANDARD PRIVILEGES

The SQL privileges defined by ANSI are *object privileges*. This means that a user has a privilege to perform a given command only on a certain object in the database. Obviously, privileges need to be able to distinguish between objects, but a privilege system based solely on object privileges cannot address all of SQL's needs, as we shall see later in this chapter.

Object privileges are associated simultaneously with both users and tables. That is to say, a privilege is given to a particular user on a particular table, either a base table or a view. You will recall that a user who creates a table (of either kind) owns that table. Among other things, this means the user has all privileges on that table and can assign them to others. These are the privileges a user can assign:

SELECT	A user with this privilege can perform queries on the table.
INSERT	A user with this privilege can perform the INSERT command on the table.
UPDATE	A user with this privilege can perform the UPDATE command on the table. You may limit this privilege to specified columns of the table.
DELETE	A user with this privilege can perform the DELETE command on the table.
REFERENCES	A user with this privilege can define a foreign key that uses one or more columns of this table as a parent key. You may limit this privilege to specified columns. (Refer to Chapter 19 for details on foreign and parent keys.)

In addition, you may encounter nonstandard object privileges, such as INDEX (the right to create an index on a table), SYNONYM (the right to create a synonym for an object, which will be explained in Chapter 23), and ALTER (the right to perform the ALTER TABLE command on a table). The mechanism SQL employs to give users these privileges is the GRANT command.

THE GRANT COMMAND

Let us say that user Diane owns the Customers table and wants to let user Adrian perform queries on it. Diane would enter the following command:

```
GRANT SELECT ON Customers TO Adrian;
```

Now Adrian can perform queries on the Customers table. Without other privileges, he can only select; he cannot perform any of the actions that affect the values in Customers (including using Customers as the parent table of a foreign key, which restricts the changes that can be made to the values in the Customers table).

When SQL receives a GRANT command, it checks the privileges of the user issuing it to determine if the GRANT is permissible. Adrian himself could not issue this command. Nor could Adrian grant SELECT to another user: the table is still owned by Diane (although we will show you shortly how Diane could enable Adrian to grant SELECT).

The syntax is the same for the granting of the other privileges. If Adrian owned the Salespeople table, he could allow Diane to enter rows into it by entering

```
GRANT INSERT ON Salespeople TO Diane;
```

Now Diane could put new salespeople into the table.

GROUPS OF PRIVILEGES, GROUPS OF USERS You do not have to restrict yourself to granting a single privilege to a single user per GRANT command. Lists of privileges or users, separated by commas, are perfectly acceptable. Stephen could either grant SELECT and INSERT on the Orders table to Adrian

```
GRANT SELECT, INSERT ON Orders TO Adrian;
```

or to both Adrian and Diane

```
GRANT SELECT, INSERT ON Orders TO Adrian, Diane;
```

When privileges and users are listed like this, all of the privileges in the list are granted to all of the users. In a strict ANSI interpretation, you cannot grant privileges on multiple tables in a single command, but some implementations may relax this somewhat, by allowing you to name several tables, separated by commas, so that all listed users get all listed privileges on all listed tables.

RESTRICTING PRIVILEGES TO CERTAIN COLUMNS

All the object privileges use the same syntax except for UPDATE and REFERENCES, which can optionally specify columns. An UPDATE privilege can be granted like the other privileges:

```
GRANT UPDATE ON Salespeople TO Diane;
```

This command would allow Diane to alter the values in any or all of the columns of the Salespeople table. However, if Adrian wanted to restrict Diane to changing commissions, he could instead enter

```
GRANT UPDATE (comm) ON Salespeople TO Diane;
```

In other words, he simply has to name the column to which the UPDATE privilege is to apply in parentheses after the table name. Multiple columns of the table can be named, in any order, separated by commas:

```
GRANT UPDATE (city, comm) ON Salespeople TO Diane;
```

REFERENCES follows this same pattern. When you grant the REFERENCES privilege to another user, he or she can create foreign keys that reference columns of your table as parent keys. Like UPDATE, the REFERENCES privilege can take a list of one or more columns to which the privilege will be limited. For example, Diane can grant Stephen the right to use the Customers table as a parent-key table with this command:

```
GRANT REFERENCES (cname, cnum)
    ON Customers TO Stephen;
```

This command gives Stephen the right to use the cnum and cname columns as parent keys to any foreign keys in his tables. Stephen has control over how this will be done. He can define (cname, cnum) or, for that matter, (cnum, cname) as a two-column parent key, matched by a two-column foreign key in one of his own tables. Or he can create separate foreign keys to reference the fields individually, provided, in either case, that Diane has appropriately constrained the parent key(s) (see Chapter 19).

There is no restriction on the number of foreign keys he could base on these parent keys, and the parent keys of various foreign keys are allowed to overlap.

As with the UPDATE privilege, you can omit the column list and thereby allow all of your columns to be usable as parent keys. Adrian could grant Diane the right to do this with the following command:

```
GRANT REFERENCES ON Salespeople TO Diane;
```

Naturally, the privilege will be usable only on columns that have the constraints required for parent keys.

USING THE ALL AND PUBLIC ARGUMENTS

SQL supports two arguments to the GRANT command that have special meaning: ALL PRIVILEGES (or simply ALL) and PUBLIC. ALL is used in place of the privilege names in the GRANT command to give the grantee all of the privileges on the table. For example, Diane could give Stephen the entire set of privileges on the Customers table with this command:

```
GRANT ALL PRIVILEGES ON Customers TO Stephen;
```

(The UPDATE and REFERENCES privileges naturally apply to all columns.) The following is an alternate way of saying the same thing:

```
GRANT ALL ON Customers TO Stephen;
```

PUBLIC is a similar sort of catch-all argument, but for users rather than privileges. When you grant privileges to the public, all users automatically receive them. Most often, this will apply to the SELECT privilege on certain base tables or views that you want to have available for anyone's perusal. To allow any user to look at the Orders table, for instance, you could enter the following:

```
GRANT SELECT ON Orders TO PUBLIC;
```

Of course, you can grant any or all privileges to the public, but this is obviously not advisable. All privileges except SELECT allow the user to change (or, in the case of REFERENCES, constrain) the content of the table. Allowing all users to change the content of your tables is inviting problems. Even if you have a small company, and it is appropriate for all of your current users to be able to perform update commands on a given table, it still may be better to grant the privileges to each user individually, rather than to the public. PUBLIC is not restricted to current users. Any new user added to your system will automatically receive all privileges assigned to PUBLIC, so if you want to restrict access to the table at all, now or possibly in the future, it is best to grant privileges other than SELECT to individual users.

GRANTING WITH THE GRANT OPTION

Sometimes, the creator of a table wants other users to be able to grant privileges on that table. This is particularly true in systems where one or a few people may create most or all of the base tables in the database and then delegate responsibility for them to those who will actually be working with them. SQL allows this through the use of the WITH GRANT OPTION clause.

If Diane wanted Adrian to have the right to grant the SELECT privilege on the Customers table to other users, she would give him the SELECT privilege and use the WITH GRANT OPTION clause:

```
GRANT SELECT ON Customers TO Adrian
 WITH GRANT OPTION;
```

Adrian would then have the right to give the SELECT privilege to third parties; he could then issue the command

```
GRANT SELECT ON Diane.Customers TO Stephen;
```

or even

```
GRANT SELECT ON Diane.Customers TO Stephen
 WITH GRANT OPTION;
```

A user with the GRANT OPTION on a particular privilege for a given table can, in turn, grant that privilege on that table, with or without the GRANT OPTION, to any other user. This does not change the ownership of the table; tables are owned by their creators. (And they must be prefixed by the authorization ID of the owner, as above, when referred to by other users. The next chapter will show you a way around this.) But a user with the GRANT OPTION on all privileges for a given table has a great deal of power over that table.

TAKING PRIVILEGES AWAY

Just as ANSI defines a CREATE TABLE command to make tables but not a DROP TABLE to get rid of them, it supports a GRANT command to allow you to give privileges to users, but doesn't define a way for you to take them back. The need to remove privileges is met by the REVOKE command, a defacto standard feature that is pretty consistent in form.

The syntax of the REVOKE command is patterned after GRANT, but with the reverse meaning. So, to take away Adrian's INSERT privilege on Orders, you could enter

```
REVOKE INSERT ON Orders FROM Adrian;
```

Lists of privileges and users are acceptable just as for GRANT, so you can also enter the following command:

```
REVOKE INSERT, DELETE ON Customers
    FROM Adrian, Stephen;
```

There is some ambiguity here, however. Who has the right to revoke a privilege? When a user with grant option on a privilege loses it, do users to whom he or she has granted the privilege lose it as well? Since this is not a standard feature, there are no authoritative answers to these questions, but the most common approach is this: Privileges are revoked by the user who granted them, and revocations will *cascade*; that is, they will automatically apply as well to all users who received the privilege from the revokee.

USING VIEWS TO FILTER PRIVILEGES

You can make the effects of privileges more precise by using views. Whenever you grant a privilege on a base table to a user, it automatically applies to all rows and, with the possible exceptions of UPDATE and REFERENCES, all columns of the table. By creating a view that references the base table and then granting privileges on the view rather than the table, you can limit these privileges in any way expressible in the query that the view contains. This greatly refines the basic capabilities of the GRANT command.

WHO CAN CREATE VIEWS? In order to create a view, you must have the SELECT privilege on all the tables that you reference in that view. If the view is updatable, any INSERT, UPDATE, and DELETE privileges that you have on the underlying table will automatically apply as well to the view. If you lack update privileges on the underlying tables, you will not have them on the views you create, even if the views themselves are updatable. Since foreign keys as such are not used in views, the REFERENCES privilege is never needed to create views. These are the restrictions defined by ANSI. Nonstandard system privileges (discussed later in this chapter) may also be involved. In the following sections we will assume that the creators of the views we discuss own or have the relevant privileges on all base tables used.

LIMITING THE SELECT PRIVILEGE TO CERTAIN COLUMNS Suppose you wanted to give user Claire the ability to see only the snum and sname columns of the Salespeople table. You could do this by putting these columns in a view

```
CREATE VIEW Clairesview
    AS SELECT snum, sname
        FROM Salespeople;
```

and granting Claire the SELECT privilege on the view, but not on the Salespeople table itself:

```
GRANT SELECT ON Clairesview to Claire;
```

You can create column-specific privileges like this using the other privileges as well, but, for the INSERT command, this will mean the insertion of default values, and, for the DELETE command, the column limitations will not be meaningful. The UPDATE and REFERENCES privileges, of course, can be made column specific without resorting to a view.

LIMITING PRIVILEGES TO CERTAIN ROWS An even more useful way to filter privileges with views is to use the view to make a privilege apply only to certain rows. You do this, naturally, by using a predicate in the view that determines which rows are included. To grant the user Adrian the UPDATE privilege on all Customers located in London, you could create this view:

```
CREATE VIEW Londoncust
    AS SELECT *
        FROM Customers
        WHERE city = 'London'
        WITH CHECK OPTION;
```

You could then grant the UPDATE privilege on it to Adrian:

```
GRANT UPDATE ON Londoncust TO Adrian;
```

This differs from a column-specific UPDATE privilege in that all of the columns of the Customers table are included, but the rows in cities other than London are left out. The WITH CHECK OPTION clause prevents Adrian from changing the city field to any value besides London.

GRANTING ACCESS ONLY TO DERIVED DATA Another possibility is to offer users access to derived data, rather than actual table values. Aggregate functions can often be handy if used this way. You can create a view that gives the counts, averages, and totals for the orders on each order date:

```
CREATE VIEW Datetotals
    AS SELECT odate, COUNT (*), SUM (amt), AVG (amt)
        FROM Orders
        GROUP BY odate;
```

Now you give user Diane SELECT on the Datetotals view:

```
GRANT SELECT ON Datetotals TO Diane;
```

USING VIEWS AS AN ALTERNATIVE TO CONSTRAINTS

One last application of this technique, mentioned in Chapter 18, is the use of views WITH CHECK OPTION as an alternative to constraints. Suppose you wanted to make sure that all city values in the Salespeople table were in one of the cities where your company currently had an office. You could place a CHECK constraint on the city column directly, but this may be difficult to change later if your company opens more offices. An alternative is to create a view that excludes incorrect city values:

```
CREATE VIEW Curcities
    AS SELECT *
        FROM Salespeople
        WHERE city IN ('London', 'Rome', 'San Jose',
          'Berlin')
        WITH CHECK OPTION;
```

Now, instead of granting users update privileges on the Salespeople table, you would grant them on the Curcities view. An advantage of this approach is that, if you need to make a change, you can drop this view, create a new one, and grant users privileges on the new view, which is often easier than changing a constraint. A disadvantage is that the owner of the Salespeople table also has to use this view if he wants to have his own mistakes rejected.

On the other hand, this approach enables the owner of the table, and any others granted update privileges on the table itself rather than the view, to make exceptions to the restriction. This is frequently desirable, and it cannot be done if you use constraints on the base table. Unfortunately, these exceptions will not be seen in the view. If you choose this approach, you may wish to create a second view containing only the exceptions:

```
CREATE VIEW Othercities
   AS SELECT *
      FROM Salespeople
      WHERE city NOT IN ('London', 'Rome', 'San Jose',
       'Berlin')
      WITH CHECK OPTION;
```

You could choose to grant users only the SELECT privilege on this view, so that they may see the excluded rows, but still not place invalid city values in the base table. In fact, users could query both views in a union and see all of the rows at once.

OTHER KINDS OF PRIVILEGES

You may have been wondering who has the right to create tables in the first place. This is an area of privilege not addressed as such by ANSI, but incapable of being ignored. All of the standard ANSI privileges emanate from this privilege; it is the creators of tables who grant the object privileges. Moreover, having all of your users creating base tables in a system of any size invites redundancy and inefficiency, to say the least. Connected with this are other concerns: Who has the right to alter, drop, or constrain tables? Should the right to create base tables be distinguished from that to create views? Should there be *superusers*—users who are generally in charge of maintaining the database and therefore have a great many or all privileges without their being individually granted?

Since ANSI doesn't address these concerns, and SQL is used in a variety of environments, we cannot offer a definitive answer to these questions. What we present here is an indication of the most common approach to these issues.

Privileges that are not defined in terms of specific data objects are called *system privileges*, or *database authorities*. At the most basic level, these will probably include the right to create data objects, probably (and desirably) distinguishing between base tables (usually created by a few users) and views (commonly created by many or all users). A system privilege to create views should supplement, rather than replace, the object privileges that ANSI requires of view creators (explained earlier in the present chapter). In addition, in a system of any size, some kind of superuser —a user who automatically has many or all privileges—will generally exist, and the superuser status may be conferred with a privilege or group of privileges. Database Administrator, or DBA, is the term most often used for such a superuser, as well as for the privilege he or she enjoys.

TYPICAL SYSTEM PRIVILEGES

The approach in common usage is to have three basic system privileges called CONNECT, RESOURCE, and DBA. To simplify a bit, *CONNECT* consists of the right to log on and the right to create views and synonyms (see Chapter 23) if granted the appropriate object privileges. *RESOURCE* consists of the right to create base tables. *DBA* is a superuser privilege giving a user virtual carte-blanche authority over the database. One or a few users with the function of administering the database will have this privilege. Some systems also have a special user, sometimes called *SYSADM* or *SYS*, who has the highest authority; these are special names, not just users with the special DBA privilege. An individual will actually log on with SYSADM as his or her authorization ID. The distinction is subtle and operates differently in different systems. For our purposes, we shall refer to highly privileged user(s) who design and control the database as DBA's, reflecting the fact that this is a function as well as a privilege.

The GRANT command, in a modified form, is usable with system as well as object privileges. Initial grants will be made by the DBA. For example, the DBA may grant the privilege to create a table to the user Rodriguez as follows:

```
GRANT RESOURCE TO Rodriguez;
```

CREATING AND DESTROYING USERS

Of course, there is also the question of how the user called Rodriguez is created. How is this authorization ID defined? In many implementations, a DBA creates a user automatically by granting the CONNECT privilege. In this case, an IDENTIFIED BY clause, indicating a password, is usually added. (If not, the operating system should determine whether you can log on to the database with a given authorization ID.) The DBA could, for example, enter

```
GRANT CONNECT TO Thelonius IDENTIFIED BY Redwagon;
```

This creates a user called Thelonius, gives him the right to log on, and assigns him the password Redwagon, all in one step. Once Thelonious is a recognized user, he or the DBA could use this same command to change the Redwagon password. Although convenient, there are limitations to this approach. It is impossible to have a user who cannot log on, even temporarily. If you want to keep a user from logging on, you have to REVOKE the CONNECT privilege, which "destroys" that user. Some implementations may allow you to create and destroy users independently of the privilege to log on.

When you grant the CONNECT privilege to a user you create that user. You must yourself have the DBA privilege to do this. If this user is to create base tables (instead of just views), she or he must also be granted the RESOURCE privilege. But this brings up another problem. If you attempted to revoke the CONNECT privilege from a user who has tables, the command would be rejected, because it would leave the tables without an owner, which is not allowed. You must drop all of a user's tables before revoking the CONNECT privilege from the user. If these tables are not empty, you will probably want to transfer their data to some other tables with an INSERT command that uses a query. You do not have to revoke the RESOURCE privilege separately; revoking CONNECT is sufficient to destroy the user.

Although the above is currently the standard approach to system privileges, it has considerable limitations. Alternative approaches are emerging that use more narrowly defined and precisely controlled system privileges.

These issues take us beyond the boundaries of the SQL standard as currently defined, and, in some implementations, may be addressed outside of SQL entirely. These things probably will not concern you much anyway, unless you are, in fact, a DBA or similar high-level user. Ordinary users need only be aware of system privileges conceptually, referring to their own documentation for specifics as needed.

SUMMARY

Privileges have enabled you to see SQL from a new angle, that of SQL actions performed by specific users in a specific database system. The GRANT command itself is simple enough: with it you grant one or more privileges on an object to one or more users. If you grant a privilege WITH GRANT OPTION to a user, that user can grant the privilege to others in turn.

You now understand the previously hinted-at uses of privileges on views—to refine privileges on the base tables, or as an alternative to constraints—and some of the advantages and disadvantages of this approach. System privileges, which are necessary but outside the realm of standard SQL, have been discussed in their most common form, so that they will be familiar when you encounter them.

Chapter 23 will continue to discuss broader issues in SQL, such as saving or reversing changes, creating your own names for other people's tables, and understanding what happens when different users attempt to access the same object at once.

Putting SQL to Work

1. Give Janet the right to change the ratings of the customers.
2. Give Stephen the right to give other users the right to query the Orders table.
3. Take the INSERT privilege on Salespeople away from Claire and all users to whom she has granted it.
4. Grant Jerry the right to insert or update the Customers table while keeping his possible rating values in the range of 100 to 500.
5. Allow Janet to query the Customers table, but restrict her access to those Customers whose rating is the lowest.

(See Appendix A for answers.)

23 Global Aspects of SQL

THIS CHAPTER DISCUSSES ASPECTS OF THE SQL language that have general relevance to the database as a whole, including the use of multiple names for data objects, the allocation of data storage, the reversing or saving of changes to the database, and the coordination of simultaneous actions by multiple users. This material enables you to configure your database, undo mistakes, and determine how one user's actions on a database will affect other users.

RENAMING TABLES

Whenever you refer in a command to a base table or view that you do not own, you must prefix it with the owner's name, so SQL knows where to look for it. Since this can, at times, be awkward, many implementations of SQL allow you to create synonyms for tables (this is not ANSI standard). A *synonym* is an alternative name, like a nickname, for a table. When you create a synonym, you own it, so there is no need to precede it with another user's authorization ID (user name).

If you have at least one privilege on one or more columns of a table, you can generally create a synonym for it. (Some implementations may have a special privilege for creating synonyms.) Adrian would create a synonym, say Clients, for Diane.Customers by using the CREATE SYNONYM command as follows:

```
CREATE SYNONYM Clients FOR Diane.Customers;
```

Now, Adrian could use the table name Clients in a command with the same effect as using Diane.Customers. The Clients synonym is owned and solely usable by Adrian.

RENAMING WITH THE SAME NAME

The user prefix is actually part of any table's name as far as SQL is concerned. Whenever you omit your own user name with a table you own, SQL fills it in for you. Therefore, two identical table names associated with different owners are actually not identical and need not lead to any confusion (at least not on SQL's part). This means that two users can create two completely unrelated tables with the same name, but it also means that one user could create a view based on and named after another user's table. This is sometimes done when the view is, for all practical purposes, to be considered the same as the table itself—for example, if the view merely uses the CHECK OPTION as a substitute for a CHECK constraint in the base table (refer to Chapter 22 for details). You can also create your own synonyms that are the same as the original table names. For example, Adrian could define Customers as his synonym for Diane.Customers like this:

```
CREATE SYNONYM Customers FOR Diane.Customers;
```

From SQL's standpoint there are now two different names for the table: Diane.Customers and Adrian.Customers. Each of the users, however, can simply refer to the table as Customers.

ONE NAME FOR EVERYBODY

If you plan to have the Customers table used by a great many users, it might be best to have them all refer to it by the same name. This will enable you, for instance, to use this name in your internal correspondence without qualification. To define a single name for all users, you create a public synonym. For example, if all users are to call the Customers table Customers, you would enter

```
CREATE PUBLIC SYNONYM Customers FOR Customers;
```

We are assuming you own the Customers table, so no user-name prefix is needed with the closing "Customers" of the command. Generally, public synonyms are created by owners of the objects or highly privileged users, such as DBA's. Users must still be granted privileges on the Customers table in order to access it. Even though the name is public, the table itself is not. Public synonyms are considered to be owned by PUBLIC, not by their creators.

DROPPING SYNONYMS

Public and other synonyms can be dropped with the DROP SYNONYM command. Synonyms are dropped by their owners, except for public synonyms, which are dropped by appropriately privileged individuals, usually DBA's. To drop his synonym Clients, now that the public synonym Customers is available, Adrian would enter

```
DROP SYNONYM Clients;
```

The Customers table itself is, of course, not affected.

HOW IS THE DATABASE ALLOCATED TO USERS?

Tables and other data objects are stored in the database in association with the particular users who own them. In a sense, you could say that they are stored in the "user's name space", although this does not neccessarily reflect any physical location, but is, like most things in SQL, strictly a logical construct. The fact is, however, that data objects have to be stored in some physical sense, and the amount of storage that can be used by a particular object or user at a given time is finite. After all, no computer has instant access to an infinite supply of media (disk, tape, or internal memory) for storing data. Moreover, SQL performance is enhanced if the logical structure of the data is reflected in some physical way that commands can take advantage of.

In larger SQL systems, a database will be divided into areas called *databasespaces* or *tablespaces*. These are areas of stored information that are arranged so that the information within them is close together for the purposes of executing commands; that is, the program does not have to search far and wide for information that is grouped in a single databasespace. Although the physical details of this are implementation dependent, it is expedient to operate on these areas within SQL itself. Systems that employ databasespaces (hereafter abbreviated as *dbspaces*) generally allow you to treat them as objects in SQL commands.

Dbspaces are created with a CREATE DBSPACE, an ACQUIRE DBSPACE, or a CREATE TABLESPACE command, depending on the implementation. One dbspace can accomodate any number of users, and a single user can have access to multiple dbspaces. The privilege to create tables, although it can be granted across the database, is often granted on a specific dbspace.

We can create a dbspace called Sampletables, with the following command:

```
CREATE DBSPACE Sampletables
    (pctindex    10,
    pctfree      25);
```

The pctindex parameter specifies what percentage of the dbspace is to be set aside to store indexes on tables. Pctfree is the percentage of the dbspace that is set aside to allow tables to expand the size of their rows (ALTER TABLE can add columns or increase the size of columns, making each row longer. This is the expansion that room is being allotted for). There are usually other parameters you can specify as well, which vary from product to product. Most products will provide automatic default values, so that you can create dbspaces without specifying parameters. The dbspace may have a specific size limitation, or it may be allowed to grow indefinitely with the tables.

Once a dbspace has been created, users are granted the right to create objects in it. You could grant Diane the right to create tables in Sampletables like this:

```
GRANT RESOURCE ON Sampletables TO Diane;
```

This enables you to allocate more specifically the data storage available. The first dbspace assigned to a given user is generally the one where all of his or her objects will be created by default. Users with access to multiple dbspaces can specify where they want a particular object to be placed.

In dividing up your database into dbspaces, you should keep in mind the types of operations that you will run frequently. Tables that you know will be joined frequently, or that have one referencing the other in a foreign key, could go well together in a dbspace.

For example, you can tell from the design of the sample tables, that the Orders table will often be joined to one or both of the other two, because the Orders table uses values from both of those tables. Other things being equal, these three tables should go on the same dbspace, regardless of who owns them. The possible presence of foreign-key constraints in the Orders table simply makes the case for sharing a dbspace stronger.

WHEN DOES A CHANGE BECOME PERMANENT?

It is easy in visualizing a database environment to picture hoards of users entering and changing data constantly, assuming that, if the system is well designed, it will function without glitches. In the real world, however, mistakes due to human or computer error happen all the time, and one of the things that good computer programmers have learned is to give people ways of undoing their actions.

A SQL command that affects the content or structure of the database—a DML update command or a DROP TABLE command, for instance—is not necessarily irreversible. You can determine after the fact whether a given group of one or more commands will effect permanent changes to the database, or be disregarded. For this purpose, commands are treated in groups called *transactions*.

A transaction is begun whenever you initiate a session with SQL. All commands you enter will be part of this same transaction, until you complete it by entering either a COMMIT WORK or a ROLLBACK WORK command. COMMIT will make all of the changes affected by the transaction permanent, and ROLLBACK will reverse them. A new transaction is begun after each COMMIT or ROLLBACK command. This process is known as transaction processing.

The syntax to make all of your changes since logging on, or since the last COMMIT or ROLLBACK, permanent is

```
COMMIT WORK;
```

The syntax to reverse them is

```
ROLLBACK WORK;
```

In many implementations, you set a parameter called something like AUTOCOMMIT. This will automatically commit all actions that execute normally. Actions that produce errors are automatically rolled back in any case. If this is offered on your system, you may choose to have all of your actions committed with a command like this:

```
SET AUTOCOMMIT ON;
```

You could return to regular transaction processing with this command:

```
SET AUTOCOMMIT OFF;
```

It is also possible for AUTOCOMMIT to be automatically set on for you by the system when you log in.

If a user session terminates abnormally—if the system crashes or the user reboots, for example—the current transaction will automatically be rolled back. This is one reason why, if you are doing your transaction processing by hand, you want to divide up your commands into many different transactions. A single transaction should not contain a lot of unrelated commands; in fact, it can frequently consist of a single command. Transactions that include an entire group of unrelated changes leave you no choice but to save or reject the whole group, when you probably want only to reverse one specific change. A good rule of thumb to follow is to have your transactions consist of single or of closely related commands.

For example, suppose you want to remove salesperson Motika from the database. Before you delete her from the Salespeople table, you first should do something with her orders and her customers. (If the foreign-key constraints are appropriately used, and your system, following ANSI, restricts parent key changes, you would have no choice but to do this. It is appropriate to do it in any case.)

One logical solution would be to set the snum on her orders to NULL, so that no salesperson receives a commission on those orders, while giving her customers to Peel. Then you could remove her from the Salespeople table:

```
UPDATE Orders
    SET snum = NULL
    WHERE snum = 1004;

UPDATE Customers
    SET snum = 1001
    WHERE snum = 1004;

DELETE FROM Salespeople
    WHERE snum = 1004;
```

If you had a problem deleting Motika (perhaps there is another foreign key referencing her that you did not know about or account for), you might want to reverse all of the changes you made until the problem could be identified and resolved. Therefore, this would be a good group of commands to treat as a single transaction. You could precede it with a COMMIT, and terminate it with a COMMIT or a ROLLBACK.

HOW SQL DEALS WITH MULTIPLE USERS AT ONCE

SQL is frequently used in multi-user environments—environments where more than one user can perform actions on the database at the same time. This creates a potential for clashes between the various actions performed. For example, suppose you are performing the following command on the Salespeople table:

```
UPDATE Salespeople
    SET comm = comm * 2
    WHERE sname LIKE 'R%';
```

While this command is executing, Diane enters this query:

```
SELECT city, AVG (comm)
   FROM Salespeople
   GROUP BY city;
```

Will the averages Diane gets reflect the changes you make to the table? It may not be important whether they do or not, but it is important that they reflect either all or none of the changed commission values. Any intermediate result is purely the accidental and unpredictable result of the order in which the values were physically altered, and the output of queries is not supposed to depend on physical details, nor should it be accidental and unpredictable.

Consider another point. Suppose you find a mistake and roll back your update after Diane gets her output. Now Diane has a series of averages based on changes that were cancelled, but she has no way of knowing her information is inaccurate.

The handling of simultaneous transactions is called *concurrency*, and there are a number of possible problems that can arise in it. Here are some examples:

- Updates can be made without regard to one another. For instance, a salesperson could query an inventory table, find ten pieces of a merchandise item on stock, and order six of them for a customer. Before this change is made, another salesperson queries the table and orders seven of this same item for one of his customers.
- Changes to the database can be rolled back after their effect has already been felt, as when you cancelled your mistake after Diane got her output.
- One action can be affected by the partial result of another action, as when Diane took averages while you were performing an update. Although this is not always a problem, in many cases functions such as aggregates should reflect the state of the database at a point of relative stability. Someone auditing the books, for example, should

be able to go back and determine that Diane's averages existed at some point in time, and could have remained the same had no further updates been made after that point. This is not the case if an update is in progress while the function is being evaluated.

- Deadlock. Two users can attempt to perform actions that interfere with one another. This can occur, for example, if two users try to change both a foreign- and its parent-key value at the same time.

There are any number of nightmare scenarios that one could envision if simultaneous transactions were uncontrolled. Luckily, SQL provides *concurrency controls* to address precisely these issues. What ANSI specifies for concurrency control is simply that all simultaneous commands shall be executed in such a way that the effect is the same as if no command were issued until the previous one was completed (including COMMIT or ROLLBACK where appropriate).

The strictest interpretation of this would simply not allow a table to be accessed by more than one transaction at a time. In many business situations, however, the need to have the database instantly accessible to multiple users requires some compromise with concurrency control. Most SQL implementations offer users options, allowing them to strike their own balance between data consistency and database accessibility. These options can be controlled by the user, the DBA, or both. Sometimes they are actually handled outside of SQL proper, even though they affect SQL operations.

The mechanisms SQL implementors use to control concurrent operations are called *locks*. Locks restrict certain operations on the database while other operations or transactions are active. The restricted operations are lined up in a queue and executed when the lock is released (some implementations give you the option of specifying NOWAIT, which will cause the command to be rejected instead of queued up, leaving you free to do something else).

Locks in multi-user systems are essential. Therefore, there will be some kind of default locking scheme that is applied to all commands on the database. This default scheme may be defined for the entire database, or your implementation may allow you to use it as a parameter in a CREATE DBSPACE or an ALTER DBSPACE command, and thereby to define it differently for different dbspaces. In addition, systems typically provide some sort of deadlock detector that finds situations where two operations have locks that are blocking one another. In this case, one of the commands will be rolled back and have its lock released.

Since the terminology and specifics of locking schemes vary from product to product, we will pattern the following discussion on IBM's database product DB2 as an example, emphasizing its most generally applicable aspects. IBM is a leader in this field (as in many others), so its approach is widely emulated. On the other hand, some implementations may vary greatly from this in syntax and in functional details, but the major effects are likely to be similar.

TYPES OF LOCKS

There are two basic kinds of locks: share locks and exclusive locks. *Share locks* (or *S-locks*) can be placed by more than one user at a time. This enables any number of users to access the data, but not to change it. *Exclusive locks* (or *X-locks*) allow no one but the owner of the lock to access the data at all. Exclusive locks are used for commands that change the content or structure of the table. They are in effect until the end of the transaction. Share locks are used for queries. How long they are in effect depends on the isolation level.

What is the *isolation level* of the lock? It is what determines how much of the table the lock ties up. In DB2, there are three isolation levels, two of which can apply to both share and exclusive locks, with the third limited to share locks. These are controlled by commands issued outside of SQL itself, so we will explain them without elaborating on exact syntax. The exact syntax of commands related to locking is different for different implementations. The following discussion is useful primarily on a conceptual level.

A *read repeatability* isolation level ensures that, within a given transaction, all records retrieved by queries will not change. As records updated in a transaction are subject to an exclusive lock until the transaction terminates, these cannot be changed in any case. With queries, on the other hand, read repeatability means that you can decide in advance which rows you want to lock and execute a query that selects them. Simply by executing the query, you ensure that no changes will be made to those rows until you terminate the current transaction. While read repeatability does protect the user who places the lock, it can also slow things up considerably.

A *cursor stability* level prevents each record from being changed while it is being read or read while it is being changed. The latter case, being an exclusive lock, applies until the change is committed or rolled back. Therefore, when you update a group of records using cursor stability, those particular records are locked until the transaction is finished, which is the same effect as read repeatability. The difference between the two is in the effect on queries. With cursor stability, rows of a table other than those a query is examining at a given time can be changed.

The third DB2 isolation level is *read only*. Read only takes a "snapshot" of the data; it doesn't really lock the table at all. Therefore, it cannot be used with update commands. Whatever the content of the table as a whole is at the moment the command is executed will be what is reflected in the query output. This is not necessarily the case with cursor stability. Read only locks ensure that your output will be internally consistent, if not necessarily up to the second, without tying up large portions of the table, as read repeatability does. Read only is handy on occasions such as when you make reports, which have to be internally consistent and are likely to access many or all rows of a table, but need not tie up the database.

OTHER WAYS OF LOCKING DATA

Some implementations do locking by page instead of row. This can either be an option under your control or something built into the design of the system. A page is a unit of memory storage, commonly 1024 bytes. A page will consist of one or more rows of a table, likely accompanied by indexes and other peripheral information, and perhaps even some rows from another table. If you lock by page instead of by row, all of the data on that page is locked just as the individual row would have been, in accordance with the isolation levels explained above.

The main advantage of this approach is in performance. When SQL doesn't have to keep locking and unlocking rows individually, it can operate faster. On the other hand, this sullies SQL's hands with implementation details that the language was designed to rise above, and arbitrarily locks rows that may not need to be locked.

A similar option available on some systems is dbspace locking. Dbspaces tend to be larger than pages, so this approach accentuates both the performance advantages and the logical disadvantages of page locking. You are generally better off to go with lower-level locking unless there seem to be noticeable performance problems attributable to it.

SUMMARY

The key things you have learned about in this chapter are:

- Synonyms, or how to create new names for data objects.
- Databasespaces (dbspaces), or how to divide up available storage in the database.
- Transaction processing, or how to save or disregard changes to the database.
- Concurrency control, or how SQL keeps commands from interfering with one another.

Synonyms are objects in the sense that they have names and (sometimes) owners, but of course they have no independent existence apart from the table whose name they replace. They can be public and therefore accessible to everyone who has access to the object, or they can be owned by a specific user.

Dbspaces are subsections of the database that are allocated to users. Related tables, such as tables that will frequently be joined, are best stored in the same dbspace.

COMMIT and ROLLBACK are the commands used to take all changes to the database since either the previous COMMIT or ROLLBACK or the beginning of the session and save or disregard them as a group.

Concurrency controls determine to what extent simultaneous commands will affect one another. These are adjustable because of the trade-off between database performance and isolation of the effects of commands.

Putting SQL to Work

1. Create a database space called "Myspace" that allocates 15 percent of its space to indexes, and 40 percent to row expansion.
2. You have been granted SELECT on Diane's Orders table. Enter a command so that you will be able to refer to this table as "Orders" without using the name "Diane" as a prefix.
3. If there is a power failure, what should happen to all changes contained in the current transaction?
4. If you cannot look at a row because a lock is in place, what kind of lock is it?
5. If you want totals, maximums, and averages for all orders, and you don't want to prevent others from using the table, which isolation level is appropriate?

(See Appendix A for answers.)

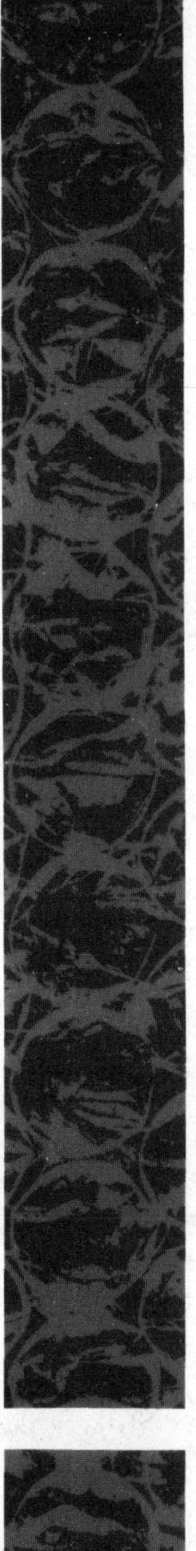

24

How a SQL Database Is Kept in Order

IN THIS CHAPTER, YOU WILL LEARN HOW A TYPICAL SQL database keeps itself organized. Not surprisingly, it is done with a relational database created and maintained by the program itself. You can access these tables yourself for information about privileges, tables, indexes, and so on. This chapter will show you some typical contents of such a database.

THE SYSTEM CATALOG

In order to operate as a SQL database, your computer system has to keep track of a lot of different things: tables, views, indexes, synonyms, privileges, users, and so on. There are various ways to do this, but clearly the most logical, efficient, sensible, and consistent way in a relational environment is to store this information in tables. This enables the computer to arrange and manipulate the information it needs, using the same procedures as it does to arrange and manipulate the data it stores for your needs.

Although this is an implementation matter, and not part of the ANSI standard as such, most SQL databases do, in fact, use a set of SQL tables for internal information. This set is called variously the *system catalog*, the *data dictionary*, or simply the *system tables*. (The term *data dictionary* can also refer to a more general repository of data, including information on the physical parameters of the database that are kept out of SQL. Therefore, there are database programs that have both a system catalog and a data dictionary.)

The tables of the system catalog are like other SQL tables: rows and columns of data. For example, one table of the catalog typically contains information about the tables in the database, with one row for each database table; another contains information about the various columns of the tables, with one row per column, and so on. The catalog tables are considered to be created and owned by the database itself, identified by a special name such as SYSTEM. The database creates these tables and updates them automatically as the system is used; catalog tables cannot be directly subjected to update commands. If this were to happen, it would greatly confuse the system and make it disfunctional.

In many systems, however, the catalog can be queried by users. This is very useful, because it enables you to find out specific things about the database you are using. Of course, all information is not generally available to all users. Like other tables, access to the catalog is restricted to users with the appropriate privileges.

Since the catalog is owned by the system itself, there is some ambiguity as to who has and can grant privileges on it. Generally, catalog privileges will be granted by a superuser, such as a system administrator logged on as SYSTEM, or a DBA. In addition, some privileges may be granted to users automatically.

A TYPICAL SYSTEM CATALOG

Let's look at some of the tables we might find in a typical system catalog:

TABLE	*INFORMATION REGARDING*
SYSTEMCATALOG	Tables (base and views)
SYSTEMCOLUMNS	Columns of tables
SYSTEMTABLES	Catalog View of SYSTEMCATALOG
SYSTEMINDEXES	Indexes on tables
SYSTEMUSERAUTH	Users of database
SYSTEMTABAUTH	Object privileges of users
SYSTEMCOLAUTH	Column privileges of users
SYSTEMSYNONS	Synonyms for tables

Now, if our DBA grants user Stephen the right to look at SYSTEMCATALOG, with this command

```
GRANT SELECT ON SYSTEMCATALOG TO Stephen;
```

Stephen can see some information about all of the tables in the database (we will assume our DBA, Chris, owns our three sample tables, and that Adrian owns the Londoncust view).

```
SELECT tname, owner, numcolumns, type, CO
    FROM SYSTEMCATALOG;
```

The output for this query is shown in Figure 24.1.

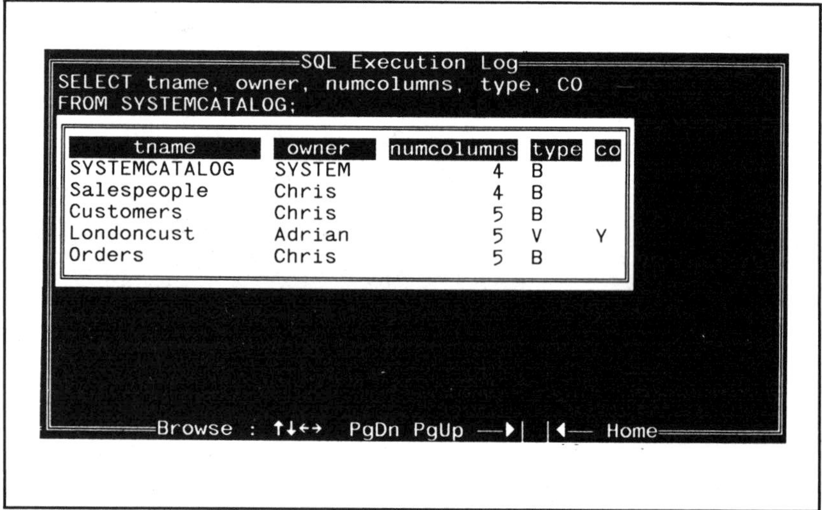

SQL Execution Log
SELECT tname, owner, numcolumns, type, CO
FROM SYSTEMCATALOG;

tname	owner	numcolumns	type	co
SYSTEMCATALOG	SYSTEM	4	B	
Salespeople	Chris	4	B	
Customers	Chris	5	B	
Londoncust	Adrian	5	V	Y
Orders	Chris	5	B	

Browse : ↑↓←→ PgDn PgUp —▸| |◂— Home

Figure 24.1: The content of the SYSTEMCATALOG table

As you can see, each row represents a table. The first column is its name; the second, the name of the user who owns it; the third, the number of columns it contains; and the fourth, a one-letter code, either B (for base table) or V (for a view). The last column is NULL unless the type is V; this column indicates whether or not check option has been specified.

Note that SYSTEMCATALOG lists itself as one of the tables present. For the sake of brevity, we have omitted the rest of the system-catalog from the output of this command. The system-catalog tables themselves ordinarily would show up in SYSTEMCATALOG.

USING VIEWS ON CATALOG TABLES

Since SYSTEMCATALOG is a table, you can use it in a view. In fact, we have assumed that there is one such view called SYSTEMTABLES. This view of SYSTEMCATALOG includes only those tables that constitute the system catalog; ordinary (database) tables, such as Salespeople, will show up in SYSTEMCATALOG, but not in SYSTEMTABLES. Let's assume that only catalog tables are owned by SYSTEM. If you wanted, you could define another view that specifically excludes the catalog tables:

```
CREATE VIEW Datatables
    AS SELECT *
        FROM SYSTEMCATALOG
        WHERE owner <> 'SYSTEM';
```

LETTING USERS SEE (ONLY) THEIR OWN OBJECTS There are other uses for views of the catalog. Suppose you want each user to be able to query the catalog for information only on the tables that he or she owns. Since the value of USER in a SQL command always stands for the authorization ID of the user issuing the command, it can be used to give users access only to their own tables. You can first create the following view:

```
CREATE VIEW Owntables
    AS SELECT *
        FROM SYSTEMCATALOG
        WHERE Owner = USER;
```

Now you can grant all users access to this view:

```
GRANT SELECT ON Owntables TO PUBLIC;
```

Each user will now be able to SELECT only those rows from SYSTEMCATALOG that show him to be the owner.

VIEWING SYSTEMCOLUMNS One possible extension of this is to allow each user to view the SYSTEMCOLUMNS table for the columns of her own tables. First, let's look at the portion of the SYSTEMCOLUMNS table that describes our sample tables (in other words, excluding the catalog itself):

tname	cname	datatype	cnumber	tabowner
Salespeople	snum	integer	1	Diane
Salespeople	sname	char	2	Diane
Salespeople	city	char	3	Diane
Salespeople	comm	decimal	4	Diane
Customers	cnum	integer	1	Claire
Customers	cname	char	2	Claire
Customers	city	char	3	Claire
Customers	rating	integer	4	Claire
Customers	snum	integer	5	Claire
Orders	onum	integer	1	Diane
Orders	odate	date	2	Diane
Orders	amt	decimal	3	Diane
Orders	cnum	integer	4	Diane
Orders	snum	integer	5	Diane

As you can see, each row of this table represents a column of a table in the database. Since each column of a given table must have a different name, as must each table of a given user, all combinations of user, table, and column names will be different from one another. Therefore the tname (table name), tabowner (table owner), and cname (column name) columns together constitute the primary key of this table. The datatype column is self-explanatory. The cnumber (column number) column indicates the placement of the column within its table. For the sake of brevity, we have omitted the column's length, precision, and scale. These indicate the size of the column, with the first applicable to character, and the others to number columns.

For reference, here is the row from SYSTEMCATALOG that refers to this table:

tname	owner	numcolumns	type	CO
SYSTEMCOLUMNS	System	8	B	

Some SQL implementations may provide you with more data than this on the columns, but these are the basics.

To illustrate the procedure suggested at the outset of this section, here is the way to allow each user to see the SYSTEMCOLUMNS information only for his own tables:

```
CREATE VIEW Owncolumns
    AS SELECT *
        FROM SYSTEMCOLUMNS
        WHERE tabowner = USER;

GRANT SELECT ON Owncolumns TO PUBLIC;
```

COMMENTING ON THE CATALOG CONTENTS

Most versions of SQL allow you to put comments in a special-remarks column of the SYSTEMCATALOG and SYSTEMCOLUMNS catalog tables; this is handy, because these tables are not always self explanatory. For the sake of simplicity, we have been omitting this column from our illustrations of these commands until now.

You use the COMMENT ON command with a string of text to label any row in one of these tables. State TABLE to comment on SYSTEMCATALOG, and COLUMN for SYSTEMCOLUMNS. For example

```
COMMENT ON TABLE Chris.Orders
    IS 'Current Customer Orders';
```

The text will be placed in the remarks column of SYSTEMCATALOG. Usually, the maximum length of remarks is 254 characters. The comment itself is specific to a particular row, the one with the tname = Orders, and owner = Chris. We see this comment in the row for the Orders table in SYSTEMCATALOG:

```
SELECT tname, remarks
    FROM SYSTEMCATALOG
    WHERE tname = 'Orders'
        AND owner = 'Chris';
```

The output for this query is shown in Figure 24.2.

SYSTEMCOLUMNS works just the same. First, we create the comment:

```
COMMENT ON COLUMN Orders.onum
    IS 'Order #';
```

Now we can select this row from SYSTEMCOLUMNS:

```
SELECT cnumber, datatype, cname, remarks
    FROM SYSTEMCOLUMNS
    WHERE tname = 'Orders'
        AND tabowner = 'Chris'
        AND cname = 'onum';
```

The output for this query is shown in Figure 24.3.

To change a comment, you simply enter a new COMMENT ON command for the same row. The old comment will be overwritten. If you want to eliminate a comment, overwrite it with an empty comment, like this:

```
COMMENT ON COLUMN Orders.onum
    IS '';
```

This empty comment will eliminate the previous remark.

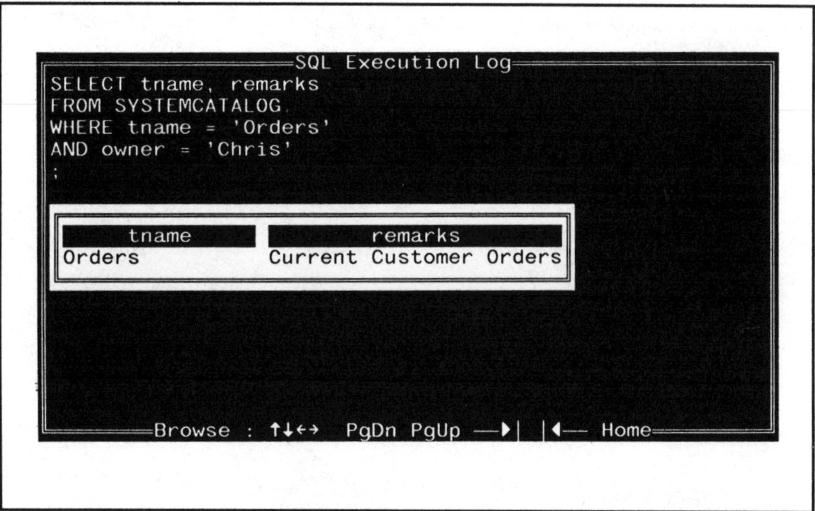

Figure 24.2: A comment on SYSTEMCATALOG

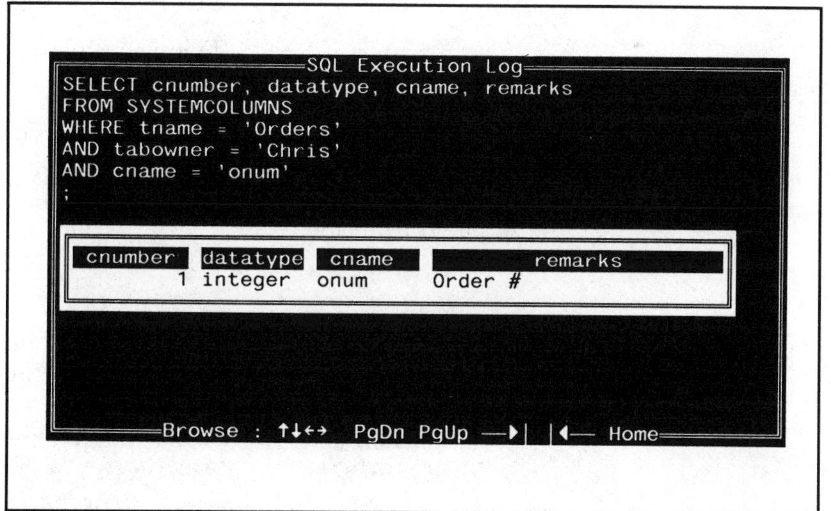

Figure 24.3: A comment on SYSTEMCOLUMNS

THE REST OF THE CATALOG

Here are the definitions of the rest of our system tables, with a sample query on each:

SYSTEMINDEXES—INDEXES IN THE DATABASE

The names of the columns in the SYSTEMINDEXES table and their descriptions are as follows:

COLUMN	DESCRIPTION
iname	The name of the index (used to drop it)
iowner	The name of the user who created the index
tname	The name of the table that contains the index
cnumber	The number of the column in the table
tabowner	The user who owns the table that contains the index
numcolumns	The number of columns in the index
cposition	The position of the current column among those in index
isunique	Whether the index is unique (Y or N)

A SAMPLE QUERY Assume a nonunique index, called salesperson, on the snum column of the Customers table:

```
SELECT iname, iowner, tname, cnumber, isunique
    FROM SYSTEMINDEXES
    WHERE iname = 'salesperson';
```

The output for this query is shown in Figure 24.4.

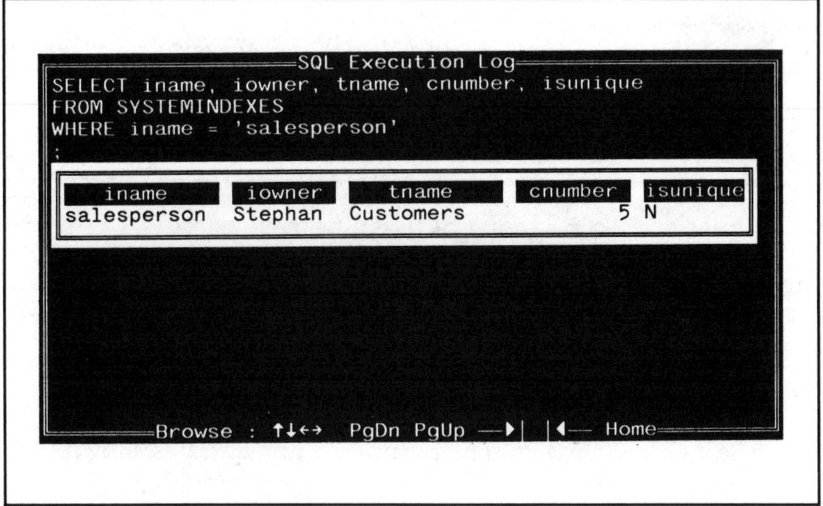
```
SQL Execution Log
SELECT iname, iowner, tname, cnumber, isunique
FROM SYSTEMINDEXES
WHERE iname = 'salesperson'
;
```

iname	iowner	tname	cnumber	isunique
salesperson	Stephan	Customers	5	N

Figure 24.4: A row from the SYSTEMINDEXES table

SYSTEMUSERAUTH—USERS AND SYSTEM PRIVLEGES IN THE DATABASE

The column names for SYSTEMUSERAUTH and their descriptions are as follows:

COLUMN	***DESCRIPTION***
username	The authorization ID of the user
password	The password the user enters to log on
resource	Whether the user has the RESOURCE privilege
dba	Whether user has the DBA privilege

We are assuming a simple system-privilege scheme such as that suggested in Chapter 22, where the three system privileges that exist are CONNECT, RESOURCE, and DBA. All users have CONNECT by definition, so it is not listed in the above table. The possible values of the resource and dba columns are Y (the user has the privilege) and N (the user does not have the privilege). The passwords are available only to highly privileged users, if any. Therefore this table can generally only be queried for information on users and system privileges.

A SAMPLE QUERY To find all users who have the RESOURCE privilege, and see which of them were DBA's, you would enter the following statement:

```
SELECT username, dba
    FROM SYSTEMUSERAUTH
    WHERE resource = 'Y';
```

The output for this query is shown in Figure 24.5.

SYSTEMTABAUTH—OBJECT PRIVILEGES THAT ARE NOT COLUMN SPECIFIC

These are the names of the columns in the SYSTEMTAB-AUTH table and their descriptions:

COLUMN	*DESCRIPTION*
username	The user who has the privileges
grantor	The user who granted privileges to username
tname	The name of table on which privileges exist
owner	The owner of tname
selauth	Whether the user has the SELECT privilege
insauth	Whether the user has the INSERT privilege
delauth	Whether the user has the DELETE privilege

The possible values for each of the object privileges listed (all of which have column names ending in "auth") are Y, N, and G. A G indicates that the user has the privilege with the grant option. In each row, at least one of these columns must have a value other than N.

Figure 24.5: Users who have the RESOURCE privilege

The first four columns of this table constitute its primary key. This means that every combination of tname, owner (remember that two different tables with different owners can have the same name), user, and grantor must be unique. Each row of this table contains all privileges (that are not column specific) granted by one specific user to another specific user on a particular object. UPDATE and REFERENCES, being privileges that can be column specific, are in a different catalog table. If a user gets privileges on a table from more than one other user, there will be separate rows created in this table. This is necessary to track cascades when privileges are revoked.

A SAMPLE QUERY To find all SELECT, INSERT, and DELETE privileges that Adrian has granted on the Customers table, you would enter the following (the output is shown in Figure 24.6):

```
SELECT username, selauth, insauth, delauth
    FROM SYSTEMTABAUTH
    WHERE grantor = 'Adrian'
        AND tname = 'Customers';
```

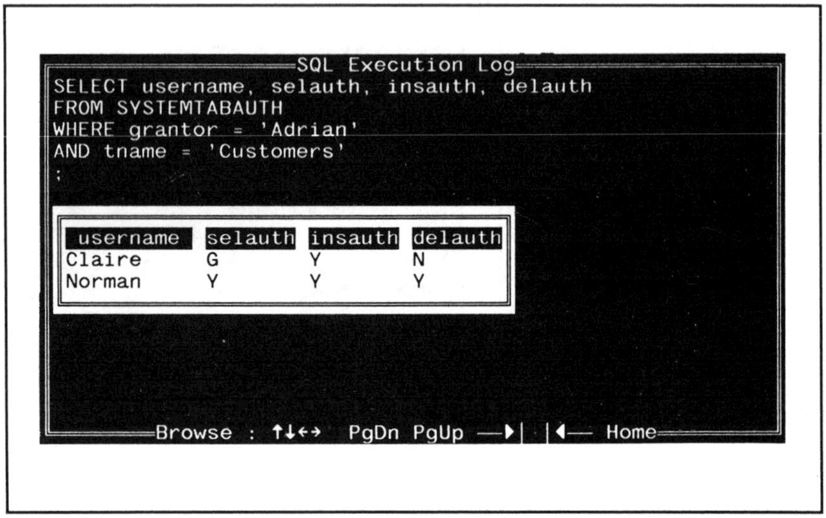

```
SQL Execution Log
SELECT username, selauth, insauth, delauth
FROM SYSTEMTABAUTH
WHERE grantor = 'Adrian'
AND tname = 'Customers'
;

 username   selauth  insauth  delauth
Claire      G        Y        N
Norman      Y        Y        Y

Browse : ↑↓←→  PgDn PgUp —▶|  |◀— Home
```

Figure 24.6: Users granted privileges on customers by Adrian

The above shows that Adrian granted Claire the INSERT and SELECT privileges on the Customers table, the latter with the grant option. To Norman, he granted SELECT, INSERT, and DELETE, but gave the grant option on none of them. If Clair had the DELETE privilege on the Customers table from some other source, it would not show up in this particular query of the table.

SYSTEMCOLAUTH

COLUMN	***DESCRIPTION***
username	The user who has the privileges
grantor	The user who granted privileges to username
tname	The name of table on which privileges exist
cname	The name of the column on which privileges exist
owner	The owner of tname

Column	*Description*
updauth	Whether the user has the UPDATE privilege on this column
refauth	Whether the user has the REFERENCES privilege on this column

Updauth and refauth can be Y, N, or G; they cannot both be N in the same row. It is the first five columns of this table that constitute the primary key. This is different from SYSTEMTABAUTH's primary key in that it includes the cname field, which specifies a particular column of the table in question to which one or both privileges apply. A separate row in this table will exist for each column of any given table on which one user has been granted column-specific privileges by another. As with SYSTEMTABAUTH, the same privilege will be listed in more than one row of this table if it has been granted by more than one user.

A SAMPLE QUERY To find out which columns of which tables you have the REFERENCES privilege on, you would enter the following (the output is shown in Figure 24.7):

```
SELECT owner, tname, cname
    FROM SYSTEMCOLAUTH
    WHERE refauth IN ('Y', 'G')
        AND username = USER
    ORDER BY 1, 2;
```

The preceding illustrates that two tables that have different owners but the same name are, indeed, two different tables (this is not the same as two synonyms for a single table).

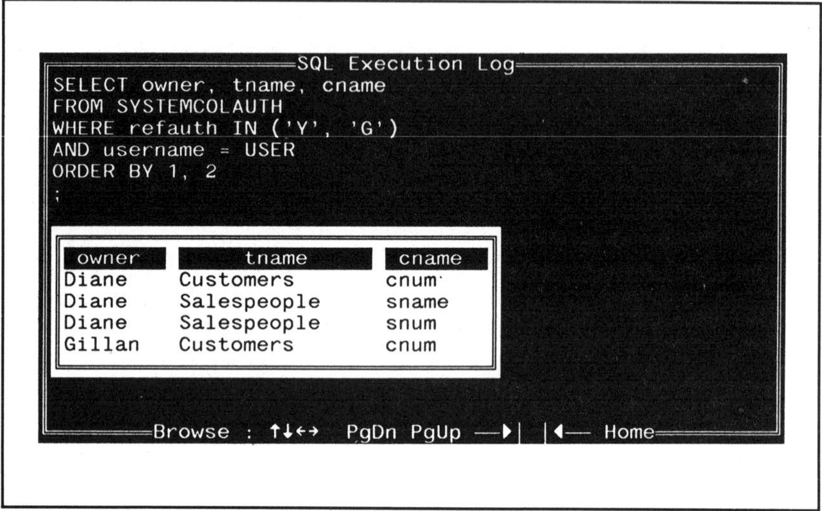

Figure 24.7: Columns that user has REFERENCES privilege on

SYSTEMSYNONS—SYNONYMS FOR TABLES IN THE DATABASE

These are the names of the columns in the SYSTEMSYNONS table and their descriptions:

COLUMN	*DESCRIPTION*
synonym	The name of the synonym
synowner	The user who owns the synonym (may be PUBLIC)
tname	The name of table as used by the owner
tabowner	The name of the user who owns the table

A SAMPLE QUERY Assume Adrian has a synonym Clients for Diane's table Customers, and that there is a public synonym Customers for the same table. You query the table for all synonyms on the Customers table (the output is shown in Figure 24.8):

```
SELECT *
    FROM SYSTEMSYNONS
    WHERE tname = 'Customers';
```

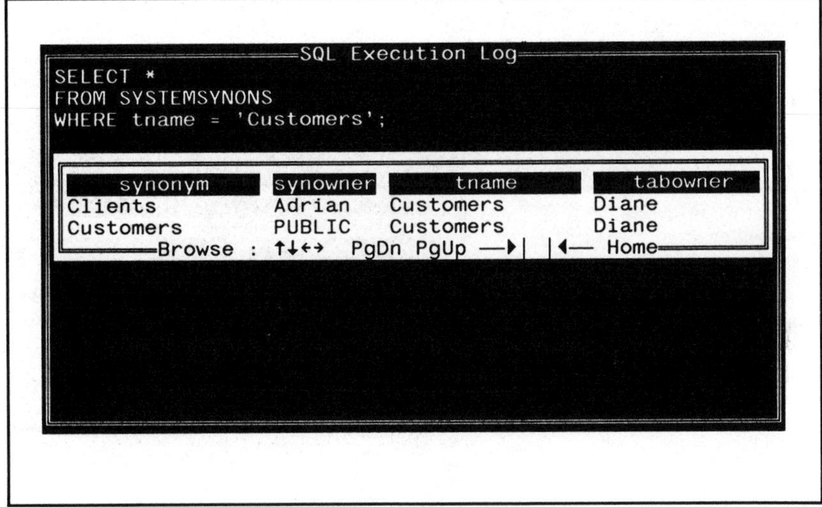

```
SELECT *
FROM SYSTEMSYNONS
WHERE tname = 'Customers';
```

synonym	synowner	tname	tabowner
Clients	Adrian	Customers	Diane
Customers	PUBLIC	Customers	Diane

Figure 24.8: Synonyms for the Customers table

OTHER USES OF THE CATALOG

Naturally, you can perform more sophisticated queries on the system catalog. Joins, for instance, can be quite handy. This command lets you see the columns of the tables and the indexes based on each (the output is shown in Figure 24.9):

```
SELECT a.tname, a.cname, iname, cposition
    FROM SYSTEMCOLUMNS a, SYSTEMINDEXES b
    WHERE a.tabowner = b. tabowner
        AND a.tname = b.tname
        AND a.cnumber = b.cnumber
    ORDER BY 3 DESC, 2;
```

This shows two indexes, one each on the Customers and Salespeople tables. The latter is a single-column index called salesno on the snum field; it was placed first because of the descending (reverse alphabetical) sort on the iname column. The other index, custsale, is used by salespeople to retrieve their customers. It is based on the combination of the snum and cnum fields within the Customers table, with the snum field coming first in the index, as shown by the cposition field.

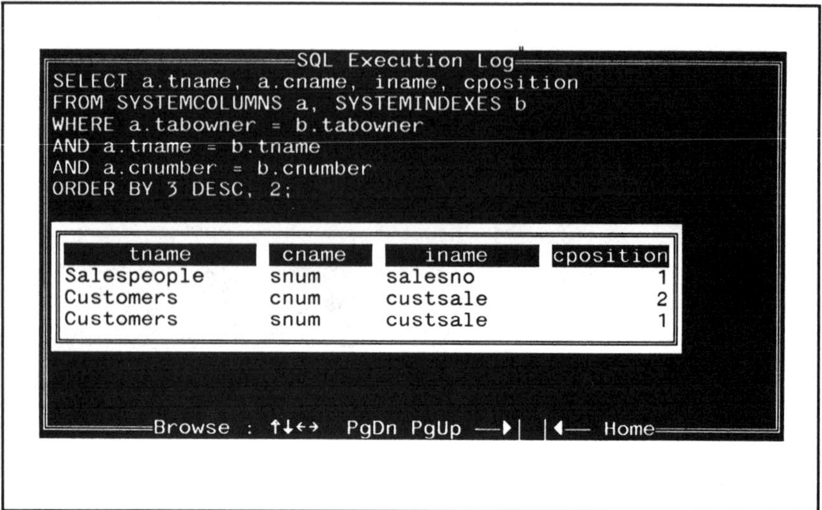

Figure 24.9: Columns and their indexes

Subqueries also can be used. Here is a way to look at the column data for columns of the catalog tables only:

```
SELECT *
   FROM SYSTEMCOLUMNS
   WHERE tname IN
      (SELECT tname
         FROM SYSTEMCATALOG);
```

In the interest of brevity, we will not illustrate the output of this command, which consists of a single entry for each column of every catalog table. You might want to place this query in a view, called, let's say, SYSTEMTABCOLS, to go with the SYSTEMTABLES view.

SUMMARY

To summarize, SQL systems use a set of tables called the system catalog to structure the database. These tables can be queried but not updated. In addition, you can add comment columns to (and remove them from) the SYSTEMCATALOG and

SYSTEMCOLUMNS tables. Creating views on these tables is an excellent way to determine exactly which information users will be able to access.

Now that you understand the catalog, you have completed your orientation to SQL as used in interactive situations. The next chapter of this book will deal with SQL as used in programs that are written primarily in other languages but are able to benefit from SQL's power and flexibility in interacting with database tables.

Putting SQL to Work

1. Query the catalog to produce, for each table with more than four columns, the table's name, the owner, and the names and data types of the columns.
2. Query the catalog to find out how many synonyms exist for each table in the database. Remember that the same synonym owned by two different users is in effect two different synonyms.
3. Find out how many tables have indexes on more than fifty percent of their columns.

(See Appendix A for answers.)

25

Using SQL With Other Lanuages (Embedded SQL)

IN THIS CHAPTER YOU WILL LEARN HOW SQL IS used to enhance programs written in other languages. Although the nonprocedural character of SQL gives it many strengths, as you have seen, it also produces a great many limitations. To overcome these limitations, you can embed SQL in programs written in one or another procedural language. For our examples, we have chosen Pascal in the belief that this language is the easiest for the uninitiated to interpret, and because Pascal is one of the languages for which ANSI has a (semiofficial) standard.

WHAT IS INVOLVED IN EMBEDDING SQL

In order to embed SQL in another language, you must be using a software package that provides support for embedded SQL in that language as well as, naturally, support for the language itself. Obviously, you have to be familiar with the language you are using. Mainly, you will be using SQL commands to operate on database tables, passing output to and taking input from the program in which it is embedded, commonly referred to as the *host program* (which may or may not get them from or pass them to a user interactively).

WHY EMBED SQL?

Although we have spent some time illustrating what SQL can do, if you are an experienced programmer, you have probably noticed that it is not, in itself, very useful for writing programs. The most immediately apparent limitation is that, while SQL can accomplish a lot with a single command, interactive SQL basically does things one command at a time. The if. . . then, for. . . do, and while. . . repeat kinds of logical constructs used to structure most computer programs are absent, so you cannot base a decision about whether, how, or how long to perform an action on the result of another action. In addition, interactive SQL cannot do much with values besides entering them into tables, locating or deriving them with queries, and outputting them directly to some device.

The more traditional languages are, however, strong in precisely these areas. They are designed so that a programmer can begin a process and, based on the results, decide to do one thing or another, or to repeat an action until some condition is met, creating logical paths and loops. Values are stored in variables that can be used and changed by any number of commands. This enables you to prompt users for input or to read it from a file, and format the output in elaborate ways (converting numeric data to diagrams, for example).

The purpose of embedded SQL is to combine these strengths, allowing you to create complex procedural programs that address the database itself through SQL—letting you set aside the complexities of operating on tables in a procedural language that is not oriented to this kind of data structure, while maintaining the strengths of a procedural language.

HOW DO YOU EMBED SQL?

SQL commands are placed in the source code of the host program preceded by the phrase EXEC SQL (think: EXECute SQL). These include some commands that are special to the embedded form of SQL, which will be introduced in this chapter. Strictly speaking, the ANSI standard does not support embedded SQL as such. It supports a concept called *modules*, which are sets of SQL procedures called from, rather than embedded in, another language. Defining an official embedded SQL syntax would involve extending the official syntax of each language in which SQL is to be embedded—a long and unrewarding task, which ANSI chose to avoid. It does, however, provide four appendices (not part of the standard proper), which define embedded SQL syntax for four languages: COBOL, Pascal, FORTRAN, and PL/I. The language C is also widely supported, and other languages are occasionally used.

When you embed SQL commands in the text of a program that is written in another language, you must *precompile* the program before you compile it. A program called a *precompiler* (or a *preprocessor*) will go through the text of your program and convert SQL commands into a form usable by the main language. You then use a compiler to convert the program from source code to executable code, as usual.

According to the module-language approach defined by ANSI, the main program calls SQL procedures. These take parameters from, and return values to, the main program. A module can contain any number of procedures, each of which consists of a single SQL command. The idea is that the procedures can function in the same way regardless of which language they are embedded in (although a module must still identify the language of the host because of differences in data types between host languages).

Implementations can (and do) conform to the standard by executing embedded SQL in such a way that the effect is the same as if modules were explicitly defined. Generally, the precompiler will create a module, called an *access module*, for this purpose. Only one module, containing any number of SQL procedures, can exist for a given program. Placing SQL statements directly in the host code is easier and more practical than directly creating the modules as such.

Programs using embedded SQL are each associated with an authorization ID when they are executed. The authorization ID associated with a program must have all the privileges to perform the SQL operations executed in the program. Generally, the embedded SQL program logs on to the database as the user executing the program. The details of this are implementor defined, but it is likely to be necessary for you to include in your program a CONNECT or similar command to fulfill this function.

USING HOST LANGUAGE VARIABLES WITH SQL

The basic way in which the SQL and host-language portions of your programs will communicate with each other is through the values in variables. Of course, different languages recognize different data types for variables. ANSI defines SQL equivalents for the four host languages it recognizes—PL/I, Pascal, COBOL, and FORTRAN; these are detailed in Appendix B. The equivalents for other languages are implementor defined. Keep in mind, of course, that types such as DATE are not recognized by ANSI; therefore no equivalent data types for host languages exist in the standard. Also, more complex host-language data types, such as matrices, may not have SQL equivalents.

You can use variables from the host program in embedded SQL statements wherever you would use value expressions. (SQL, when used in this chapter, will refer to embedded SQL, unless otherwise indicated.) The current value of the variable will be the value used in the command. Host variables must

- Be declared in a SQL DECLARE SECTION (discussed shortly)
- Be of a compatible data type for their function in the SQL command (for example, a numeric type if they are to be inserted into a numeric field)
- Be assigned a value at the time they are used in the SQL command, unless the SQL command itself will assign a value
- Be preceded by a colon (:) when referred to in the SQL command

Since host variables are distinguished from SQL column names by a colon, you can use variables with the same names as your columns, if desired.

Suppose you have four variables in your program, called id_num, salesperson, loc, and comm. These contain values that you want to insert into the Salespeople table. You could embed the following SQL command in your program:

```
EXEC SQL INSERT INTO Salespeople
     VALUES (:id_num, :salesperson, :loc, :comm)
```

The current values of these variables would be put into the table. As you can see, the comm variable has the same name as the column its value is being inserted into; the rest of the variables do not. You will also notice that the semicolon at the end of the command has been omitted. That is because the proper termination for an embedded SQL command varies with the language.

For Pascal and PL/I, it is the semicolon; for COBOL, it is the word END-EXEC; and for FORTRAN, no termination mark is used. Other languages depend on the implementation, but we will use the semicolon for the sake of consistency with interactive SQL and with Pascal. Pascal terminates both embedded SQL and its own commands with a semicolon.

The way to make a command such as the above powerful is to enclose it in a loop and iterate it repeatedly with different values in the variables, such as in the following example:

```
while not end-of-file (input) do
    begin
    readln (id_num, salesperson, loc, comm);
    EXEC SQL INSERT INTO Salespeople
        VALUES (:id_num, :salesperson, :loc, :comm);
    end;
```

This Pascal program fragment defines a loop that will read values from a file, store them in the four named variables, store the values of those variables in the Salespeople table, and then read the next four values, repeating the process until the entire input file has been read. It assumes that each set of values is terminated with a carriage return (for those unfamiliar with Pascal, the readln function reads input and moves to the next line of the source). This gives you an easy way to transfer data from text files into a relational structure. Naturally, you can first process the data in whatever ways are possible in your host language, such as excluding commission under .12:

```
while not end-of-file (input) do
    begin
    readln (id_num, salesperson, loc, comm);
    if comm >= .12 then
    EXEC SQL INSERT INTO Salespeople
        VALUES (:id_num, :salesperson, :loc, :comm);
    end;
```

Only rows that meet the comm >= .12 condition are inserted. This shows how you can use both loops and conditions as normal in the host language.

DECLARING VARIABLES

All variables that are to be referenced in SQL statements must first be declared in a SQL DECLARE SECTION, using the ordinary host-language syntax. You may have any number of these sections in a program, and they may be located anywhere in code before the variable is used, subject to restrictions defined by the host language. The declare sections will begin and end with the embedded SQL commands BEGIN DECLARE SECTION and END DECLARE SECTION, preceded, as usual, with EXEC SQL. To declare the variables used in the previous example, you could enter the following:

```
EXEC SQL BEGIN DECLARE SECTION;
Var
    id-num:          integer;
    Salesperson:     packed array (1 . . 10) of char;
    loc:             packed array (1 . . 10) of char;
    comm:            real;
EXEC SQL END DECLARE SECTION;
```

For those unfamiliar with Pascal, Var is a heading that precedes a series of variable declarations, and packed (or unpacked) arrays are variables holding a series of values distinguished by parenthesized numbers (for example, the third character of loc would be loc(3)). The use of a semicolon after each variable definition is a Pascal, not a SQL, requirement.

RETRIEVING VALUES INTO VARIABLES

In addition to putting the values of variables into tables using SQL commands, you can use SQL to obtain values for those variables. One way to do this is with a variation of the SELECT command that contains an INTO clause. Let's reverse our previous example and put Peel's row from the Salespeople table into our host-language variables.

```
EXEC SQL SELECT snum, sname, city, comm
    INTO :id_num, :salesperson, :loc, :comm
    FROM Salespeople
    WHERE snum = 1001;
```

The values selected are placed in the variables named in the INTO clause in order. Naturally, the variables named in the INTO clause must be of the proper types to receive these values, and there must be a variable for each column selected.

Except for the presence of the INTO clause, this query is like any other. The INTO clause adds a considerable restriction to the query, however. It must retrieve no more than one row. If it retrieves multiple rows, they cannot all be inserted into the same variables at the same time. The command will fail. For this reason, SELECT INTO should be used only under the following conditions:

- When you use the predicate to test for a value that you know will be unique, as in this example. The values that you know will be unique are those that have a constraint forcing uniqueness or a unique index, as discussed in Chapters 17 and 18.
- When you use one or more aggregate functions and do not use GROUP BY.
- When you use SELECT DISTINCT on a foreign key with a predicate referencing a single value of the parent key (provided your system enforces referential integrity), as in the following example:

```
EXEC SQL SELECT DISTINCT snum
     INTO :salesnum
     FROM Customers
     WHERE snum =
          (SELECT snum
               FROM Salespeople
               WHERE sname = 'Motika');
```

Assuming Salespeople.sname and Salespeople.snum are unique and primary keys, respectively, of that table, and that Customers.snum is a foreign key referencing Salespeople.snum, you can rely on this query to produce a single row.

There are other cases where you will know that a query should produce a single row of output, but these are relatively obscure and, in many cases, rely on your data having an integrity that cannot be enforced with constraints. It is not good to rely on this. You are creating a program that is likely to be used for some time, and it is best to play it safe with regard to potential failures. At any rate, there is no need to grope for queries that produce single rows, as SELECT INTO is only a convenience. As you will see, you can deal with queries that produce multiple rows of output by using a cursor.

THE CURSOR

One of SQL's strengths is its ability to operate on all rows of a table that meet certain criteria as a unit without foreknowledge of how many such rows there may be. If ten rows satisfy a predicate, a query will output ten rows. If ten million rows qualify, ten million rows are produced. This does make things difficult, however, when you try to interface to other languages. How can you assign the output of a query to variables when you don't know how much output there will be? The solution is to use what is called a cursor.

You are probably familiar with the cursor as that blinking item that marks your place on the computer screen. You can think of a SQL cursor as a device that, similarly, marks your place in the output of a query, although the analogy is strained. Really, the designers of SQL should have come up with a name that did not already have another meaning.

A *cursor* is a kind of variable that is associated with a query. The value of this variable will be each row, in turn, of that query's output. Like host variables, cursors must be declared before they are used. This is done with the DECLARE CURSOR command, as follows:

```
EXEC SQL DECLARE CURSOR Londonsales FOR
     SELECT *
          FROM Salespeople
          WHERE city = 'London';
```

The query is not executed immediately; this is only a definition. Cursors are somewhat similar to views, in that the cursor contains a query, and the content of the cursor is whatever the output of the query is at the time the cursor is opened (explained shortly). Unlike base tables or views, however, the rows of a cursor are ordered: there is a first, second ... last row of a cursor. This order can either be explicitly controlled with an ORDER BY clause in the query, be arbitrary, or follow an implementor-defined default ordering scheme.

When you reach the point in your program where you are ready to execute the query, you open the cursor with the following command:

```
EXEC SQL OPEN CURSOR Londonsales;
```

The values in the cursor will be those present when you execute this command, not the previous DECLARE command nor any subsequent FETCH commands. Next, you use the FETCH command to extract the output from this query, one row at a time.

```
EXEC SQL FETCH Londonsales INTO :id_num,
  :salesperson, :loc, :comm;
```

This will put the values from the first row selected into the variables. Another FETCH command will produce the next set of values. The idea is to put the FETCH command inside a loop, so that you fetch a row, do whatever you want to with the values from that row, and loop back to fetch the next set of values into the same variables. For example, perhaps you want to write the output, one row at a time, prompting the user to see if she wants to advance to the next row

```
Look_at_more := True;
     EXEC SQL OPEN CURSOR Londonsales;
      while Look_at_more do
          begin
          EXEC SQL FETCH Londonsales
          INTO :id_num, :Salesperson, :loc, :comm;
          writeln (id_num, Salesperson, loc, comm);
          writeln ('Do you want to see more data? (Y/N)');
          readln (response);
          if response = 'N' then Look_at_more := False
          end;
     EXEC SQL CLOSE CURSOR Londonsales;
```

In Pascal, : = means "is assigned the value of", whereas = by itself still has the usual meaning. The writeln function writes its output, and then starts a new line. The single quotes around character values in the second writeln and in the if. . .then statement are a Pascal convention that happens to duplicate SQL.

The effect of this fragment is to set a Boolean variable called Look_at_more to true, open the cursor, and enter the loop. Within the loop, a row is fetched from the cursor and output to the screen. Then the user is prompted to see if she wants to look at the next row. Unless she responds with N for No, the loop is repeated, and the next row of values is fetched. Although Look_at_more and response must be declared as Boolean and char, respectively, in a Pascal variable declaration section, they need not be included in a SQL declare section, because they are not used in the SQL commands.

As you can see, the colons before the variable names are not used for the nonSQL statements. Also notice that there is a CLOSE CURSOR statement corresponding to the OPEN CURSOR statement. This, as you may have guessed, empties the cursor of values, so that the query will have to be reexecuted, with an OPEN CURSOR statement before more values can be fetched. It is not necessary for all rows selected by the query to have been fetched in order to close the cursor, although this is the usual procedure. Once the cursor is closed, SQL does not keep track of which rows were fetched. If you open the cursor again, the query is reexecuted at that point, and you start over from scratch.

This example does not provide any automatic exit from the loop when all the rows have been fetched. When FETCH has no more rows to retrieve, it simply does not change the values in the variables of the INTO clause. Therefore, once the data is exhausted, these variables will be repeatedly output with the same values as long as the user fails to terminate the loop with an entry of N.

SQLCODE

It would be nice to know when the data was exhausted, so we could tell the user this and exit the loop automatically. It is even more important that we know if a SQL command has produced an error. The SQLCODE (called SQLCOD in FORTRAN) variable is provided to meet these functions. This must be defined as a host-language variable and must be of the data type in that host language that corresponds to one of SQL's exact numeric types as shown in Appendix B. The value of SQLCODE is set each time a SQL command is executed. There are basically three possibilities:

1. The command was executed without error, but did not have any effect. This is defined for various commands as follows:

   a) For SELECT, no rows were selected by the query.

   b) For FETCH, the last row had already been fetched, or no rows were selected by the query in the cursor.

   c) For INSERT, no rows were inserted (this implies that a query was used to generate values for the insert, and that it failed to retrieve any rows).

   d) For UPDATE and DELETE, no rows met the predicate's condition, and therefore no change was made to the table.

   In any of these cases, SQLCODE will be set to 100.

2. The command executed normally without any of the above conditions being true. In this case, SQLCODE will be set to 0.

3. The command generated an error. If this happens, any changes made to the database by the current transaction will be rolled back (see Chapter 23). In this case, SQLCODE will be set to some negative number that is implementor defined. The purpose of this number is to identify the problem as precisely as possible. Generally, your system will provide a subprogram to execute, which will have information about the meaning of the negative numbers your implementor has defined. Some error message will be generated to a screen or file, and the program will roll back changes from the current transaction, disconnect from the database, and exit.

USING SQLCODE TO CONTROL LOOPS

Now we can refine our previous example to exit the loop automatically if the cursor is empty, all rows have been fetched, or an error is produced:

```
Look_at_more := True;
EXEC SQL OPEN CURSOR Londonsales;
    while Look_at_more
    and SQLCODE = 0 do
        begin
        EXEC SQL FETCH Londonsales
            INTO :id_num, :Salesperson, :loc, :comm;
        writeln (id_num, Salesperson, loc, comm);
        writeln ('Do you want to see more data? (Y/N)');
        readln (response);
        if response = 'N' then Look_at_more := False;
        end;
EXEC SQL CLOSE CURSOR Londonsales;
```

WHENEVER

This is fine for exiting when all rows have been fetched, but if you produce an error, you need to do something about it, as mentioned in the third case, above. For this purpose, SQL supports GOTO statements. In fact, it allows you to define these globally, so that the program will execute a GOTO command automatically if a certain SQLCODE value occurs. You do this with the WHENEVER clause. Here are a couple of examples:

```
EXEC SQL WHENEVER SQLERROR GOTO Error_handler;
EXEC SQL WHENEVER NOT FOUND CONTINUE;
```

SQLERROR is another way of saying SQLCODE < 0; NOT FOUND is another way of saying SQLCODE = 100. (Some implementations also call the latter case SQLWARNING.) Error_handler is a name for a place in the program that execution will jump to if an error occurs (GOTO can be either one or two words). It is defined in whatever manner is appropriate for the host language, such as a label in Pascal or a section name or paragraph name in COBOL (hereafter we shall use the term label). This will most likely identify a standard procedure intended by the implementor to be included in all programs.

CONTINUE means not to do anything special for the SQLCODE value. This is also the default if you do not use a WHENEVER command specifying that SQLCODE value. However, having this inactivity defined as an action gives you the ability to switch back and forth between taking and not taking action at various points in your program.

For example, if your program includes a series of INSERT commands using queries that really should produce values, you might want to print a special message or do something to indicate that the queries are coming back empty, and no values are being inserted. In this case, you could enter the following:

```
EXEC SQL WHENEVER NOT FOUND GOTO No_rows;
```

No_rows is a label on some code containing an appropriate action. On the other hand, if you are doing a fetch later in the program, you will want to enter the following at that point

```
EXEC SQL WHENEVER NOT FOUND CONTINUE;
```

because performing a fetch repeatedly until all rows are retrieved is the normal procedure and does not require or want special handling.

UPDATING CURSORS

Cursors can also be used to select a group of rows from a table that can then be updated or deleted one by one. This enables you to get around some of the restrictions of the predicates used in the UPDATE and DELETE commands. Specifically, you can refer to the table being affected in the predicate of the cursor's query or any of its subqueries, which you cannot do in predicates of these commands themselves. As pointed out in Chapter 16, standard SQL does not accept an attempt in the following form to delete all customers with ratings below average:

```
EXEC SQL DELETE FROM Customers
    WHERE rating <
        (SELECT AVG (rating)
            FROM Customers);
```

However, you could get this effect by using a query to select the appropriate rows, storing these in a cursor, and performing the DELETE using the cursor. First you would declare the cursor, like this:

```
EXEC SQL DECLARE Belowavg CURSOR FOR
    SELECT *
        FROM Customers
        WHERE rating <
            (SELECT AVG (rating)
                FROM Customers);
```

Then you could create a loop to delete all the customers selected by the cursor:

```
EXEC SQL WHENEVER SQLERROR GOTO Error_handler;
EXEC SQL OPEN CURSOR Belowavg;
while not SQLCODE = 100 do
    begin
    EXEC SQL FETCH Belowavg INTO :a, :b, :c, :d, :e;
    EXEC SQL DELETE FROM Customers
        WHERE CURRENT OF Belowavg;
    end;
EXEC SQL CLOSE CURSOR Belowavg;
```

The WHERE CURRENT OF clause means that the DELETE applies to the row currently retrieved by the cursor. This implies that the cursor and the DELETE command both reference the same table and, therefore, that the query in the cursor is not a join. The cursor must also be updatable. To be updatable, a cursor must satisfy the same criteria as a view (see Chapter 21). In addition, ORDER BY and UNION, which are not allowed in views, are permitted in cursors, but prevent the cursor from being updatable. Notice, in the above example, that we still had to fetch the rows from the cursor into a set of variables, even though we did not use these variables. This is required by the syntax of the FETCH command.

UPDATE works in the same way. You can increase the commission of all salespeople who have customers with a rating of 300, in the following way. First you declare the cursor:

```
EXEC SQL DECLARE CURSOR High_Cust AS
    SELECT *
        FROM Salespeople
        WHERE snum IN
            (SELECT snum
                FROM Customers
                WHERE rating = 300);
```

Then you perform the updates in a loop:

```
EXEC SQL OPEN CURSOR High_cust;
while SQLCODE = 0 do
    begin
    EXEC SQL FETCH High_cust
        INTO :id_num, :salesperson, :loc, :comm;
    EXEC SQL UPDATE Salespeople
        SET comm = comm + .01
        WHERE CURRENT OF High_cust;
    end;
EXEC SQL CLOSE CURSOR High_cust;
```

Note: some implementations require you to specify in a cursor definition that the cursor will be used to perform UPDATE commands on certain columns. This is done by concluding the cursor definition with a FOR UPDATE OF <*column list*>. To declare the High_cust cursor in this manner, so that you could UPDATE the comm column, you would enter this statement:

```
EXEC SQL DECLARE CURSOR High_Cust AS
    SELECT *
        FROM Salespeople
        WHERE snum IN
```

```
    (SELECT snum
        FROM Customers
        WHERE rating = 300)
FOR UPDATE OF comm;
```

This provides a measure of security against accidental updates, which can be quite destructive.

INDICATOR VARIABLES

NULLS are special markers defined by SQL. They cannot be placed into host variables. Attempting to insert a NULL into a host variable is incorrect, because host languages do not support NULLS as defined in SQL. Although the result of an attempt to insert a NULL into a host variable is implementor defined, the result most consistent with database theory is to produce an error: SQLCODE will be set to a negative number, and an error-handling routine will be called. You will usually want to avoid this. Frequently, you may select NULLs along with valid values without it being a reason for your program to crash. Even if the program does not crash, the values in the host variables will be incorrect because they will not be NULLs. Providing an alternative method of dealing with this situation is a function of indicator variables.

Indicator variables are declared in the SQL declare section, like other variables. They will be of the host-language type that corresponds to a SQL exact numeric type. Whenever you perform an operation that might place a NULL in a host-language variable, you should use an indicator variable as a safeguard. You place the indicator in the SQL command directly after the host-language variable you want to protect, without an intervening blank or comma, although you may optionally insert the word INDICATOR.

An indicator variable in a command is initially assigned a value of 0. If a NULL is produced, however, the indicator variable is set to a negative number. You may then test the indicator to see if a NULL value was found. Let's assume the city and comm fields of the Salespeople table do not have NOT NULL constraints, and that we have declared, in the SQL declare section, two Pascal variables of the integer type, i_a and i_b. (There is nothing in the declare section itself that would mark these as indicator variables. They become indicator variables when used as such.) Here is one possibility:

```
EXEC SQL OPEN CURSOR High_cust;
while SQLCODE = 0 do
    begin
    EXEC SQL FETCH High_cust
        INTO :id_num, :salesperson,
            :loc:i_a, :commINDICATOR:i_b;
    If i_a >= 0 and i_b >= 0 then
                {no NULLs produced}
        EXEC SQL UPDATE Salespeople
            SET comm = comm + .01
            WHERE CURRENT OF High_cust;
    Else
                {one or both NULL}
    begin
        If i_a < 0 then
            writeln ('salesperson ', id_num, ' has no city');
        If i_b < 0 then
            writeln ('salesperson ', id_num, ' has no
             commission');
    end;
                {else}
    end; {while}
EXEC SQL CLOSE CURSOR High_cust;
```

As you can see, we chose to include the keyword INDICATOR in one case and exclude it in the other for the sake of illustration; the effect is the same in either case. Each row is fetched, but the UPDATE is performed only if NULLs were not found. If NULLs were produced, the else part of the program is executed, which will print a warning message identifying where each NULL was found. Note: indicators should be tested in the host language, as above, rather than in the WHERE clause of a SQL command. The latter is not illegal, but the results are often unexpected.

USING INDICATOR VARIABLES TO EMULATE SQL NULLS

Another possibility is to treat the indicator variable associated with each host-language variable in a special way so as to emulate the behavior of SQL NULLs. Whenever you use one of these values in your program, for example in an if...then statement, you can check the associated indicator variable first to see if the value is actually a NULL. If so, you treat the variable differently. For example, if a NULL value were retrieved from the city field for the host variable city, which is associated with the indicator variable i_city, you could set city equal to a series of blanks. This would only be necessary if you wanted to print it; its value should make no difference to your program logic. Of course, i_city is automatically set to a negative value. Suppose you had the following if...then construct in your program:

```
if city = 'London' then
     comm := comm + .01
else comm := comm - .01;
```

Any value entered into the city variable will either be equal to 'London' or it will not. Therefore, the commission will be either incremented or decremented in every case. However, the equivalent commands in SQL operate differently:

```
EXEC SQL UPDATE Salespeople
     SET comm = comm + .01
     WHERE city = 'London';
```

and

```
EXEC SQL UPDATE Salespeople
     SET comm = comm - .01;
     WHERE city <> 'London';
```

(Of course, the Pascal version operates only on single values, whereas the SQL version operates on entire tables.) If the city value in the SQL version were NULL, both of the predicates would be unknown, and the comm value would therefore not be changed in either case. You could use the indicator variable to make the behavior of your host language consistent with this by defining a condition that excludes the NULLs:

```
If i_city >= 0 then
     begin
     If city = 'London' then
          comm := comm + .01
     else comm := comm - .01;
     end;
     {begin and end needed only for clarity in this case}
```

In a more complex program, you may want to set a Boolean variable to true to indicate that city is NULL. Then you could simply test this variable whenever appropriate.

OTHER USES OF INDICATOR VARIABLES

Indicator variables can also be used to assign NULL values. Simply append them to a host-variable name in an UPDATE or INSERT command in the same way you would in a SELECT command. If the indicator variable has a negative value, a NULL will be placed in the field. For example, the following command will place NULLs in the city and comm fields of the Salesperson table whenever the indicators i_a or i_b are negative; otherwise it will place the values of the host variables there:

```
EXEC SQL INSERT INTO Salespeople
     VALUES (:id_num, :salesperson, :loc:i_a, :comm:i_b);
```

Indicator variables are also used to indicate string truncation. This occurs if you insert a SQL character value into a host variable that is not large enough to contain all of the characters. This is especially a problem with the nonstandard VARCHAR and LONG data types (refer to Appendix C). In this case, the variable will be filled with the beginning characters of the string, and the trailing characters will be lost. If an indicator variable is used, it will be set to a positive number indicating the length of the string before truncation, thereby letting you know how much text was lost. You will test for this case by seeing if the indicator is > 0 rather than < 0.

SUMMARY

SQL commands are embedded in procedural languages in order to combine the strengths of the two approaches. Some extensions to SQL are necessary to make this work. Embedded SQL commands are translated by a program called a precompiler to a form usable by the compiler of the host language, basically as procedure calls to subprograms that the precompiler creates, called access modules. ANSI supports, in a roundabout way, embedded SQL in these languages: Pascal, FORTRAN, COBOL, and PL/I. Other languages are used by implementors as well, most notably C.

In an attempt to describe embedded SQL in a nutshell, here are the most important points in this chapter:

- All embedded SQL commands begin with the words EXEC SQL and end in a manner that is dependant upon the host language used.
- All host variables to be accessed in SQL commands must be declared in a SQL declare section before they are used.
- All host variables must be preceded by a colon when they are used in a SQL command.
- Queries can store their output directly in host variables using the INTO clause if and only if they select a single row.
- Cursors can be used to store the output of a query and access it one row at a time. Cursors are declared (which defines the query they shall contain), opened (which executes said query), and closed (which removes the query's output from the cursor). While a cursor is open, the FETCH command is used to advance it to each row of the query's output in turn.

- Cursors are updatable or read-only. To be updatable, a cursor must satisfy all of the criteria that a view must satisfy; in addition, it must not use ORDER BY or UNION, clauses that views cannot use in any case. A cursor that is not updatable is read-only.
- If a cursor is updatable, it can be used to control which rows are affected by embedded UPDATE and DELETE commands through the WHERE CURRENT OF clause. The DELETE or UPDATE must be against the same table that the cursor accesses in its query.
- SQLCODE must be declared as a variable of an exact numeric type for every program that will use embedded SQL. Its value is set automatically after the execution of every SQL command.
- If a SQL command executed normally but it did not produce output or the normally expected change to the database, SQLCODE will equal 100. If the command produced an error, SQLCODE will equal some implementor-defined negative number that describes the error. Otherwise, SQLCODE will equal 0.
- The WHENEVER clause can be used to define an action to be taken as soon as a SQLCODE of 100 (NOT FOUND) or a negative number (SQLERROR) occurs. The action can be either to go to some target point in the program (GOTO <label>) or to do nothing (CONTINUE). Naturally, doing nothing is the default.
- Exact numeric variables can also be used as indicator variables. Indicator variables follow another variable name in a SQL command, without any intervening characters except for the (optional) word INDICATOR.
- Normally, the value of an indicator variable is 0. If a SQL command attempts to place a NULL into a host variable that uses an indicator, the indicator will be set to a negative number. This fact can be used to prevent

errors and to flag SQL NULLs for special treatment in the host program.

- Indicator variables can be used to insert NULLs in SQL INSERT or UPDATE commands. They can also take positive numbers to indicate string truncation.

Putting SQL to Work

Note: The answers for these exercises are written in psuedocode, which is an English language description of the logic that the program should follow. This is done to help the readers who may not be familiar with Pascal (or any other language that could be used). It also keeps the focus on the concepts involved, rather than on the particulars of one or another language. For the sake of consistency with the examples, the style of the pseudocode will be similar to Pascal. We will omit from the programs everything that is extraneous to the matters at hand (such as definitions of input/output devices, connections to a database, and so on). Naturally, there is more than one way to do these exercises; nor is mine necessarily the best (probably not).

1. Design a simple program that selects all snum and cnum combinations from both the Orders and Customers tables and checks to see that all such combinations in the former are the same as in the latter. If a combination in the Orders table is not found in the Customers table, the snum value for that row is changed to match. You may assume that a cursor with a subquery is updatable (an ANSI restriction, also applicable to views, that is not widely enforced), and that the basic integrity of the database, other than the error you are checking for, is sound (primary keys are unique, all cnums in the Orders table are correct, and so on). Include a declare section, and be sure also to declare any cursors used.
2. Suppose your program does enforce the ANSI prohibition against allowing cursors or views employing subqueries to be updatable. How would you have to modify the above program?
3. Design a program that prompts the user to change the city values of the salespeople, automatically increasing com-

missions by .01 for salespeople transferred to Barcelona and decreasing them by .01 for salespeople transferred to San Jose. In addition, salespeople currently in London will lose .02 off their commission regardless of whether their city is changed, while salespeople not currently in London will have theirs increased by .02. The changes in commission based on whether a salesperson is in London will be applied independently of those based on where they are being transferred to. Either the city or comm field can contain NULLS, and these should be treated as they would be in SQL. Warning: this is a slightly more convoluted program.

(See Appendix A for answers.)

A

Answers to Exercises

CHAPTER 1

1. cnum
2. rating
3. Record is another word for row. Field is another word for column.
4. Because the rows are, by definition, in no particular order.

CHAPTER 2

1. Character (or text) and number
2. No
3. Data Manipulation Language (DML)
4. A word recognized by SQL as having a special instructive meaning

CHAPTER 3

1. ```
   SELECT onum, amt, odate
       FROM Orders;
   ```
2. ```
   SELECT *
       FROM Customers
       WHERE snum = 1001;
   ```
3. ```
   SELECT city, sname, snum, comm
       FROM Salespeople;
   ```
4. ```
   SELECT rating, cname
       FROM Customers
       WHERE city = 'San Jose';
   ```
5. ```
   SELECT DISTINCT snum
       FROM Orders;
   ```
   ```

CHAPTER 4

1. **SELECT * FROM Orders WHERE amt > 1000;**

2.
```
SELECT sname, city
    FROM Salespeople
    WHERE city = 'London'
        AND comm > .10;
```

3.
```
SELECT *
    FROM Customers
    WHERE rating > 100
        OR city = 'Rome';
```

   or

```
SELECT *
    FROM Customers
    WHERE NOT rating <= 100
        OR city = 'Rome';
```

   or

```
SELECT *
    FROM Customers
    WHERE NOT (rating <= 100
        AND city <> 'Rome');
```

   There may be other solutions as well.

4.

onum	amt	odate	cnum	snum
3001	18.69	10/03/1990	2008	1007
3003	767.19	10/03/1990	2001	1001
3005	5160.45	10/03/1990	2003	1002
3009	1713.23	10/04/1990	2002	1003
3007	75.75	10/04/1990	2004	1002
3008	4723.00	10/05/1990	2006	1001
3010	1309.95	10/06/1990	2004	1002
3011	9891.88	10/06/1990	2006	1001

5.

onum	amt	odate	cnum	snum
3001	18.69	10/03/1990	2008	1007
3003	767.19	10/03/1990	2001	1001

onum	amt	odate	cnum	snum
3006	1098.16	10/03/1990	2008	1007
3009	1713.23	10/04/1990	2002	1003
3007	75.75	10/04/1990	2004	1002
3008	4723.00	10/05/1990	2006	1001
3010	1309.95	10/06/1990	2004	1002
3011	9891.88	10/06/1990	2006	1001

6.
```
SELECT *
   FROM Salespeople;
```

CHAPTER 5

1.
```
SELECT *
   FROM Orders
   WHERE odate IN (10/03/1990, 10/04/1990);
```
and
```
SELECT *
   FROM Orders
   WHERE odate BETWEEN 10/03/1990 AND 10/04,1990;
```

2.
```
SELECT *
   FROM Customers
   WHERE snum IN (1001, 1004);
```

3.
```
SELECT *
   FROM Customers
   WHERE cname BETWEEN 'A' AND 'H';
```
Note: In an ASCII based system, this will not produce Hoffman because of the trailing blanks after the H. For the same reason the second boundary cannot be G, as this would not produce the names of Giovanni and Grass. G could be used if followed with a Z, so as to follow other letters in alphabetical order, rather than preceding them as blanks do.

4.
```
SELECT *
   FROM Customers
   WHERE cname LIKE 'C%';
```

5.
```
SELECT *
     FROM Orders
     WHERE amt <> 0
          AND (amt IS NOT NULL);
```

or

```
SELECT *
     FROM Orders
     WHERE NOT (amt = 0
          OR amt IS NULL);
```

CHAPTER 6

1.
```
SELECT COUNT(*)
     FROM Orders
     WHERE odate = 10/03/1990;
```

2.
```
SELECT COUNT (DISTINCT city)
     FROM Customers;
```

3.
```
SELECT cnum, MIN (amt)
     FROM Orders
     GROUP BY cnum;
```

4.
```
SELECT MIN (cname)
     FROM Customers
     WHERE cname LIKE 'G%';
```

5.
```
SELECT city,
  MAX (rating)
     FROM Customers
     GROUP BY city;
```

6.
```
SELECT odate, count (DISTINCT snum)
     FROM Orders
     GROUP BY odate;
```

CHAPTER 7

1.
```
SELECT onum, snum, amt * .12
     FROM Orders;
```

2. ```
   SELECT 'For the city ', city, ', the highest rating is ',
    MAX (rating)
       FROM Customers
       GROUP BY city;
   ```

3. ```
   SELECT rating, cname, cnum
       FROM Customers
       ORDER BY rating DESC;
   ```

4. ```
   SELECT odate, SUM (amt)
       FROM Orders
       GROUP BY odate
       ORDER BY 2 DESC;
   ```

CHAPTER 8

1. ```
   SELECT onum, cname
       FROM Orders, Customers
       WHERE Customers.cnum = Orders.cnum;
   ```

2. ```
   SELECT onum, cname, sname
       FROM Orders, Customers, Salespeople
       WHERE Customers.cnum = Orders.cnum
           AND Salespeople.snum = Orders.snum;
   ```

3. ```
   SELECT cname, sname, comm
       FROM Salespeople, Customers
       WHERE Salespeople.snum = Customers.snum
           AND comm > .12;
   ```

4. ```
   SELECT onum, comm * amt
       FROM Salespeople, Orders, Customers
       WHERE rating > 100
           AND Orders.cnum = Customers.cnum
           AND Orders.snum = Salespeople.snum;
   ```

CHAPTER 9

1. ```
   SELECT first.sname, second.sname
       FROM Salespeople first, Salespeople second
       WHERE first.city = second.city
           AND first.sname < second.sname;
   ```

   The aliases need not have these particular names.

2. ```
   SELECT cname, first.onum, second.onum
        FROM Orders first, Orders second, Customers
        WHERE first.cnum = second.cnum
             AND first.cnum = Customers.cnum
             AND first.onum < second.onum;
   ```

   There are a few variations of this that are possible, but your answer should have all the same logical components.

3. ```
   SELECT a.cname, a.city
        FROM Customers a, Customers b
        WHERE a.rating = b.rating
             AND b.cnum = 2001;
   ```

CHAPTER 10

1. ```
   SELECT *
        FROM Orders
        WHERE cnum =
             (SELECT cnum
             FROM Customers
             WHERE cname = 'Cisneros');
   ```

   or

   ```
   SELECT *
        FROM Orders
        WHERE cnum IN
             (SELECT cnum
                  FROM Customers
                  WHERE cname = 'Cisneros');
   ```

2. ```
   SELECT DISTINCT cname, rating
        FROM Customers, Orders
        WHERE amt >
             (SELECT AVG (amt)
                  FROM Orders)
             AND Orders.cnum = Customers.cnum;
   ```

3. ```
   SELECT snum, SUM (amt)
        FROM Orders
        GROUP BY snum
        HAVING SUM (amt) >
             (SELECT MAX (amt)
        FROM Orders);
   ```
   ```

CHAPTER 11

1.
```
SELECT cnum, cname
     FROM Customers outer
     WHERE rating =
          (SELECT MAX (rating)
               FROM Customers inner
               WHERE inner.city = outer.city);
```

2. Correlated Subquery Solution:
```
SELECT snum, sname
     FROM Salespeople main
     WHERE city IN
          (SELECT city
               FROM Customers inner
               WHERE inner.snum <> main.snum);
```
   Join Solution:
```
SELECT DISTINCT first.snum, sname
     FROM Salespeople first, Customers second
     WHERE first.city = second.city
          AND first.snum <> second.snum;
```
   The correlated subquery finds all customers not serviced by a given salesperson and checks to see if any of them are located in his or her city. The join solution is simpler and more intuitive. It finds cases where the city fields match and the snums do not. Therefore a join is a more elegant solution to this problem, given what we have studied up till now. There is a more elegant subquery solution that we will encounter later.

CHAPTER 12

1.
```
SELECT *
     FROM Salespeople first
     WHERE EXISTS
          (SELECT *
          FROM Customers second
               WHERE first.snum = second.snum
                    AND rating = 300);
```

2.
```
SELECT a.snum, sname, a.city, comm
    FROM Salespeople a, Customers b
    WHERE a.snum = b.snum
        AND b.rating = 300;
```

3.
```
SELECT *
    FROM Salespeople a
    WHERE EXISTS
        (SELECT *
            FROM Customers b
            WHERE b.city = a.city
                AND a.snum <> b.snum);
```

4.
```
SELECT *
    FROM Customers a
    WHERE EXISTS
        (SELECT *
            FROM Orders b
            WHERE a.snum = b.snum
                AND a.cnum <> b.cnum)
```

CHAPTER 13

1.
```
SELECT *
    FROM Customers
    WHERE rating > = ANY
        (SELECT rating
            FROM Customers
            WHERE snum = 1002);
```

2.

cnum	cname	city	rating	snum
2002	Giovanni	Rome	200	1003
2003	Liu	San Jose	200	1002
2004	Grass	Berlin	300	1002
2008	Cisneros	San Jose	300	1007

3.
```
SELECT *
    FROM Salespeople
    WHERE city <> ALL
        (SELECT city
            FROM Customers);
```

```
or
SELECT *
    FROM Salespeople
    WHERE NOT city = ANY
        (SELECT city
            FROM Customers);
```

4.
```
SELECT *
    FROM Orders
    WHERE amt > ALL
        (SELECT amt
            FROM Orders a, Customers b
            WHERE a.cnum = b.cnum
                AND b.city = 'London');
```

5.
```
SELECT *
    FROM Orders
    WHERE amt >
        (SELECT MAX (amt)
            FROM Orders a, Customers b
            WHERE a.cnum = b.cnum
                AND b.city = 'London');
```

CHAPTER 14

1.
```
SELECT cname, city, rating, 'High Rating'
    FROM Customers
    WHERE rating >= 200

    UNION

SELECT cname, city, rating, ' Low Rating'
    FROM Customers
    WHERE rating < 200;

or
SELECT cname, city, rating, 'High Rating'
    FROM Customers
    WHERE rating >= 200

    UNION

SELECT cname, city, rating, ' Low Rating'
    FROM Customers
    WHERE NOT rating >= 200;
```

The difference between these two statements is in the form of the second predicate. Notice that, in both cases, the string 'Low Rating' has an extra blank at the beginning, so that it will match 'High Rating' for length.

2.
```
SELECT cnum, cname
     FROM Customers a
     WHERE 1<
          (SELECT COUNT (*)
               FROM Orders b
               WHERE a.cnum = b.cnum)
     UNION
SELECT snum, sname
     FROM Salespeople a
     WHERE 1<
          (SELECT COUNT (*)
               FROM Orders b
               WHERE a.snum = b.snum)
     ORDER BY 2;
```

3.
```
SELECT snum
     FROM Salespeople
     WHERE city = 'San Jose'
     UNION
(SELECT cnum
     FROM Customers
     WHERE city = 'San Jose'
     UNION ALL
SELECT onum
     FROM Orders
     WHERE odate = 10/03/1990);
```

CHAPTER 15

1.
```
INSERT INTO Salespeople (city, cname, comm, cnum)
     VALUES ('San Jose', 'Blanco', NULL, 1100);
```

2.
```
DELETE FROM Orders WHERE cnum = 2006;
```

3. ```
   UPDATE Customers
       SET rating = rating + 100
       WHERE city = 'Rome';
   ```

4. ```
   UPDATE Customers
       SET snum = 1004
       WHERE snum = 1002;
   ```

CHAPTER 16

1. ```
   INSERT INTO Multicust
       SELECT *
           FROM Salespeople
           WHERE 1 <
           (SELECT COUNT (*)
               FROM Customers
               WHERE Customers.snum =
                Salespeople.snum);
   ```

2. ```
   DELETE FROM Customers
       WHERE NOT EXISTS
           (SELECT *
               FROM Orders
               WHERE cnum = Customers.cnum);
   ```

3. ```
   UPDATE Salespeople
       SET comm = comm + (comm * .2)
       WHERE 3000 <
           (SELECT SUM (amt)
               FROM Orders
               WHERE snum = Salespeople.snum);
   ```

   A more sophisticated version of this command might make sure the commission did not exceed 1.0 (100%):

   ```
   UPDATE Salespeople
       SET comm = comm + (comm * .2)
       WHERE 3000 <
           (SELECT SUM (amt)
               FROM Orders
               WHERE snum = Salespeople.snum)
       AND comm + (comm * .2) < 1.0;
   ```

   These problems may have other solutions as well.
   ```

CHAPTER 17

1.
```
CREATE TABLE Customers
      (cnum     integer,
      cname    char(10),
      city     char(10),
      rating   integer,
      snum     integer);
```

2. **CREATE INDEX Datesearch ON Orders(odate);**

   (All index names used in these answers are arbitrary.)

3. **CREATE UNIQUE INDEX Onumkey ON Orders(onum);**

4. **CREATE INDEX Mydate ON Orders(snum, odate);**

5. **CREATE UNIQUE INDEX Combination ON Customers(snum, rating);**

CHAPTER 18

1.
```
CREATE TABLE Orders
      (onum     integer NOT NULL PRIMARY KEY,
      amt      decimal,
      odate    date NOT NULL,
      cnum     integer NOT NULL,
      snum     integer NOT NULL,
      UNIQUE (snum, cnum));
```

   or

```
CREATE TABLE Orders
      (onum     integer NOT NULL UNIQUE,
      amt      decimal,
      odate    date NOT NULL,
      cnum     integer NOT NULL,
      snum     integer NOT NULL,
      UNIQUE (snum, cnum));
```

   The first solution is preferable.

2.
```
CREATE TABLE Salespeople
      (snum     integer NOT NULL PRIMARY KEY,
      sname    char(15) CHECK (sname BETWEEN 'AA'
                 AND 'MZ'),
```

```
        city      char(15),
        comm      decimal NOT NULL DEFAULT = .10);
```

3. CREATE TABLE Orders

```
        (onum     integer NOT NULL,
        amt       decimal,
        odate     date,
        cnum      integer NOT NULL,
        snum      integer NOT NULL,
        CHECK ((cnum > snum) AND (onum > cnum)));
```

CHAPTER 19

1. CREATE TABLE Cityorders

```
        (onum     integer NOT NULL PRIMARY KEY,
        amt       decimal,
        cnum      integer,
        snum      integer,
        city      char (15),
    FOREIGN KEY (onum, amt, snum)
            REFERENCES Orders (onum, amt, snum),
    FOREIGN KEY (cnum, city)
            REFERENCES Customers (cnum, city) );
```

2. CREATE TABLE Orders

```
        (onum     integer NOT NULL,
        amt       decimal,
        odate     date,
        cnum      integer NOT NULL,
        snum      integer,
        prev      integer,
    UNIQUE (cnum, onum),
    FOREIGN KEY (cnum, prev) REFERENCES Orders (cnum,
     onum) ); 9
```

CHAPTER 20

1. CREATE VIEW Highratings

```
        AS SELECT *
            FROM Customers
```

```
WHERE rating =
     (SELECT MAX (rating)
          FROM Customers);
```

2.
```
CREATE VIEW Citynumber
     AS SELECT city, COUNT (DISTINCT snum)
          FROM Salespeople
          GROUP BY city;
```

3.
```
CREATE VIEW Nameorders
     AS SELECT sname, AVG (amt), SUM (amt)
          FROM Salespeople, Orders
          WHERE Salespeople.snum = Orders.snum
          GROUP BY sname;
```

4.
```
CREATE VIEW Multcustomers
     AS SELECT *
          FROM Salespeople a
          WHERE 1 <
               (SELECT COUNT (*)
                    FROM Customers b
                    WHERE a.snum = b.snum);
```

CHAPTER 21

1. #1 is not updatable because it uses DISTINCT.
   #2 is not updatable because it uses a join, an aggregate function, and GROUP BY.
   #3 is not updatable because it is based on #1, which is not updatable.
   #4 is updatable.

2.
```
CREATE VIEW Commissions
     AS SELECT snum, comm
          FROM Salespeople
          WHERE comm BETWEEN .10 AND .20
          WITH CHECK OPTION;
```

3.
```
CREATE TABLE Orders
     (onum    integer NOT NULL PRIMARY KEY,
     amt      decimal,
     odate    date DEFAULT VALUE = CURDATE,
     snum     integer,
     cnum     integer);
```

```
CREATE VIEW Entryorders
    AS SELECT onum, amt, snum, cnum
        FROM Orders;
```

CHAPTER 22

1. **GRANT UPDATE (rating) ON Customers TO Janet;**
2. **GRANT SELECT ON Orders TO Stephen WITH GRANT OPTION;**
3. **REVOKE INSERT ON Salespeople FROM Claire;**
4. Step 1:
```
CREATE VIEW Jerrysview
    AS SELECT *
        FROM Customers
        WHERE rating BETWEEN 100 AND 500
        WITH CHECK OPTION;
```
   Step 2: **GRANT INSERT, UPDATE ON Jerrysview TO Jerry;**
5. Step 1:
```
CREATE VIEW Janetsview
    AS SELECT *
        FROM Customers
        WHERE rating =
            (SELECT MIN (rating)
                FROM Customers);
```
   Step 2: **GRANT SELECT ON Janetsview TO Janet;**

CHAPTER 23

1.
```
CREATE DBSPACE Myspace
    (pctindex    15,
     pctfree     40);
```
2. **CREATE SYNONYM Orders FOR Diane.Orders;**
3. They should be rolled back.
4. An Exclusive Lock.
5. Read Only.

CHAPTER 24

1. ```
   SELECT a.tname, a.owner, b.cname, b.datatype
       FROM SYSTEMCATALOG a, SYSTEMCOLUMNS b
       WHERE a.tname = b.tname
           AND a.owner = b.owner
           AND a.numcolumns > 4;
   ```

   Note: because most of the column names of the joined tables are different, not all of the uses of aliases a and b in the above command are strictly neccessary. They are provided for clarity.

2. ```
   SELECT tname, synowner, COUNT (ALL synonym)
       FROM SYTEMSYNONS
       GROUP BY tname, synowner;
   ```

3. ```
   SELECT COUNT (*)
       FROM SYSTEMCATALOG a
       WHERE numcolumns/2 <
           (SELECT COUNT (DISTINCT cnumber)
               FROM SYSTEMINDEXES b
               WHERE a.owner = b.tabowner
                   AND a.tname = b.tname);
   ```

CHAPTER 25

1. ```
   EXEC SQL BEGIN DECLARE SECTION;
       SQLCODE:integer;
   {always required}
       cnum        integer;
       snum        integer;
       custnum:    integer;
       salesnum:   integer;
   EXEC SQL END DECLARE SECTION;
   EXEC SQL DECLARE Wrong_Orders AS CURSOR FOR
       SELECT cnum, snum
           FROM Orders a
           WHERE snum <>
               (SELECT snum
                   FROM Customers b
                   WHERE a.cnum = b.cnum);
   ```

```
{We are still using SQL to do the main work here. The
query above locates the rows of the Orders table that are
not in agreement with the Customers table.}
EXEC SQL DECLARE Cust_assigns AS CURSOR FOR
     SELECT cnum, snum
          FROM Customers;
{This cursor is used to provide the correct snum values.}
begin {main program}
EXEC SQL OPEN CURSOR Wrong_Orders;
while SQLCODE = 0 do
{Loop until Wrong_Orders is empty}
     begin
     EXEC SQL FETCH Wrong_Orders INTO
      (:cnum, :snum);
     if SQLCODE = 0 then
          begin
{If Wrong_Orders is empty, we don't want this loop to do
anything.}
     EXEC SQL OPEN CURSOR Cust_Assigns;
          repeat
               EXEC SQL FETCH Cust_Assigns
                    INTO (:custnum, :salesnum);
          until :custnum = :cnum;
{The repeat FETCH until. . . command will go through the
Cust_Assigns cursor until the row that matches the
current cnum of Wrong_Orders is found.}
          EXEC SQL CLOSE CURSOR Cust_assigns;
{So that we will start out fresh next time through the
loop. The value we need from this cursor is stored in the
salesnum variable.}
          EXEC SQL UPDATE Orders
               SET snum = :salesnum
               WHERE CURRENT OF Wrong_Orders;
          end; {If SQLCODE = 0}
     end; {While SQLCODE. . .do}
EXEC SQL CLOSE CURSOR Wrong_Orders;
end; {main program}
```

2. Given the program I used, the solution would be to simply include onum, the primary key of the Orders table, in the Wrong_Orders cursor. In the UPDATE command, you would then use a WHERE onum = :ordernum predicate (assuming a declared integer variable odernum), instead of a WHERE CURRENT OF Wrong_Orders. The resulting program would look like this (most comments from previous version omitted):

```
EXEC SQL BEGIN DECLARE SECTION;
     SQLCODE:     integer;
     odernum      integer;
     cnum         integer;
     snum         integer;
     custnum:     integer;
     salesnum:    integer;
EXEC SQL END DECLARE SECTION;
EXEC SQL DECLARE Wrong_Orders AS CURSOR FOR
     SELECT onum, cnum, snum
          FROM Orders a
          WHERE snum <>
               (SELECT snum
                    FROM Customers b
                    WHERE a.cnum = b.cnum);
EXEC SQL DECLARE Cust_assigns AS CURSOR FOR
     SELECT cnum, snum
          FROM Customers;
begin {main program}
EXEC SQL OPEN CURSOR Wrong_Orders;
while SQLCODE = 0 do {Loop until Wrong_Orders is
  empty}
     begin
     EXEC SQL FETCH Wrong_Orders
          INTO (:odernum, :cnum, :snum);
     if SQLCODE = 0 then
          begin
          EXEC SQL OPEN CURSOR Cust_Assigns;
          repeat
               EXEC SQL FETCH Cust_Assigns
                    INTO (:custnum, :salesnum);
          until :custnum = :cnum;
```

```
            EXEC SQL CLOSE CURSOR Cust_assigns;
            EXEC SQL UPDATE Orders
                 SET snum = :salesnum
                 WHERE CURRENT OF Wrong_Orders;
            end; {If SQLCODE = 0}
       end; {While SQLCODE. . .do}
   EXEC SQL CLOSE CURSOR Wrong_Orders;
   end; {main program}
```

3.

```
EXEC SQL BEGIN DECLARE SECTION;
     SQLCODE       integer;
     newcity       packed array[1 . . 12] of char;
     commnull      boolean;
     citynull      boolean;
     response      char;
EXEC SQL END DECLARE SECTION;
EXEC SQL DECLARE CURSOR Salesperson AS
     SELECT * FROM SALESPEOPLE;
begin {main program}
EXEC SQL OPEN CURSOR Salesperson;
EXEC SQL FETCH Salesperson
     INTO (:snum, :sname, :city:i_cit, :comm:i_com);
{Fetch first row.}
while SQLCODE = 0 do
{While there are rows in Salesperson.}
     begin
     if i_com < 0 then commnull : = true;
     if i_cit < 0 then citynull : = true;
{Set boolean flags that will indicate NULLS.}
     if citynull then
          begin
          write ('No current city value for salesperson ',
          snum, ' Would you like to provide one? (Y/N)');
{Prompt indicates city is NULL.}
          read (response);
{The response will be used later.}
          end {if citynull}
```

```
    else {not citynull}
        begin
        if not commnull then
{To perform comparison and operations only on nonNULL
comm values.}
            begin
            if city = 'London' then comm := comm - .02
                else comm := comm + .02;
            end;
{If not commnull, begin and end are for clarity.}
        write ('Current city for salesperson ',
            snum, ' is ', city,
            Do you want to change it? (Y/N)');
```

3. Note: Salespeople not currently assigned a city will not have their commissions changed on the basis of whether they reside in London.

```
        read (response);
{Response now has a value regardless of whether
citynull is true or false.}
        end; {else not citynull}
    if response = 'Y' then
        begin
        write ('Enter new city value: ');
        read (newcity);
        if not commnull then
{This operation can be performed only on nonNULL
values.}
            case newcity of:
                begin
                'Barcelona': comm := comm + .01,
                'San Jose': comm := comm -.01
                end; {case and if not commnull}
        EXEC SQL UPDATE Salespeople
            SET city = :newcity, comm = :comm:i_com
            WHERE CURRENT OF Salesperson;
{Indicator variable will put a NULL in comm if
appropriate.}
```

```
            end; {If response = 'Y', if response <> 'Y', no
             change is made.}
            EXEC SQL FETCH Salesperson
                INTO (:snum, :sname, :city:i_cit,
                 :comm:i_com);
{fetch next row}
    end; {while SQLCODE = 0}
EXEC SQL CLOSE CURSOR Salesperson;
end; {main program}
```

B

SQL Data Types

THE DATA TYPES RECOGNIZED BY ANSI CONSIST OF CHAR and several types of number values, which can be catagorized as exact numeric and approximate numeric. The exact numeric types are numbers, with or without decimal points, in conventional notation. The approximate numeric types are numbers in exponential (base 10) notation. Other than this, the distinctions between these types are sometimes subtle.

Sometimes data types use an argument, which I have called the size argument, whose exact format and meaning varies from type to type. Defaults are provided for all types if the size argument is omitted.

ANSI TYPES

These are the ANSI data types (names in parentheses are synonyms):

TEXT

DATA TYPE	DESCRIPTION
CHAR (or CHARACTER)	A string of text in an implementor-defined format. Here the size argument is a single nonnegative integer that refers to the maximum length of the string. Values of this type must be enclosed in single quotes, such as 'text'. Two adjacent single quotes ('') inside the string will represent one single quote (').

EXACT NUMERIC

DATA TYPE	DESCRIPTION
DEC (or DECIMAL)	A decimal number; that is, a number that can have a decimal point in it. Here the size argument has two parts: precision and scale. The scale cannot exceed the precision. Precision comes first, and a comma must separate it from the scale argument. The precision indicates how many (significant) digits the number is to have. The maximum number of digits for the number is an implementation-determined value equal to or greater than this number. The scale indicates the maximum number of digits to the right of the decimal point. A scale of zero makes the field the equivalent of an integer.
NUMERIC	Same as DECIMAL except that the maximum number of digits may not exceed the precision argument.
INT (or INTEGER)	A number without a (shown) decimal point. Equivalent to a DECIMAL with no digits to the right of the decimal point, that is, with a scale of 0. The size argument is not used (it is automatically set to an implementation-dependent value).
SMALLINT	Same as INTEGER except that, depending on implementation, the default size may (or may not) be smaller than INTEGER.

APPROXIMATE NUMERIC

DATA TYPE	DESCRIPTION
FLOAT	A floating point number in base 10 exponential notation. The size argument consists of a single number specifying the minimum precision.
REAL	Same as FLOAT, except that no size argument is used. The precision is set to an implementation-dependent default.
DOUBLE PRECISION (or DOUBLE)	Same as REAL, except that the implementation-defined precision for DOUBLE PRECISION must exceed the implementation-defined precision of REAL.

EQUIVALENT DATA TYPES IN OTHER LANGUAGES

When embedding SQL in other languages, the values used in and produced by SQL commands are normally stored in host-language variables (see Chapter 25). These variables must be of compatible data types with the SQL values they will hold. In its annexes, which are not part of the offical SQL standard, ANSI provides support for use of embedded SQL with four languages: Pascal, PL/I, COBOL, and FORTRAN. Among other things, this involved defining SQL equivalents for data types of variables used in these languages. Here are the equivalents in the four ANSI-defined languages:

PL/I

SQL TYPE	PL/I EQUIVALENT
CHAR	CHAR
DECIMAL	FIXED DECIMAL
INTEGER	FIXED BINARY
FLOAT	FLOAT BINARY

COBOL

SQL TYPE	COBOL EQUIVALENT
CHAR (<*integer*>)	PIC X(<*integer*>)
INTEGER	PIC S(<*nines*>) USAGE COMPUTATIONAL
NUMERIC	PIC S(<*nines with embedded V*>) DISPLAY SIGN LEADING SEPARATE

PASCAL

SQL TYPE	PASCAL EQUIVALENT
INTEGER	INTEGER
REAL	REAL
CHAR (<*length*>)	PACKED ARRAY [1..<*length*>] OF CHAR

FORTRAN

SQL TYPE	FORTRAN EQUIVALENT
CHARACTER	CHARACTER
INTEGER	INTEGER
REAL	REAL
DOUBLE PRECISION	DOUBLE PRECISION

C

Some Common Nonstandard SQL Features

THERE ARE A NUMBER OF FEATURES OF THE SQL language that, while not defined as part of the ANSI or ISO standard, are common to numerous implementations because they have been found to be useful in practice. This appendix outlines a number of these features. Naturally, these features vary from product to product, and this discussion is intended only to introduce some common approaches.

DATA TYPES

The data types supported by the SQL standard are outlined in Appendix B. They amount to CHARACTER and a variety of numeric types. Implementations can, in fact, be greatly more sophisticated than this in terms of the types that they actually can use. We will discuss a variety of these nonstandard data types here.

DATE AND TIME TYPES

As mentioned in Chapter 2, the DATE data type is widely supported, even though it is not part of the standard. We have used this type in our Orders table, assuming a format of mm/dd/yyyy. This is the IBM standard format for the U.S. Other formats are, of course, possible, and implementations often support a variety of formats, allowing you to choose the one that best suits your needs. An implementation that offers this feature should be able to convert dates from one format to another automatically. Here are some other major date formats you may encounter:

STANDARD	*FORMAT*	*EXAMPLE*
International Standards Organization (ISO)	yyyy-mm-dd	1990-10-31
Japanese Industrial Standard (JIS)	yyyy-mm-dd	1990-10-31
IBM European Standard (EUR)	dd.mm.yyyy	10.31.1990

Having a special type defined for dates enables you to perform date arithmetic. For example, you can add a number of days to a date and produce another date, with the program itself keeping track of the number of days in months, leap years, and so on. Dates can also be compared; for example, date A < date B means that date A precedes date B chronologically.

In addition to dates, many programs define a special type for times, which can also be presented in a variety of formats including the following:

STANDARD	*FORMAT*	*EXAMPLE*
International Standards Organization (ISO)	hh-mm-ss	21.04.37
Japanese Industrial Standard (JIS)	hh-mm-ss	21.04.37
IBM European Standard (EUR)	hh-mm-ss	21.04.37
IBM USA Standard (USA)	hh.mm AM/PM	9.04 PM

Times can be added or compared accurately just as dates can, with the correct number of seconds in a minute or hours in a day automatically accounted for. In addition, special built-in constants indicating the current date or time (CURDATE or CURTIME) are common. These are like the constant USER in that their value will continually change with the context.

Can you include time and date in a single field? Some implementations define the DATE type finely enough to include times. Alternatively, a third type, such as TIMESTAMP, can be defined as a combination of the two.

TEXT STRING TYPES

ANSI supports one type to represent text. This is the CHAR type. Any field of this type is defined to have a specific length. If the string inserted into the field is less than that length, it is padded with blanks; the string cannot be longer than the field length. Although convenient from the implementor's point of view, this definition has some limitations for the user. For instance, the character fields have to be of the same length in order to undergo a UNION.

Many implementors support strings of varying length through the data types VARCHAR and LONG VARCHAR (usually just called LONG). Whereas a field of the CHAR type always allocates memory storage for the maximum number of characters that can be stored in the field, a VARCHAR field of either variety will allocate only enough memory to store the actual contents of the field, although SQL will have to set aside some associated memory space to keep track of the field's current length. VARCHAR fields can be any length up to an implementor-defined maximum. This maximum can vary from 254 to 2048 characters for VARCHAR, and up to 16K characters for LONG. LONG is generally used for text of an explanatory nature or for data that cannot be easily compressed into simple field values; VARCHAR can be used for any text string whose length will vary.

It is not always a good idea to use VARCHAR instead of CHAR, by the way. Retrieving and updating VARCHAR fields is more complex, and therefore slower, than retrieving and updating CHAR fields. In addition, some of the memory VARCHAR saves is used to store the length of the string anyway. You should appraise how much the values of a field are likely to vary in length as well as whether they may need to undergo unions with other fields before deciding whether to use CHAR or VARCHAR. Frequently, the LONG type can also be used to store binary data. Of course, the LONG field's unwieldy size limits the SQL operations you can perform on it. Consult your manual for details.

THE FORMAT COMMAND

As we pointed out in Chapter 7, the processing of output provided in standard SQL is rather limited. Although many implementations include SQL in packages that have other features to handle this function, some also use a command such as FORMAT within SQL to impose certain forms, structures, or limitations on query output. Among the possible functions of the FORMAT command are

- To specify the width of columns (as printed).
- To specify how NULLs will be represented.
- To provide (new) headings for columns.
- To provide top- or bottom-of-page titles for printed output.
- To impose appropriate, or modify given, formats for fields containing date, time, or money values.
- To calculate totals and subtotals without excluding the field being totaled, as SUM does. (An alternative approach to this problem in some products is the COMPUTE clause.)

The FORMAT command can be entered immediately before or after the query to which it will apply, depending on the implementation. One FORMAT command usually will apply to only one query, although any number of FORMAT commands can apply to the same query. Here are some typical FORMAT commands:

```
FORMAT NULL '_______';
FORMAT BTITLE 'Orders Grouped by Salesperson';
FORMAT EXCLUDE (2, 3);
```

The first of these will have NULL values printed as '_______' in the output; the second will insert the title 'Orders Grouped by Salesperson' at the bottom of each page; the third will exclude the second and third columns of the previous query's output. You might possibly use the last of these if you only selected certain columns to use them in an ORDER BY clause, sequencing your output. Which specific functions FORMAT can perform varies, so a complete illustration of its different applications is beyond our scope here.

There are other commands that may be used to fufill these fucntions. The SET command is similar to FORMAT; it can either be an alternative or a supplemental command that will apply to all queries in the current user session, rather than a single query. Another implementation begins its commands with the keyword COLUMN rather than FORMAT, as follows:

```
COLUMN odate FORMAT dd-mon-yy;
```

This imposes a 10-Oct-90 format on the date field for the purpose of the query's output.

The COMPUTE clause, mentioned previously, is inserted into a query, as follows:

```
SELECT odate, amt
    FROM Orders
    WHERE snum = 1001
    COMPUTE SUM (amt);
```

This will produce all of Peel's orders, with the date and amount, and then total the amounts. Another implementation produces subtotals using COMPUTE as a command. First, it defines a break:

```
BREAK ON odate;
```

This divides the output of the above query on the page into groups, so that all odate values in a group are the same. Now you could enter the following statement:

```
COMPUTE SUM OF amt ON odate;
```

The column in the ON clause must previously have been used in a BREAK command.

FUNCTIONS

In ANSI standard SQL, you can apply aggregate functions to columns or use their values in scalar expressions, such as comm * 100. There are many other useful functions that you are likely to encounter in practice. Here is a list of some common SQL functions other than the standard aggregates. They can be used in the SELECT clause of queries, just like aggregate functions, but these functions operate on single values instead of groups. In the following list they are categorized according to the types of data they operate on. Unless otherwise indicated, variables in this list stand for any value expression of the proper type that could be used in a SELECT clause:

MATHEMATICAL FUNCTIONS

These functions are applied to numbers.

FUNCTION	*MEANING*
ABS(X)	Absolute value of X (converts negative or positive to positive).
CEIL(X)	X is a decimal value that will be rounded upwards.
FLOOR(X)	X is a decimal value that will be rounded downwards.
GREATEST(X,Y)	Returns the larger of the two values.
LEAST(X,Y)	Returns the lesser of the two values.
MOD(X,Y)	Returns the remainder of X / Y.
POWER(X,Y)	Returns X to the power of Y.
ROUND(X,Y)	Rounds X to Y decimal places. If Y is omitted, rounds to integer.
SIGN(X)	Returns a minus if X < 0, a plus otherwise.
SQRT(X)	Returns the square root of X.

CHARACTER FUNCTIONS

These functions can be applied to strings of text, either from columns of a text data type, literal text strings, or a combination of the two.

<table>
<tr><th>FUNCTION</th><th>MEANING</th></tr>
<tr><td>LEFT(<<em>string</em>>,X)</td><td>Returns the leftmost X characters of the string.</td></tr>
<tr><td>RIGHT(<<em>string</em>>,X)</td><td>Returns the rightmost X characters of the string.</td></tr>
<tr><td>ASCII(<<em>string</em>>)</td><td>Returns the ASCII code that represents the string in the computer's memory.</td></tr>
<tr><td>CHR(<<em>ASCII code</em>>)</td><td>Returns the printable characters the ASCII code represents.</td></tr>
<tr><td>VALUE(<<em>string</em>>)</td><td>Returns a mathematical value for the string. Assumes that the string is of the CHAR or VARCHAR type but consists of numbers. VALUE('3') will produce a 3 of the integer type.</td></tr>
<tr><td>UPPER(<<em>string</em>>)</td><td>Converts the string to all uppercase letters.</td></tr>
<tr><td>LOWER(<<em>string</em>>)</td><td>Converts the string to all lowercase letters.</td></tr>
<tr><td>INITCAP(<<em>string</em>>)</td><td>Converts the string to initial caps. Called PROPER in some implementations.</td></tr>
<tr><td>LENGTH(<<em>string</em>>)</td><td>Returns the number of characters in the string.</td></tr>
<tr><td><<em>string</em>>||<<em>string</em>></td><td>Combines the two strings in the output, so that the first will be followed immediately by the</td></tr>
</table>

second. (|| is called the concatenate operator.)

LPAD(<*string*>,X,'*')	Pads the string on the left with the '*', or whatever character is indicated, to make it X characters long.
RPAD(<*string*>,X,'*')	Same as LPAD, except that the padding is done on the right.
SUBSTR(<*string*>,X,Y)	Extracts Y letters from the string beginning at position X.

DATE AND TIME FUNCTIONS

These functions operate on valid date or time values.

FUNCTION	***MEANING***
DAY(<*date*>)	Extracts the day of the month from the date. Similar functions exist for MONTH, YEAR, HOUR, SECOND, and so on.
WEEKDAY(<*date*>)	Derives the day of the week from the date.

OTHER

This function can apply to any data type.

FUNCTION	***MEANING***
NVL(<*column*>,<*value*>)	NVL (NULL Value) will substitute <*value*> for any NULL found in <*column*>. If the current value of <*column*> is not NULL, NVL has no effect.

INTERSECT AND MINUS

The UNION command, as you have seen in Chapter 14, unites two queries by merging their output into one. Two other commonly found ways of combining seperate queries are INTERSECT and MINUS. INTERSECT outputs only rows produced by both of the queries intersected, whereas MINUS outputs rows that are produced by one but not the other. Therefore, the following two queries

```
SELECT *
    FROM Salespeople
    WHERE city = 'London'
    INTERSECT
SELECT *
    FROM Salespeople
    WHERE 'London' IN
        (SELECT city
            FROM Customers
            WHERE Customers.snum =
             Salespeople.snum);
```

would output the rows produced by both of the queries, producing all salespeople in London who had at least one customer located there as well. On the other hand

```
SELECT *
    FROM Salespeople
    WHERE city = 'London'
    MINUS
SELECT *
    FROM Salespeople
    WHERE 'London' IN
        (SELECT city
            FROM Customers
            WHERE Customers.snum =
             Salespeople.snum);
```

would remove rows selected by the second query from the output of the first, and thereby produce all salespeople in London who did not have customers there. MINUS is sometimes called DIFFERENCE.

AUTOMATIC OUTER JOINS

In Chapter 14, we discussed the outer join and showed you how to implement it using the UNION command. Some database programs have more direct ways of implementing outer joins. In some implementations, a parenthesized plus sign (+) after the predicate will produce rows that satisfy the condition as well as rows that do not. The predicate condition will contain a field that is being matched in both tables, and NULLS will be inserted where no match was found. For example, suppose you wanted to see your salespeople matched to their customers, without excluding those salespeople who were not currently assigned any customers (although there are none in the sample tables as given, this is still a possibility):

```
SELECT a.snum, sname, cname
    FROM Salespeople a, Customers b
    WHERE a.snum = b.snum (+);
```

This is the equivalent of the following UNION:

```
SELECT a.snum, sname, cname
    FROM Salespeople a, Customers b
    WHERE a.snum = b.snum
    UNION
SELECT snum, sname, '__________'
    FROM Salespeople
    WHERE snum NOT IN
        (SELECT snum
            FROM Customers);
```

We are assuming underscores to be the current representation of NULL (see the FORMAT command earlier in this appendix on representation of NULL).

KEEPING TRACK OF ACTIONS

Your SQL implementation is likely, if it accessed by multiple users, to provide some way of keeping track of actions performed on the database. There are two major forms of this: Journaling and Auditing. These forms differ in purpose.

Journaling, as we use the term here, is done for the purpose of protecting your data if the system crashes. You first use an implementation-dependent procedure to backup the current contents of your database, so that an extra copy of these contents is stored somewhere. You then journal the changes to the database. This stores in some memory area other than the main database memory, preferably a different device, each command that made a change in the structure or content of the database. If you have a problem and lose the current contents of your database, you can reexecute all changes logged in the journal on the backed up copy, and recreate the database in the state it was as of the last journal entry. A typical command to begin journaling changes would be the following:

```
SET JOURNAL ON;
```

Auditing is done for security purposes. It keeps track of who performs which actions on the database, and stores this information in a table accessible only to one or a few highly privileged users. Naturally, you seldom want to audit every action, because this would soon take up a lot of memory. You can set auditing for particular users, particular actions or particular data objects. Here is one form of an AUDIT command:

```
AUDIT INSERT ON Salespeople BY Diane;
```

Either the ON or BY clauses could have been omitted, resulting in an audit of all objects or users, respectively. AUDIT ALL, in place of AUDIT INSERT, would have tracked all Diane's actions involving Salespeople.

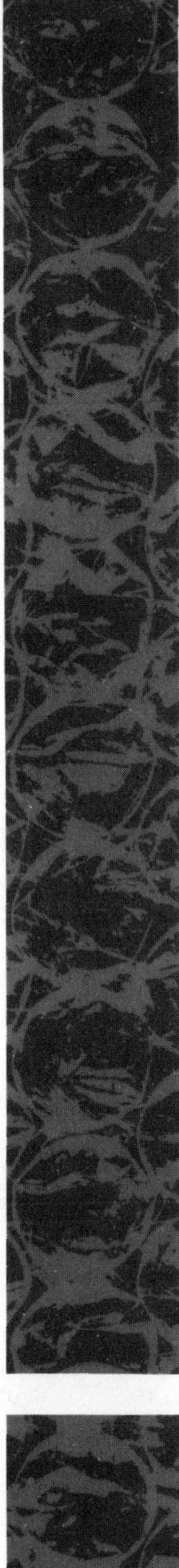

D

Syntax and Command Reference

THIS APPENDIX CONTAINS A MORE CONCISE DEFINITION of the various SQL commands. Its purpose is to give you a quick and precise SQL reference and definition. The first section of this appendix defines the elements used to construct SQL commands; the second details the syntax and offers a concise explanation of the commands themselves.

The following standard conventions are observed (these are called BNF conventions):

- Keywords are in all uppercase letters.
- SQL and other special terms are in angle brackets and italicized (< *and* >).
- Optional portions of a command are in square brackets ([and]).
- Elipses (. . .) indicate that the preceding portion of the command may be repeated any number of times.
- A vertical bar (|) indicates that whatever precedes it may optionally be replaced by whatever follows it.
- Braces ({ and }) indicate that everything within them is to be regarded as a whole for the purpose of evaluating other symbols (for example, vertical bars or ellipses).
- Double colon equals (:: =) means that what follows is the definition of what precedes it.

In addition, we will use the following sequence (.,. .) to indicate that the preceding may be repeated any number of times with the individual occurances separated by commas. Attributes that are not part of the official standard will be marked (*nonstandard*) in the explanation.

NOTE: the terminology we use here is not the official ANSI terminology. The official terminology can get quite labyrinthian, so we have simplified things somewhat. For this reason, we sometimes use different terms than ANSI, or even use the same terms somewhat differently. For example, our definition of <*predicate*> combines what the standard calls a <*predicate*> with what is there called a <*search condition*>. We have eliminated the need for the latter.

SQL ELEMENTS

This section defines the elements of SQL commands. These are divided for our purposes into two categories: the basic language elements, and the functional language elements. The basic elements are the building blocks of the language; when SQL examines a command, it first evaluates each character in the text of the command in terms of these elements. The <*separator*>'s divide one part of a command from another; whatever is between <*separator*>'s is treated as a unit. On the basis of this division, SQL interprets the command.

The functional elements are the various things (other than keywords) that these units will be interpreted as. They are portions of a command, delineated by <*separator*>'s, that have special meaning to SQL. Some are specific to particular commands and are discussed with those commands later in this appendix. The ones listed here are common elements to multiple commands. Functional elements can be defined in terms of each other or even in terms of themselves. For example, the <*predicate*>, our final and most complex case, contains <*predicate*> in its own definition. This is because a <*predicate*> using AND or OR can contain any number of <*predicate*>'s that could stand alone.

We have given the <*predicate*> a separate section in this appendix because of the variety and complexity of this functional language element. It will follow the discussion of the other functional parts of commands.

BASIC LANGUAGE ELEMENTS

ELEMENT	DEFINITION
<*separator*>	<*comment*> | <*space*> | <*newline*>
<*comment*>	--<*string*><*newline*>
<*space*>	space character
<*newline*>	implementor-defined end of line character
<*identifier*>	<*letter*>[{<*letter or digit*> | <*underscore*}. . .] NOTE: In strict ANSI standard, letters must be uppercase, and <*identifier*>'s must be no longer than 18 characters.

<table>
<tr><th>ELEMENT</th><th>DEFINITION</th></tr>
<tr><td><underscore></td><td>_</td></tr>
<tr><td><percent sign></td><td>%</td></tr>
<tr><td><delimiter></td><td>any of the following: , ( ) < > . : = + * – / <> >= <= or a <string></td></tr>
<tr><td><string></td><td>[any printable text in single quotes]
NOTE: In <string>'s, two consecutive single quotes ('') will be interpreted as one.</td></tr>
<tr><td><SQL term>
(*embedded only*)</td><td>host-language dependent statement terminator.</td></tr>
</table>

FUNCTIONAL ELEMENTS

The following table shows the functional elements of SQL commands and their definitions:

<table>
<tr><th>ELEMENT</th><th>DEFINITION</th></tr>
<tr><td><query></td><td>SELECT statement</td></tr>
<tr><td><subquery></td><td>Parenthesized SELECT statement within another statement, which is, in effect, evaluated separately for each candidate row of the other statement</td></tr>
<tr><td><value expression></td><td><primary>
| <primary><operator><primary>
| <primary><operator><value expression></td></tr>
<tr><td><operator></td><td>any of the following: + – / *</td></tr>
<tr><td><primary></td><td><column name>
| <literal>
| <aggregate function>
| <built-in constant>
| <nonstandard function></td></tr>
<tr><td><literal></td><td><string> | <mathematical expression></td></tr>
</table>

Element	***Definition***
<*built-in constant*>	USER | <*implementation-defined constant*>
<*table name*>	<*identifier*>
<*column spec*>	[<*table name*> | <*alias*>.]<*column name*>
<*grouping column*>	<*column spec*> | <*integer*>
<*ordering column*>	<*column spec*> | <*integer*>
<*colconstraint*>	NOT NULL | UNIQUE | CHECK (<*predicate*>) | PRIMARY KEY | REFERENCES <*table name*>[(<*column name*>)]
<*tabconstraint*>	UNIQUE (<*column list*>) | CHECK (<*predicate*>) | PRIMARY KEY (<*column list*>) | FOREIGN KEY (<*column list*>) REFERENCES <*table name*>[(<*column list*>)]
<*defvalue*>	DEFAULT VALUE = <*value expression*>
<*data type*>	Legal data type (See Appendix B for those supported by ANSI or Appendix C for other common ones.)
<*size*>	Meaning depends on <*data type*> (See Appendix B.)
<*cursor name*>	<*identifier*>
<*index name*>	<*identifier*>
<*synonym*>	<*identifier*>(*nonstandard*)
<*owner*>	<*Authorization ID*>
<*column list*>	<*column spec*> .,..
<*value list*>	<*value expression*> .,..
<*table reference*>	{ <*table name*> [<*alias*>] } .,..

PREDICATES

The following definition of <predicate> lists the various types that will be explained in the following pages:

```
<predicate> :: = [NOT]
                 { <comparison predicate>
                 | <in predicate>
                 | <null predicate>
                 | <between predicate>
                 | <like predicate>
                 | <quantified predicate>
                 | <exists predicate> }
                 [AND | OR  <predicate>]
```

A *<predicate>* is an expression that can be true, false, or unknown, with the exceptions of the *<exists predicate>* and the *<null predicate>*, which can be only true or false. Unknown occurs if NULL values prevent a definitive answer from being produced. This will be the case whenever a NULL is compared to any value. The standard Boolean operators—AND, OR, and NOT—may be used with a *<predicate>*. NOT true is false, NOT false is true, and NOT unknown is unknown. AND and OR have the effects on a combination of predicates illustrated in the following tables:

AND

AND	**true**	**false**	**unknown**
true	true	false	unknown
false	false	false	false
unknown	unknown	false	unknown

OR

OR	**true**	**false**	**unknown**
true	true	true	true
false	true	false	unknown
unknown	true	unknown	unknown

These tables are read in a manner similar to multiplication tables: you combine the true, false, or unknown values from the rows with those of the columns to get the result indicated where that column intersects that row. In the AND table for example, the third column (unknown) and the first row (true) intersect at the upper left showing unknown—the value of true AND unknown.

The order of precedence is determined by parentheses. Whenever these are not present, NOT will be evaluated first, followed by AND and OR. The various types of <*predicate*>'s are considered separately in the following sections.

<comparison predicate>

Syntax

<**value expression**> <**relational op**> <**value expression**> |
<**subquery**>

<**relational op**> :: =
=
| <
| >
| <
| >=
| <>

If either <*value expression*> is NULL, the <*comparison predicate*> is unknown; otherwise, it is true if the comparison is true and false if it is not. The <*relational op*>'s have the standard mathematical meanings for numeric values; for other types of values, its meaning is implementation defined. The two <*value expression*>'s must be of comparable data types. If a <*subquery*> is used, it must contain a single <*value expression*> in the SELECT clause, whose value will replace the second <*value expression*> in the <*comparison predicate*>, each time the <*subquery*> is effectively executed.

<between predicate>

Syntax

<**value expression**> **[NOT] BETWEEN** <**value expression**>
AND <**value expression**>

The <*between predicate*> A BETWEEN B AND C has the same value as the <*predicate*> (A > = B AND A < = C). The <*between predicate*> A NOT BETWEEN B AND C has the same value as NOT (A BETWEEN B AND C). <*value expression*>'s may be produced by <*subquery*>'s (*non-standard*).

<in predicate>

Syntax

<*value expression*> [NOT] IN <*value list*> | <*subquery*>

The <*value list*> will consist of one or more enumerated values, parenthesized and separated by commas, that are of a comparable data type with the <*value expression*>. If a <*subquery*> is used, it must contain only one <*value expression*> in its SELECT clause (more may be possible, but this is not standard). The <*subquery*> will, in effect, be executed separately for each candidate row of the main query, and the values that it outputs will constitute the <*value list*> for that row. In either case, the <*in predicate*> will be true if the <*value expression*> is present in the <*value list*>, unless NOT is specified. A NOT IN (B, C) is equivalent to NOT (A IN (B, C)).

<like predicate>

Syntax

<*charvalue*> [NOT] LIKE <*pattern*>[ESCAPE <*escapechar*>]

<*charvalue*> is any <*value expression*> of an alphanumeric type (*nonstandard*). (<*charvalue*> can be only <*column spec*> in standard.) <*pattern*> consists of a <*string*> that will be tested to see if it matches <*charvalue*>. <*escapechar*> is a single alphanumeric character. A match will exist if the following conditions are true:

- For every <*underscore*> in <*pattern*> that is not immediately preceded by <*escapechar*>, there is one corresponding character in <*charvalue*>.

- For every <*percent sign*> in <*pattern*> that is not immediately preceded by <*escapechar*>, there are zero or more corresponding characters in <*charvalue*>.
- For every <*escapechar*> in <*pattern*> that is not immediately preceded by another <*escapechar*>, there is no corresponding character in <*charvalue*>.
- For every other character in <*pattern*>, the same character is present at the corresponding point in <*charvalue*>.

If a match exists, the <*like predicate*> is true, unless NOT was specified. A NOT LIKE 'text' is equivalent to NOT (A LIKE 'text'.)

<null predicate>

Syntax

<*column spec*> IS [NOT] NULL

<*column spec*> IS NULL if the NULL value is present in that column. This will make the <*null predicate*> true unless NOT was specified. <*column spec*> IS NOT NULL has the same result as NOT (<*column spec*> IS NULL).

<quantified predicate>

Syntax

<*value expression*><*relational op*>
<*quantifier*><*subquery*>

<quantifier> ::= ANY | ALL | SOME

The SELECT clause of the <*subquery*> must include one and only one <*value expression*>. All of the values produced by the <*subquery*> constitute the <*result set*>. The <*value expression*> is compared, using the <*relational operator*>, to every member of the <*result set*>. This comparison is evaluated as follows:

- If <*quantifier*> = ALL, and every member of the <*result set*> makes the comparison true, the <*quantified predicate*> is true.

- If <*quantifier*> = ANY, and there is at least one member of the <*result set*> that makes the comparison true, the <*quantified predicate*> is true.
- If the <*result set*> is empty, the <*quantified predicate*> is true if the <*quantifier*> is ALL and false otherwise.
- If the <*quantifier*> is SOME, the effect is the same as ANY.
- If the <*quantified predicate*> is neither true nor false, it is unknown.

<exists predicate>

Syntax

```
EXISTS (<subquery>)
```

If the <*subquery*> produces one or more rows of output, the <*exists predicate*> is true; otherwise it is false.

SQL COMMANDS

This section details the syntax of the various SQL commands. It enables you to quickly look up a command, find its syntax and a brief description of how it works.

NOTE: Commands that begin with EXEC SQL, as well as commands or clauses that end with <*SQL term*> can be used only in embedded SQL.

BEGIN DECLARE SECTION

Syntax

```
EXEC SQL BEGIN DECLARE SECTION<SQL term>
 <host-language variable declarations>
 EXEC SQL END DECLARE SECTION<SQL term>
```

This command creates a section of the host-language program for the declaration of host variables that will be used in embedded SQL statements. The variable SQLCODE must be included as one of the host-language variable declarations.

CLOSE CURSOR

Syntax

EXEC SQL CLOSE CURSOR <*cursor name*><*SQL term*>;

This command defines the CURSOR as closed, so that no values may be FETCHED from it until it is opened once more.

COMMIT (WORK)

Syntax

COMMIT WORK;

This command makes permanent all changes to the values in the database since the beginning of the transaction, ending the current, and beginning a new, transaction.

CREATE INDEX (*NONSTANDARD*)

Syntax

CREATE [UNIQUE] INDEX <*index name*>
ON <*table name*> (<*column list*>);

This command creates a fast-access path to make retrievals of rows containing the indicated columns more efficient. If UNIQUE is specified, the table may not contain duplicate values in those columns.

*CREATE SYNONYM (*NONSTANDARD*)*

Syntax

CREATE [PUBLIC] SYNONYM <*synonym*> FOR <*owner*>.<*table name*>;

This command creates an alternate name for a table. The synonym is owned by its creator, and the table itself is normally one that is owned by another user. By using the synonym, its owner does not have to refer to the table by its full (including owner) name. If PUBLIC is specified, synonym is owned by SYSTEM and accessible to all users.

CREATE TABLE

Syntax

CREATE TABLE <*table name*>
({<*column name*> <*data type*>[<*size*>]
[<*colconstraint*>. . .]
[<*defvalue*>]} .,. . <*tabconstraint*> .,. .);

CREATE TABLE creates a table in the database. This table will be owned by its creator. The columns are considered to be in the order named. The <*data type*> defines the kind of data the column will hold. The standard <*data type*>'s are described in Appendix B; other commonly used <*data type*>'s are discussed in Appendix C. The meaning of <*size*> depends on the <*data type*>. <*colconstraint*>'s and <*tabconstraint*>'s impose limitations on the values that can be entered into the columns. <*defvalue*> defines a value that will automatically be inserted if no other value is indicated for that row. (See Chapter 17 for details on the CREATE TABLE command itself and Chapters 18 and 19 for details on the constraints and on <*defvalue*>).

CREATE VIEW

Syntax

```
CREATE VIEW <table name>
     AS <query>
     [WITH CHECK OPTION];
```

The view is treated as any other table in SQL commands. When a command references the <*table name*>, the <*query*> is performed, and its output constitutes the content of the table for the duration of that command. Some views can be updated, which means update commands can be performed on them and transferred to the table referenced in the <*query*>. If WITH CHECK OPTION is specified, these updates must also satisfy that <*query*>'s <*predicate*>.

DECLARE CURSOR

Syntax

```
EXEC SQL DECLARE <cursor name> CURSOR FOR
 <query><SQL term>
```

This command associates the <*cursor name*> with the <*query*>. When the cursor is opened (See OPEN CURSOR), the <*query*> is performed, and its output can be FETCHED. If the cursor is updatable, the table referenced in the <*query*> can have its content changed by update operations on the cursor (See Chapter 25 on updatability of cursors).

DELETE

Syntax

```
DELETE FROM <table name>
     {   [WHERE <predicate>] ;}
     | WHERE CURRENT OF <cursor name><SQL term>
```

If the WHERE clause is absent, all rows of the table are removed. If the WHERE clause uses a <*predicate*>, rows that satisfy the <*predicate*> are removed. If the WHERE clause has a CURRENT OF <*cursor name*> argument, the row of <*table name*> currently referenced by <*cursor name*> is removed. The WHERE CURRENT OF form may be used only in embedded SQL, and only with updatable cursors.

EXEC SQL

Syntax

```
EXEC SQL <embedded SQL command> <SQL term>
```

EXEC SQL is used to begin all SQL commands embedded in another language.

FETCH

Syntax

```
EXEC SQL FETCH <cursor name>
     INTO <host-variable list><SQL term>
```

FETCH takes the output of the current row of the <*query*>, inserts it into the <*host-variable list*>, and moves the cursor to the next row. The <*host-variable list*> may optionally include indicator as well as target variables (See Chapter 25.)

GRANT

Syntax (standard)

```
GRANT ALL [PRIVILEGES]
     | {SELECT
     |  INSERT
     |  DELETE
     |  UPDATE [(<column list>)]
     |  REFERENCES [(<column list>)] } .,..
```

```
ON <table name> .,..
TO PUBLIC | <Authorization ID> .,..
[WITH GRANT OPTION];
```

ALL, with or without PRIVILEGES, includes every privilege in the above list. PUBLIC includes all users present and future. This command enables the grantee(s) to perform the said actions on the table(s) named. REFERENCES allows the grantee(s) to use the columns in <*column list*> as a parent to a foreign key. The other privileges consist of the right to perform the commands for which the privileges are named on the table. UPDATE, like REFERENCES, can be restricted to certain columns. GRANT OPTION confers the ability to give these privileges to other users in turn.

Syntax (common nonstandard)

```
GRANT  DBA
   |   RESOURCE
   |   CONNECT .,..
   TO <Authorization ID> .,..
   [IDENTIFIED BY> password>
```

CONNECT gives the grantee the right to log on and a few other limited rights. RESOURCE gives the user the right to create tables. DBA gives the grantee almost unlimited rights. IDENTIFIED BY is used with CONNECT to define or change user's password.

INSERT

Syntax

```
INSERT INTO <table name> [ (<column list>) ]
    VALUES (<value list>) | <query>;
```

INSERT creates one or more new rows in <*table name*>. If the VALUES clause is used, those values are inserted into <*table name*>. If a <*query*> is specified, each row of its output will be inserted into <*table name*>. If the <*column list*> is omitted, all columns of <*table name*>, in order, are assumed.

OPEN CURSOR

Syntax

```
EXEC SQL OPEN CURSOR <cursor name><SQL term>
```

OPEN CURSOR executes the query associated with <*cursor name*>. The output can now be retrieved one row at a time with the FETCH command.

*REVOKE (*NONSTANDARD*)*

Syntax

```
REVOKE { ALL [PRIVILEGES]
    |   <privilege> .,..} [ON <table name>]
    FROM { PUBLIC
    |   <Authorization ID> .,..};
```

The <*privilege*> can be any of those outlined in the GRANT command. The user issuing the REVOKE must be the same as the user who issued the GRANT. The ON clause will be used if the privilege is of a type specific to a particular object.

ROLLBACK (WORK)

Syntax

```
ROLLBACK WORK;
```

The comand cancels all changes to the database made during the current transaction. It also ends the current, and begin a new, transaction.

SELECT

Syntax

```
SELECT {[DISTINCT | ALL] <value expression> .,..} | *
    [INTO <host variable list> (*embedded only*)]
```

FROM <*table reference*> .,. .
[WHERE <*predicate*>]
[GROUP BY <*grouping column*> .,. .]
[HAVING <*predicate*>]
[ORDER BY <*ordering column*> [ASC | DESC] .,. .];

This statement constitutes a query and outputs values from the database (see Chapters 3–14). The following rules and definitions apply:

- If neither ALL nor DISTINCT is specified, ALL is assumed.
- A <*value expression*> consists of a <*column spec*>, an <*aggregate funct*>, a <*nonstandard function*>, a <*constant*>, or any combination of these along with operators into a valid expression.
- A <*table reference*> consists of the name of a table, including the owner prefix if current user is not owner, or a synonym (*nonstandard*) for a table. The table can either be a base table or a view. Optionally, an alias can be specified, which is a synonym for the table usable only for the duration of the current command. A table name or synonym must be separated from an alias by one or more <*separator*>'s.
- If GROUP BY is used, all <*column spec*>'s used in the SELECT clause must be used as <*grouping column*>'s, unless they are contained in <*aggregate funct*>'s. All <*grouping column*>'s must be present among the <*value expressions*>'s in the SELECT clause. For each distinct combination of <*grouping column*> values, there shall be one and only one row of output.
- If HAVING is used, the <*predicate*> is applied to every row of output produced by the GROUP BY clause, and those rows that make it true are output.
- If ORDER BY is used, the output has a definite sequence. Each <*column identifier*> refers to a specific <*value expression*> in the SELECT clause. If that <*value

expression> is a <*column spec*>, the <*column identifier*> can be that same <*column spec*>. Otherwise the <*column identifier*> will be a positive integer indicating the place of the <*value expression*> in the SELECT clause sequence. The output will be arranged so as to place the values contained in the <*column identifier*> in ascending order, unless DESC is specified. The <*column identifier*>'s named first in the ORDER BY clause take precedence over those named later in determining output sequence.

A SELECT statement evaluates each candidate row of the table(s) on which it is drawn independently. A *candidate row* is defined as follows:

- If only one <*table reference*> is included, each row of that table in turn is the candidate row.
- If more than one <*table reference*> is included, each row of every table shall be combined in turn with every combination of rows from all the other tables. Every such combination shall in turn be the candidate row.

Each candidate row produces values that make the <*predicate*> in the WHERE clause true, false, or unknown. Unless GROUP BY is used, each <*value expression*> is applied in turn to each candidate row whose values make the predicate true, and the results of this operation are the output. If GROUP BY is used, the candidate rows are combined using aggregate functions. If no <*predicate*> is included, each <*value expression*> is applied to every candidate row or to every group. If DISTINCT is specified, duplicate rows are eliminated from the output.

UNION

Syntax

```
<query> {UNION [ALL] <query> }...;
```

The output of the two or more <*query*>'s is merged. Each <*query*> must contain the same number of <*value expression*>'s in its SELECT clause and in such an order that the 1..nth of each is compatible in <*data type*> and <*size*> with the 1..nth of all others.

UPDATE

Syntax

```
UPDATE <table name>
    SET { <column name> =<value expression> } .,..
    {[  WHERE <predicate>] ; }
    |        {[WHERE CURRENT OF <cursor name>]
              <SQL term>]}
```

UPDATE changes the values in each <*column name*> to the corresponding <*value expression*>. If the WHERE clause uses a <*predicate*>, only rows of the tables whose current values make that <*predicate*> true will be changed. If WHERE uses a CURRENT OF clause, the values in the row of <*table name*> currently in the <*cursor name*> are changed. The WHERE CURRENT OF form is usable only in embedded SQL, and only with updatable cursors. In the absense of a WHERE clause, all rows are changed.

WHENEVER

Syntax

```
EXEC SQL WHENEVER <SQLcond> <action> <SQL
 term>

<SQLcond> ::= SQLERROR | NOT FOUND | SQLWARNING
 (the latter is not standard)

<action> ::= CONTINUE | GOTO <target> | GO TO
 <target>

<target> ::= host language dependent.
```

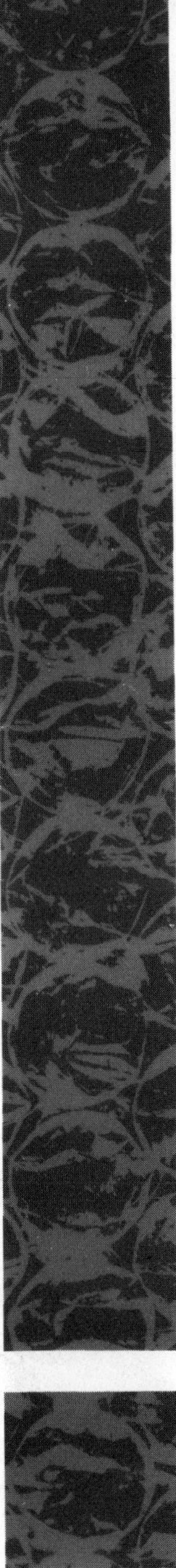

E

Tables Used in Examples

TABLE 1: SALESPEOPLE

snum	sname	city	comm
1001	Peel	London	.12
1002	Serres	San Jose	.13
1004	Motika	London	.11
1007	Rifkin	Barcelona	.15
1003	Axelrod	New York	.10

TABLE 2: CUSTOMERS

cnum	cname	city	rating	snum
2001	Hoffman	London	100	1001
2002	Giovanni	Rome	200	1003
2003	Liu	San Jose	200	1002
2004	Grass	Berlin	300	1002
2006	Clemens	London	100	1001
2008	Cisneros	San Jose	300	1007
2007	Pereira	Rome	100	1004

TABLE 3: ORDERS

onum	amt	odate	cnum	snum
3001	18.69	10/03/1990	2008	1007
3003	767.19	10/03/1990	2001	1001
3002	1900.10	10/03/1990	2007	1004
3005	5160.45	10/03/1990	2003	1002
3006	1098.16	10/03/1990	2008	1007
3009	1713.23	10/04/1990	2002	1003
3007	75.75	10/04/1990	2004	1002
3008	4723.00	10/05/1990	2006	1001
3010	1309.95	10/06/1990	2004	1002
3011	9891.88	10/06/1990	2006	1001

INDEX

B

C

D

E

J

K

L

S

T

TO JOIN THE SYBEX MAILING LIST OR ORDER BOOKS
PLEASE COMPLETE THIS FORM

NAME ______________________ COMPANY ______________________

STREET ______________________ CITY ______________________

STATE ______________________ ZIP ______________________

☐ PLEASE MAIL ME MORE INFORMATION ABOUT **SYBEX** TITLES

ORDER FORM (There is no obligation to order)

PLEASE SEND ME THE FOLLOWING:

TITLE	QTY	PRICE
______________________	______	______
______________________	______	______
______________________	______	______
______________________	______	______
TOTAL BOOK ORDER	______	$______

SHIPPING AND HANDLING PLEASE ADD $2.00 PER BOOK VIA UPS ______

FOR OVERSEAS SURFACE ADD $5.25 PER BOOK PLUS $4.40 REGISTRATION FEE ______

FOR OVERSEAS AIRMAIL ADD $18.25 PER BOOK PLUS $4.40 REGISTRATION FEE ______

CALIFORNIA RESIDENTS PLEASE ADD APPLICABLE SALES TAX ______

TOTAL AMOUNT PAYABLE ______

☐ CHECK ENCLOSED ☐ VISA
☐ MASTERCARD ☐ AMERICAN EXPRESS

ACCOUNT NUMBER ______________________

EXPIR. DATE ______ DAYTIME PHONE ______________

CUSTOMER SIGNATURE ______________________________________

CHECK AREA OF COMPUTER INTEREST:

☐ BUSINESS SOFTWARE

☐ TECHNICAL PROGRAMMING

☐ OTHER: ______________________

THE FACTOR THAT WAS MOST IMPORTANT IN YOUR SELECTION:

☐ THE SYBEX NAME

☐ QUALITY

☐ PRICE

☐ EXTRA FEATURES

☐ COMPREHENSIVENESS

☐ CLEAR WRITING

☐ OTHER ______________________

OTHER COMPUTER TITLES YOU WOULD LIKE TO SEE IN PRINT:

____

____

OCCUPATION

☐ PROGRAMMER ☐ TEACHER

☐ SENIOR EXECUTIVE ☐ HOMEMAKER

☐ COMPUTER CONSULTANT ☐ RETIRED

☐ SUPERVISOR ☐ STUDENT

☐ MIDDLE MANAGEMENT ☐ OTHER:

☐ ENGINEER/TECHNICAL ______________

☐ CLERICAL/SERVICE

☐ BUSINESS OWNER/SELF EMPLOYED

CHECK YOUR LEVEL OF COMPUTER USE

☐ NEW TO COMPUTERS

☐ INFREQUENT COMPUTER USER

☐ FREQUENT USER OF ONE SOFTWARE PACKAGE:

NAME ______________________________

☐ FREQUENT USER OF MANY SOFTWARE PACKAGES

☐ PROFESSIONAL PROGRAMMER

OTHER COMMENTS:

____

____

____

____

____

____

____

PLEASE FOLD, SEAL, AND MAIL TO SYBEX

SYBEX, INC.
2021 CHALLENGER DR. #100
ALAMEDA, CALIFORNIA USA
94501

SEAL